SEVENTH EDITION

OFF THE BEATEN PATH®
ARIZONA

A GUIDE TO UNIQUE PLACES

CARRIE MINER FRASURE

gpp®
travel

Guilford, Connecticut

All the information in this guidebook is subject to change. We recommend that you call ahead to obtain current information before traveling.

To buy books in quantity for corporate use
or incentives, call **(800) 962-0973**
or e-mail **premiums@GlobePequot.com**.

Layout: Joanna Beyer
Text design: Linda R. Loiewski
Maps: Equator Graphics © Morris Book Publishing, LLC

ISSN 1540-1197
ISBN 978-0-7627-5021-4

Printed in the United States of America
10 9 8 7 6 5 4 3 2 1

This book is dedicated to those adventurers in life who seek out new experiences by taking the road less traveled.

Page

NORTHERN ARIZONA

Chinle

Bullhead City Kingman

Williams

Flagstaff

Winslow

Holbrook

WESTERN ARIZONA

Lake Havasu City

Prescott

Sedona
Camp Verde

Payson

Show Low

Pinetop-Lakeside

Wickenburg

Phoenix

EASTERN ARIZONA

CENTRAL ARIZONA

Safford

Casa Grande

Yuma

SOUTHERN ARIZONA

Tucson

Willcox

Tombstone

Sierra Vista

Nogales

Bisbee

N

Contents

Introduction

Arizona is perhaps best known as the home of one of the world's most gorgeous gorges, the Grand Canyon. It has also gained a well-deserved reputation as a prime winter playground for snowbirds seeking sunshine and pampering. Indeed, it is all that—plus so much more.

Veer off the interstates or the main drags of Arizona's diverse communities, and you'll find hidden treasures that the Sunday travel sections often overlook. From secluded inlets on massive Lake Powell and stunning swimming holes in little-traveled regions of the Grand Canyon to an annual jousting fest in the desert and a folklore preserve tucked into a wildlife-rich canyon, Arizona holds more curiosities than any weeklong vacation itinerary could even begin to include (there's even skiing!).

Far from a cultural desert, Arizona has just about any arts-related diversion visitors might wish to enjoy, including Broadway-style shows; resident symphony, ballet, and theatrical companies; and venues for rock concerts and jazz jams. Add to this a generous supply of top-notch museums—showcasing Native American heritage, contemporary fine art, lifestyles of long-gone civilizations, and the flora and fauna of the enigmatic Sonoran Desert—and you'll quickly discover that there is infinitely more here than is often believed.

Sports fans will find their nirvana in Phoenix, the nation's fifth largest city, with professional teams wearing the uniforms of nearly every league imaginable—from the NBA's Phoenix Suns and the major league's Arizona Diamondbacks to the NHL's Phoenix Coyotes and the NFL's Phoenix Coyotes. Fans can even root for their own home teams during spring-training exhibition games that bring the boys of summer to sites throughout the state every

Elevations and Temperatures

One of the most surprising facts about Arizona is the variety of climates and landscapes. It's not all desert; it's not all lowland. In fact, the terrain ranges from 70 feet above sea level at Yuma to 12,643 feet and alpine terrain atop the San Francisco peaks. Even Phoenix is at a higher elevation than you might imagine at 1,117 feet. The ride through the center of the state is a nice surprise as it climbs to 7,000 feet at Flagstaff where the great plateau of the Grand Canyon and the Navajo-Hopi Reservations begins. In early March, high temperatures in the state can range from a low of forty-seven degrees Fahrenheit in Flagstaff to a high of seventy-seven degrees in Yuma (with Phoenix at seventy-one degrees).

March. Longtime local favorites include the Arizona State University Phoenix Coyotes and their rivals to the south, the University of Arizona Wildcats. For an even wilder sport, visitors should check out one of the many rodeos that are staged each year, demonstrating the best skills that area cowboys have to offer!

Let Arizona's hospitable residents pamper you at the day's end. Nowhere will you find your accommodations as diverse or—in many cases—luxurious. City slickers can relive their childhood fantasies at one of the many authentic guest ranches, and those in search of the ultimate in service and style can choose from dozens of top-rated resort hotels that offer activities ranging from their own water parks and European-style spas to horseback riding and championship golf. And if a day on the links is your idea of heaven, Arizona has a course for nearly every day of the year.

Even film buffs will find a fascinating array of locations that include working movie sets to scenic vistas that have served as studio "back lots" for decades. Wander among the landscapes that John Wayne galloped through, or visit the western theme park that was built for the classic film *Arizona.*

Some of the destinations in this book will have you traveling on the main road; some will take you out where the tour buses don't run. The thing about Arizona is, as film hero Buckaroo Banzai used to say, "No matter where you go, there you are."

Arizona Climate at a Glance

(Average daily high/low temperatures by month and region)

Month	Deserts	Mountains	Month	Deserts	Mountains
January	66/41	43/16	July	106/81	82/50
February	71/45	46/19	August	104/79	80/49
March	76/49	50/23	September	98/73	74/42
April	85/55	58/27	October	88/61	63/31
May	94/64	68/34	November	75/49	51/22
June	104/73	79/41	December	66/42	44/17

Note: Temperatures in degrees Fahrenheit.

Greater Phoenix Average Temperatures

Month	Highs	Lows	Month	Highs	Lows
January	65.2	39.4	July	105.0	79.5
February	69.7	42.5	August	102.3	77.5
March	74.5	46.7	September	98.2	70.9
April	83.1	53.0	October	87.7	59.1
May	92.4	61.5	November	74.3	46.9
June	102.3	70.6	December	66.4	40.2

Average high: 85.1

Average low: 57.3

Note: Temperatures in degrees Fahrenheit.

Tucson Average Temperatures

Month	Highs	Lows	Month	Highs	Lows
January	65	37	July	101	74
February	69	40	August	98	72
March	74	43	September	95	67
April	82	50	October	86	55
May	90	57	November	74	44
June	100	67	December	66	38

Average annual days of sunshine: 350

Note: Temperatures in degrees Fahrenheit.

For Further Information about Arizona

Arizona Office of Tourism (Administration Office)
Grand Canyon State Information Center
1110 W. Washington St., Ste. 155
Phoenix, AZ 85007

Flagstaff Average Temperatures

Month	Highs	Lows	Month	Highs	Lows
January	43	17	July	82	50
February	46	19	August	80	49
March	50	23	September	74	42
April	58	27	October	63	31
May	68	34	November	51	22
June	79	41	December	44	17

Average annual days of sunshine: 228

Average annual precipitation: 22.91 inches

Average annual snowfall: 108.80 inches

Note: Temperatures in degrees Fahrenheit.

(602) 364-3700 or (866) 275-5816 (toll-free)

www.arizonaguide.com

Downtown Phoenix Visitor Information Center

125 N. Second Street, Suite 120

Phoenix, AZ 85004

Flagstaff Convention and Visitors Bureau

One E. Rte. 66

Flagstaff, AZ 86001

(928) 774-9541 or (800) 842-7293 (toll-free)

www.flagstaffarizona.org

Greater Phoenix Convention and Visitors Bureau (Administration Office)

One Arizona Center

400 E. Van Buren St., Ste. 600

Phoenix, AZ 85004-2290

(602) 254-6500 or (877) CALL-PHX (toll-free)

www.phoenixcvb.com

The Four Corners: Arizona as Part of a Southwest Itinerary

In so many ways Arizona is the heart of the Southwest. It is home to more Indian tribes than any other state in the union, and it is bordered by several major national parks, monuments, and recreation areas. Traveling from New Mexico in the east, you can develop an itinerary that might include several national monuments and national historic parks (El Morro and El Malpais between Albuquerque and Gallup, Gila Cliffs west of Truth or Consequences, White Sands near Las Cruces, or Aztec Ruins and Chaco Culture near Farmington in the northwest corner). In western Colorado you can visit Curacanti National Recreation Area and Black Canyon of the Gunnison National Park between Montrose and Gunnison, then continue through the western Colorado ski country to Durango and visit Mesa Verde National Park and Canyons of the Ancients National Monument near Four Corners. In southern Utah you'll find the beginning of the extensive chain of national parks, monuments, and recreation areas that stretches from Utah through northern Arizona to southern Nevada and includes Arches, Canyonlands, Capitol Reef, Glen Canyon/Lake Powell, Grand Canyon National Park, and Lake Mead/Hoover Dam; also in southern Utah are Zion and Bryce Canyon national parks. In southern Nevada, adjacent to Lake Mead, you'll find the popular Red Rocks and Valley of Fire State Parks. Finally, to the west in California are the Joshua Tree and Death Valley National Parks, and the Mohave National Preserve and Imperial Sand Dunes Recreation Area.

New Mexico

Navajo and Zuni Reservations (both are partly in New Mexico and partly in Arizona)

Bisti Badlands Natural Area

El Morro National Monument

El Malpais National Monument

Gila Cliff Dwellings National Monument

Chaco Culture National Historic Park

Aztec Ruins National Monument

White Sands National Monument

Colorado

Curecanti National Recreation Area

Black Canyon of the Gunnison National Park

Canyons of the Ancients National Monument

Mesa Verde National Park

Utah

Arches National Park

Canyonlands National Park

Capitol Reef National Park

Natural Bridges National Monument

Glen Canyon National Recreation Area

Nevada

Red Rocks State Park

Valley of Fire State Park

Lake Mead National Recreation Area

California

Joshua Tree National Park

Mojave Desert National Preserve

Death Valley National Park

Imperial Sand Dunes Recreation Area

Tucson Visitor Center and Administration Offices

100 S. Church Ave.
Tucson, AZ 85701
(520) 624-1817 or (800) 638-8350 (toll-free)
www.visittucson.org

Web Sites

Official site of the Arizona Office of Tourism, with links to many cities and attractions: www.arizonaguide.com

Arizona Bureau of Land Management: www.az.blm.gov

Arizona Game & Fish: www.gf.state.az.us

Arizona Department of Commerce: (including individual community profiles on every city and town throughout the state): www.azcommerce.com

Arizona Department of Transportation: www.dot.state.az.us

Arizona Highways **magazine:** www.arizonahighways.com

Arizona's Home Page (The Arizona Republic): www.azcentral.com

Arizona Humanities Council: www.arizonaheritagetraveler.org

Arizona State Parks: www.pr.state.az.us

U.S. Fish and Wildlife Services: www.fws.gov/southwest

ARIZONA'S TOP TEN VISITOR ATTRACTIONS

Grand Canyon National Park
(4,413,668)

South Mountain Park
(3,000,000)

Saguaro National Park
(2,647,313)

Tempe Town Lake
(2,782,000)

Chase Field
(2,699,178)

Glen Canyon National Recreation Area
(1,894,114)

Lake Mead National Recreation Area
(1,824,297)

London Bridge
(1,500,000)

The Phoenix Zoo
(1,474,000)

US Airways Center (formerly America West Arena)
(1,392,526)

(according to 2007 attendance figures)

Dining and Lodging Fees

Arizona dining and lodging vary greatly throughout the state and change seasonally. Restaurants listed as *Places to Eat* are open for lunch and dinner unless otherwise noted. Pricing for rooms under *Places to Stay* is for double occupancy during high season.

PLACES TO EAT

Up to $12   Inexpensive

$13 to $25   Moderate

$26 and up   Expensive

PLACES TO STAY

Up to $100   Inexpensive

$101 to $200   Moderate

$201 and up   Expensive

Arizona Strip

If you'd like to visit a community that is short in the way of tourist amenities but long on history, you might want to make a stop in **Colorado City** (928-875-2646), on AZ 389 immediately south of the Utah state line. The town, called Short Creek until 1958, has been around since the 1860s, when it was a Mormon settlement. When the Church of Jesus Christ of Latter Day Saints outlawed polygamy in 1890, church members who decided they'd rather fight than switch headed for Short Creek. This tiny agro-community became known to church officials and Arizona law enforcement officers as a haven for polygamists, and Mormons continue to be thus characterized by Hollywood and other less-informed folk.

Over the next forty to fifty years, there were several arrests for polygamy, and some questionable detective work was done by agents investigating the populace by posing as filmmakers. On July 26, 1953, the town's male population was rounded up and taken to the schoolhouse (which still stands today), where they were arrested, and the children were led away in the custody of the state. The families were eventually

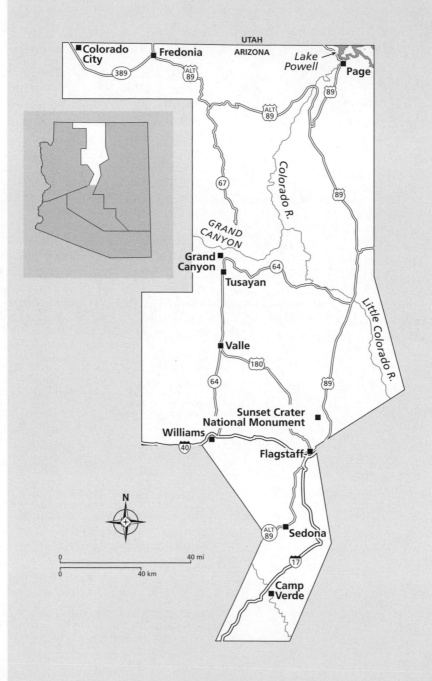

Colorado
City

Fredonia

UTAH

ARIZONA

Lake
Powell

Page

389

ALT
89

89

ALT
89

Colorado R.

67

GRAND
CANYON

Grand
Canyon

64

Tusayan

Little Colorado R.

Valle

180

64

89

Sunset Crater
National Monument

Williams

40

Flagstaff

N

Sedona

ALT
89

17

0   40 mi
0   40 km

Camp
Verde

reunited—even in a conservative state like Arizona, the meat-hook approach to law enforcement didn't go over well. The governor responsible for the raid (conservative Republican Howard Pyle) was defeated for reelection, partly because of public disapproval of his methods in this case.

From all appearances polygamy (which court rulings have declared is legal as a religious doctrine) is still practiced in Colorado City. For decades following the raid, outsiders were not especially welcome in town, and one can hardly blame residents. Though the gingham gowns, spit curls, and many other trappings of a simpler time still abound, the community is changing enough to make a genuine effort to accommodate travelers. Visitors report that people here are friendly and more than willing to give you directions or chat about what there is to see and do in the area.

One of the favorite activities here is hiking, as there are many wild areas to the north just across the Utah border. The vegetation here is typical of the high desert—junipers, sagebrush, some piñon pines—and there are distinct seasonal changes in temperature: High double- to triple-digit readings are common in the summer, and during the winter the community experiences three or four good snowfalls.

If you get hungry while visiting Colorado City, the **Vermillion Cliffs Candy Shop & Deli** (928-875-8093) at Arizona Avenue and Richard Street is open from 5 a.m. to 3 p.m. and has a full breakfast menu, along with every type of sandwich imaginable. They also make their own candy—including toffee, caramels, chocolate-covered peanuts, and date balls—and bake coffee cake, brownies, pies, and other goodies on the premises. Currently there are no motels in Colorado City; the nearest lodging is either in Hurricane, Utah, or Fredonia, Arizona.

One of the most spectacular nearby sights is **Toroweap Point** (spelled

AUTHOR'S TOP PICKS IN NORTHERN ARIZONA

Antelope Canyon	Museum of Northern Arizona
Antelope Point Marina	Pink Jeep Tours
El Tovar Lodge	Papillon Grand Canyon Helicopters
Glen Canyon National Recreation Area	Sunset Crater Volcano National Monument
Grand Canyon National Park—North Rim	Wupatki National Monument

TOP ANNUAL EVENTS IN NORTHERN ARIZONA

FEBRUARY

International Film Festival

Sedona

International independent cinema, documentary, and animation, panel discussions featuring leading film professionals.

(928) 282-1177 or (888) 399-FILM; www .sedonafilmfestival.com

Winterfest

Flagstaff

Sled-dog races, llama games, winter sports, snow sculpture, parade, concerts, theater, art shows, historic tours, workshops, and winter stargazing.

(928) 774-4505; www.flagstaffchamber .com

MARCH

Grand Canyon State Winter Games

Flagstaff

Arizona Snowbowl, slalom and giant slalom races, all ages, 5K Nordic ski race, and ice hockey. Other games and activities are held in Phoenix and Tucson.

(928) 773-9707 or (480) 517-9700; www.gcsg.org

MAY

Rendezvous Days

Williams

Parade, black powder shoot, carnival, street dances, crafts, and music.

(928) 635-4061; www.williamschamber .com

Zuni Festival of Arts and Culture

Flagstaff

Zuni artists, dancers, and flute players perform at this festival at the Museum of Northern Arizona in partnership with the A:shiwi A:wan Museum and Heritage Center.

(928) 774-5213; www.musnaz.org

JUNE

Wool Festival

Flagstaff

Sheep shearing, spinning and weaving demonstrations, and livestock competition at the Arizona Historical Society Pioneer Museum.

(928) 774-6272; www.arizonahistorical society.org

JULY

Arizona Highland Celtic Festival

Flagstaff

Celtic celebration honoring the people of Brittany, Cornwall, Scotland, and Wales.

(928) 774-9541; www.nachs.info

Hopi Festival of Arts and Culture

Flagstaff

Hopi artists, demonstrations, tribal dances, storytelling, and children's activities at the Museum of Northern Arizona.

(928) 774-5213; www.musnaz.org

Western Arts Day

Grand Canyon National Park North Rim

Cowboy poetry readings, musical performances, and arts and crafts demonstrations.

(928) 638-7888; www.nps.gov/grca

AUGUST

August Native American Heritage Days

Grand Canyon National Park North Rim

Craft demonstrations, educational lectures, guided hikes, Indian arts and crafts, and Native American song and dance.

(928) 638-7888; www.nps.gov/grca

Cool Country Cruise-In and Route 66 Festival

Williams

1950s-style fun with a classic car show, battle of the bands, and a sock hop.

(928) 635-1418; www.williamschamber .com

Navajo Festival of Arts and Culture
Flagstaff
Navajo artists, demonstrations, storytellers, hoop dancing, and music at the Museum of Northern Arizona.
(928) 774-5213; www.musnaz.org

SEPTEMBER
Apple Festival
Oak Creek
Pick apples from an orchard planted in 1912, birding, history tours, arts and crafts, and kids' games at Slide Rock State Park.
(928) 282-3034; www.azstateparks.com

Coconino County Fair
Flagstaff
Northern Arizona's largest county fair features educational exhibits, livestock, live entertainment, a demolition derby, and carnival at the Fort Tuthill Coconino County Fairgrounds.
(928) 679-8004 or (800) 559-9289; www.coconino.az.gov

Festival of Science
Flagstaff
Promotes science awareness and enthusiasm through field trips, exhibits, and lectures.
(800) 842-7293; www.scifest.org

Fiesta del Tlaquepaque
Sedona
Mexican-style celebration; piñatas, mariachi bands, folklorico dance groups, and flamenco/classical guitarists.
(928) 282-4838; www.tlaq.com

Grand Canyon Music Festival
Grand Canyon National Park South Rim Shrine of the Ages Auditorium, musicians from around the country, jazz to classical.
(928) 638-9215 or (800) 997-8285; www.grandcanyonmusicfest.org

Jazz on the Rocks Benefit Festival
Sedona
Radisson Poco Diablo Resort, internationally known jazz festival.
(928) 282-1985; www.sedonajazz.com

Labor Day PRCA Rodeo
Williams
(928) 635-4061; www.williamschamber.com

Pine Country Pro Rodeo
Flagstaff
PRCA approved, purse of $50,000 plus, chili cook-off, fashion show, parade, and barn dances.
(928) 526-3556 or (800) 842-7293; www.pinecountryprorodeo.com

OCTOBER
Celebraciónes de la Gente
Flagstaff
Diá de los Muertos (Day of the Dead) celebration at the Museum of Northern Arizona. Hispanic artists, Latin music, Aztec fire dancing, storytelling, mariachis, and ballet folklorico performances.
(928) 774-5213; www.musnaz.org

Fort Verde Days
Camp Verde
March to the beat of a different drum and learn about Arizona's military history with flag ceremonies, living history presentations, cavalry drills, and a vintage baseball game.
(928) 567-3275; www.azstateparks.com

NOVEMBER
Polar Express
Williams
Take a journey to the "North Pole" on this special evening train ride held through Dec. The magical adventure takes its cue from the classic children's book *The Polar Express* by Chris Van

continued

Allsburg and includes hot chocolate, cookies, caroling, storytelling, and a visit from Santa Claus.
(800) THE-TRAIN; www.thetrain.com

Red Rock Fantasy of Lights
Sedona
Holiday lights, themed displays, and holiday music through the first week of Jan.
(928) 282-1777 or (800) 521-3131; www.redrockfantasy.com

DECEMBER
Festival of Lights Parade
Page
Check out the boats all dressed up for the holiday at Wahweap marina and

enjoy the parade of lights through Page after the sun goes down.
(928) 645-2741; www.pagechamber .com

Parade of Lights
Williams
Carolers, luminaries, fine-arts show, shopping, and hot chocolate.
(928) 635-4061; www.williamschamber .com

Tuweep on some maps), about 60 miles from Colorado City off AZ 389 down a lengthy stretch of graded (unpaved) road. The primary access point, also known as the Sunshine Route, is on BLM Road 109, which leaves the highway about 7 miles west of Fredonia. The Clayhole Route travels along BLM Road 5, which leaves the highway at Colorado City. Allow two to three hours to travel to Toroweap and be aware that the routes may be impassable when wet. The point juts out over the Colorado River, which lies about 3,000 feet below. Because it's closer to the river than many areas of the Grand Canyon are, you get both a spectacular view and a real sense of the power of the Colorado. There is no charge for day use or the nine primitive campsites at the rim. At Toroweap, the Lava Falls Route drops 2,500 feet down a steep 1.5-mile trail to the Colorado River. Be aware that the trail is poorly marked and is exposed to the sun, making it one of the most strenuous trails into the canyon. A lot of visitors either don't know about Toroweap Point or decide that they'd rather see the Colorado from the South Rim of the Grand Canyon, so chances are you can spend as long as you like at Toroweap and not get elbowed aside by other visitors.

A hop and skip east is ***Pipe Spring National Monument*** (928-643-7105; www.nps.gov/pisp) on AZ 389, where an original Mormon fort (constructed of brick and wood) sits surrounded by high-desert vegetation and trees fed by underground springs. The name Pipe Spring comes from a locally famous feat of marksmanship executed by settler William Hamblin, who shot the bottom off a tobacco pipe. During the summer months there are costumed re-creations of pioneer life, but year-round you can feed the ducks in the duck pond and enjoy the serenity of this remote area. You will also learn about the little-known Paiute Indians at the Pipe Spring National Monument–Kaibab Band of Paiute Indians Visitor Center and Museum. Admission is $5 for ages fifteen and older and is good for seven days. Farther east off AZ 389 is **Steamboat Mountain,** a natural outcropping of red stone that perfectly resembles its name. Though there are no picnic areas around the rock, weather permitting, it makes a nice 2-mile hike.

The quaint community of **Fredonia** (928-643-7241), also within spitting distance of the Utah border, was founded more than one hundred years ago by Mormon settlers. Some folks say the town's name is a combination of "free" and the Spanish word *doña,* meaning "lady." Accounts collected by the Daughters of the Pioneers claim that Mormons residing in Kanab would send their extra wives over the state line into the Arizona border town in an attempt to evade U.S. marshals cracking down on polygamy.

officialarizona

State gem: Turquoise

State fossil: Petrified wood

State mammal: Ringtail

State reptile: Arizona ridge-nosed rattlesnake

State fish: Apache trout

State amphibian: Arizona tree frog

State butterfly: Two-tailed swallowtail

State song: The "Arizona March Song"

State colors: Blue and old gold

State tree: Paloverde

State bird: Cactus wren

State flower: Saguaro cactus blossom

State motto: *Ditat Deus* (God Enriches)

Official state neckwear (yes, there really is one): Bola tie

Arizona's largest newspaper: *The Arizona Republic,* Phoenix

Two newspapers in Tucson: *The Arizona Daily Star* (morning) and the *Tucson Citizen* (afternoon)

It's really the natural beauty of this area and evidence of ancient Anasazi cultures that draw visitors. Less than a two-hour drive from the city limits are Zion National Park and Bryce Canyon National Park (both in Utah), as well as Lake Powell and the North Rim of Grand Canyon. There are a multitude of solitary trails for hiking in the 68,340-acre **Kanab Creek Wilderness Area** and the 40,610-acre **Saddle Mountain Wilderness Area,** both of which are south of Fredonia and are managed by the North Kaibab Ranger District (928-

643-7295; www.fs.fed.us/r3/kai). Information on the trails and wilderness area conditions can also be found at the Jacob Lake Visitor Center (928-643-8167) at the juncture of US 89 and AZ 67 in Jacob Lake.

Taking US 89A southeast from Fredonia leads you over the Kaibab Plateau to the *Vermillion Cliffs,* which John Wesley Powell described as "a long bank of purple cliffs plowed from the horizon high into the heavens." There are several pullouts and one scenic overlook so you can stop and take pictures of these bright-red walls of rock. At the base of the cliffs are some easy hiking trails. One difficult and unmaintained trail—known as Sandhill Crack—actually goes up the cliff.

Just south of the cliffs is a marked, gravel road that leads to *House Rock Ranch,* a state-managed ranch where buffalo roam free. This road is passable most times of the year in an ordinary vehicle, although it's a bit bumpy in places and has been known to get washed out. Call the North Kaibab Ranger District (928-643-7395; www.fs.fed.us/r3/kai) for information on road conditions. The ranch, founded in the 1920s as part of a buffalo-raising venture that failed, is now operated by the Arizona Game and Fish Department. There are also antelope, deer, and bighorn sheep in the House Rock Valley area, though they can all be rather elusive. The best wildlife-watching advice from locals is to drive south of the ranch on the 26-mile road until you come to the end. Then get out and walk around a bit.

Continuing east on US 89A past the Vermillion Cliffs will take you to *Marble Canyon.* In 1995 the state built a new bridge for car traffic over the Colorado River at Marble Canyon while retaining the older Navajo bridge, which is about 200 feet away from the new one, as a pedestrian crossing. This gives you the opportunity to actually walk out and stand nearly 500 feet over the river that carved the Grand Canyon.

There are several lodges near Marble Canyon, including the *Marble Canyon Lodge* (928-355-2225 or 800-726-1789) and the *Cliff Dwellers Lodge* (928-355-2228 or 800-962-9755; www.cliffdwellerslodge.com). Marble Canyon Lodge is a sixty-room facility that has a restaurant that's open from 6 a.m. to 9 p.m., a convenience store, a small trading post, a gas station, a post office, and a coin-operated laundry. The rate for double occupancy ranges from $54 to $134 depending on the season. The Cliff Dwellers Lodge has twenty-two rooms, a small convenience store, a gas station, a fly-fishing guide service and fly-fishing shop, and a restaurant that's open from morning through the evening hours. The rate for double occupancy is $80 to $95.

Make sure to bring your rod and reel. This stretch of ice-cold, crystal-clear water at Lees Ferry below Glen Canyon Dam provides arguably the best trout fishing in the Southwest.

Grand Canyon National Park: North Rim

Named a national park by President Woodrow Wilson in 1919, **Grand Canyon National Park** (928-638-7888; www.nps.gov/grca) remains the crown jewel of Arizona's tourism offerings. Drawing more than 4.4 million visitors a year, this natural wonder is a jaw-dropper no matter how many times you peer over its edge. Each time of day and each season brings a distinct palette of hues to the canyon, providing its own unique panorama. A word of caution though: The only thing separating the gazers from the gorge is a low stone wall. Unfortunately, it's not at all unusual for a hapless tourist to discover the laws of gravity a little too late. Enjoy the view, but respect the potential danger that exists—particularly for the careless.

Though many tourists choose to limit their exploration of the canyon to the views from the South Rim, there is another, very different side to this spectacular locale. The **North Rim** of the canyon is about 1,200 feet higher than the South Rim, and during the winter it gets snowed in (the only access road, AZ 67, is closed every year from mid-Oct to mid-May). It doesn't have as many amenities as the South Rim has, and it isn't as accessible. Admission to the park is $25 and is good for seven days at both the North and South Rims.

Located on the Kaibab Plateau, the North Rim is significantly lusher than the South Rim. It also has spectacular views without the crowds found on the more popular South Rim. Only 10 percent of the total number of visitors to the canyon travel to the North Rim, so solitude is easy to find. If you want to stay in the park on the North Rim, your only choice is the **Grand Canyon Lodge** (928-638-2611 or 877-386-4383 from May through Oct and 928-645-6865 from Nov through Apr; www.grandcanyonforever.com) or at the **North Rim Campground** (877-444-6777; www.recreation.gov). Fortunately, the Grand Canyon Lodge is a nice place to stay, and the main building (constructed of native pine logs and limestone slabs) is built right on the edge of the North Rim not far from **Bright Angel Point.** The view out the windows of the dining room of this 1937 National Historic Landmark is unparalleled. In addition to the dining

grandcanyon funfacts

Age: 2 billion years old

Depth: South Rim inner canyon—4,500 feet; North Rim inner canyon—5,700 feet

Width: 10 miles average

Length: 277 miles

Area: 1,904 square miles

Elevation: North Rim—8,200 feet; South Rim—7,000 feet

Visitors: more than 4.4 million per year

room (which serves traditional western fare such as prime rib, steaks, and seafood, with some vegetarian items thrown in), the main lodge also has a lobby, sunroom, gift shop, saloon, and cafeteria. The National Park Service offers evening programs on different canyon topics in the lodge's old ballroom.

Accommodations range from historical log cabins to basic motel rooms, which once served as lodgings for on-site personnel. Two miles down the road, near the North Rim campground, you will find a gas station, a general store, and a coin-operated laundry.

After checking in, take the 23-mile paved road to **Cape Royal.** Nearly 3 miles along Cape Royal Road, a spur to the left leads to **Point Imperial** (which, at an elevation of 8,803 feet, is the highest lookout on either rim). This popular viewpoint offers a grand view of the Vermillion Cliffs to the north, the Painted Desert to the east, the Little Colorado River Canyon to the southeast, and Navajo Mountain to the northeast. Picnic tables at the viewpoint make this a convenient place to stop for a picnic lunch. It is also the only viewpoint, other than Cape Royal, that has bathroom facilities. The most remote of the viewpoints on Cape Royal Road is **Cape Final,** which can only be accessed by a 2-mile hike along an old jeep trail through a ponderosa pine forest. The viewpoint features panoramic views of the northern canyon, the Palisades of the Desert, and the impressive spectacle of Juno Temple. Additional lookouts along the rest of the drive offer views of such legendary landmarks as Freya Castle, Vishnu Temple, and Wotan's Throne.

While the viewpoints along Cape Royal Road are definitely worth visiting, those seeking even more solitude should head out to **Point Sublime.** The 17-mile dirt road winds through gorgeous high country and dead-ends at what is arguably the most scenic viewpoint on the either rim. The road is only intended for use by high-clearance vehicles and will take at least two hours to travel one way. Camping is allowed at this solitary viewpoint as long as you procure a permit from the Backcountry Office (928-638-7875; Mon through Fri between 1 and 5 p.m.) ahead of time.

There are several trails leading through the forest to remote viewpoints accessible only by foot. The best of the bunch is the 9.8-mile round-trip **Widforss Trail.** The trailhead is accessed across from the North Kaibab Trail parking lot and leads to Widforss Point at 7,900 feet, where you will be able to see five of the canyon's temples—Zoroaster, Brahma, Deva, Buddha, and Manu. Although there are several hiking trails in the vicinity, the **North Kaibab Trail** is the only trail on the North Rim leading into the canyon. The long, steep path descends 5,840 feet over 14.5 miles to the Colorado River and Phantom Ranch. Park rangers suggest Roaring Springs (5,020 feet) as the turnaround point for day hikers. For a fee, a shuttle takes hikers to the North Kaibab trailhead twice daily from Grand Canyon Lodge.

If you'd rather have someone else do all the hard work, hitch a ride with **Canyon Trail Rides** (435-679-8665; www.canyonrides.com). This outfitter, with an information desk in the Grand Canyon Lodge, offers everything from one-hour rides on rim trails to full-day trips down the North Kaibab Trail to Roaring Springs.

If you're up for an adventure, legend has it that John Doyle Lee, the Mormon pioneer who is famous for **Lees Ferry** and infamous for his participation in the murder of more than 120 travelers at Mountain Meadows, supposedly found a gold mine somewhere on the North Rim. In the more than a century since Lee's death, numerous searchers have combed the canyon, starting at **Soap Creek** just south of Lees Ferry, and heading west as far as **Vulcan's Throne.** If Lee's contemporaries are to be believed, the gold is still out there. *Note:* Mining isn't allowed in Grand Canyon National Park, so if you do stumble across the treasure you'll have to settle for being famous but not rich!

Die-hard adventurers can find even more solitude by hiking, snowshoeing, or cross-country skiing to the North Rim after AZ 67 closes at Jacob Lake, which is usually in mid-October or early November after the first heavy snows. Winter visitors must obtain a backcountry permit for overnight use during the winter season (mid-Oct through mid-May).

Keep in mind that the Grand Canyon National Park's North Rim is surrounded by **Kaibab National Forest** (928-643-7395; www.fs.fed.us/r3/kai). The North District Ranger Office can supply you with maps of hiking trails, scenic drives, and camping sites outside the park boundaries. Cyclists in particular might be glad to learn the route of the Rainbow Rim Trail, an 18-mile, one-way trail that begins at Parissawampitts Point at the end of FR 214 and ends at Timp Point on FR 271. Cycling within park boundaries is limited to the Bridle Trail, making this alternative ride through a ponderosa pine forest and high mountain meadows a real treat. Best of all, the trail stops at three other Grand Canyon viewpoints—Fence, Locust, and North Timp. The trail is also open to hikers.

Although the North Rim of the Grand Canyon is fairly remote, true solitude seekers should head east to the **Grand Canyon-Parashant National Monument.** In January 2000, President Bill Clinton set aside more than one million acres of land along the northern edge of the Grand Canyon in the northwest corner of Arizona. The isolated area is seldom visited and is comanaged by the National Park Service and the U.S. Bureau of Land Management. There are no facilities at the monument. Camping is primitive and hikers should expect wilderness hiking conditions. For maps and information on the national monument, check with the Interagency Information Center (435-688-3246 or 435-688-3200; www.nps.gov/para) at 345 E. Riverside Dr. in St. George, Utah. You can also gather informational materials at the Pipe Springs National Monument Visitor Center on AZ 389.

Lake Powell to Sunset Crater

It may be difficult to imagine Arizona as an aquatic play park (particularly because the state is more famous for its giant cacti and desert sunsets), but the truth is that this state has a plethora of lakes and rivers that are perfect for any activity from relaxing float trips to shooting the rapids.

On the border with Utah sits **Lake Powell,** in the **Glen Canyon National Recreation Area**. Lake Powell began to flow into life in 1963 with the closing of the gates on **Glen Canyon Dam** on the Colorado River. Nine years later, 186 river miles had filled about one hundred canyons, creating a playground that includes 1,960 miles of shoreline and boating opportunities galore. Admission is $15 per vehicle for seven days.

From the Arizona side, Lake Powell can be reached by driving on US 89 to Page, near the southern tip of the lake or at Antelope Point off AZ 98.

The Glen Canyon Dam and the **Carl Hayden Visitors Center** (928-608-6404; www.nps.gov/glca) are located off US 89 about 2 miles north of Page. These attractions provide travelers with the opportunity to learn some of the area's history (even prehistory—dinosaur footprints, taken from the canyon, are on display), as well as tour the massive dam and witness its energy-producing prowess. The second-highest dam in the United States, Glen Canyon Dam has a maximum power output of 1,320 megawatts, enough power for a city of more than one million inhabitants. The power is sold to independent companies that utilize it in southern Arizona, Las Vegas, and as far away as Los Angeles.

Less than 5 miles northwest on US 89 is the **Wahweap Lodge and Marina** (928-645-2433 or 800-528-6154; www.lakepowell.com). The marina rents houseboats and other watercraft, and the lodge provides comfortable accommodations for travelers. Its dining room features an eclectic blend of American dishes and occasionally stages live entertainment. Located off AZ 98, the newer **Antelope Point Marina** (928-645-5900 or 800-255-5561; www .antelopepointlakepowell.com) also rents houseboats and personal watercraft. If you want to experience a houseboat for just a night or two, the marina rents them as hotel rooms. Luggage service, a floating restaurant and general store, and the popular wakeboard winch make Antelope Point Marina a welcome addition to Lake Powell's offerings.

One of the most popular ways to enjoy the lake is to rent a houseboat and live on the water for a week or a weekend. These floating motel rooms range from 44 to 75 feet and can sleep as many as twelve passengers. Necessities and amenities such as refrigerators, range-ovens, toilets, showers, and gas grills are available to help you have a great vacation. Some of the more deluxe rigs even offer options like TVs and VCRs, swim slides, hot tubs, and multi-speaker CD players.

> ## trivia
>
> Lake Powell, along the northern Arizona–Utah border, has more miles of shoreline than the entire Pacific coast of the United States.

You can rent houseboats at Wahweap, Antelope Point, and three other marinas that form an elliptical ring around Lake Powell. For reservations and information on Wahweap Lodge and Marina, Hall's Crossing Marina, Bullfrog Resort and Marina, or Hite Marina contact **Lake Powell Resorts & Marinas** (800-528-6154; www.lakepowell.com). The latter three marinas are located on the Utah side of the border. Prices range from $2,245 for three days on a 44-foot boat during the budget season (wintertime) to $12,120 for seven days in the summer season on the spiffy 75-foot Odyssey Class boat that sports a top deck with flying-bridge controls. For reservations at Antelope Point Marina, contact Forever Resorts (800-255-5561; www.antelopepointlakepowell.com). Prices range from $2,910 for three days on a 59-foot Deluxe XT houseboat during off-season to $14,798 for seven days on a 75-foot Silver XTreme during the busy summer months.

If you want to check out the other side of the dam and would prefer not to do your own piloting, guides from **Wilderness River Adventures** (800-528-6154; www.riveradventures.com) can take you from Lake Powell on a 15-mile float trip aboard a large raft. The journey starts at the base of the Glen Canyon Dam and makes a stop where you can get a close-up view of Anasazi petroglyphs; *Anasazi* (Ah–nah–*sah*–zee) is a Navajo word that translates as "ancient ones" and relates to a northern Arizona Indian tribe that vanished centuries ago. The float trip concludes at **Lees Ferry,** where Mormon pioneers used to cross the Colorado River on their way back to Utah to get married. Still standing near the ferry crossing are cabins erected by settlers. There are also picnic areas and restrooms.

The beauty of the Glen Canyon area is astounding: clear mountain vistas of sand-sculpted and water-worked stones, high-desert vegetation, and sunsets of breathtaking dimensions. Over the years the region's majesty has attracted many film companies. Notable movies filmed here include *Planet of the Apes, Maverick* and Hong Kong director John Woo's *Broken Arrow.*

One of Glen Canyon's most famous examples of nature's creative power is *Rainbow Bridge,* which the Navajos call *Nááts'íílid Na'nízhoozhí*—meaning "rainbow extends across"—and consider sacred. At 290 feet, it's the world's tallest stone arch. Some of the lake excursion packages offered by the marinas include visits to this marvel, which can only be reached on foot or horseback. Another natural landmark not to be missed is *Antelope Canyon.* There are several tour operators (no one can enter the canyon without a guide due to potential flash flooding), but the best of the bunch is *Antelope Canyon Tours* (928-645-9102 or 866-645-9102; www.antelopecanyon.com). Seven days a week, Carolene Ekis and her Navajo guides take visitors on a stunning tour of one of the most gorgeous sandstone slot canyons in the country. Photographers get special attention and workshop tips for capturing the sweeping sandstone walls in the Photographer's Tour.

South on US 89 you'll cross the Little Colorado River and soon arrive at the *Wupatki National Monument* (928-679-2365; www.nps.gov/wupa) near the San Francisco peaks. The monument, about 40 miles north of Flagstaff, is composed of more than 800 ruins of structures built by the ancient Sinagua Indians, who moved into the area around A.D. 1066. The ruins include a kind of handball court and a warm-air "blowhole" that releases a constant stream from deep underground. Seasonal mini-lectures are offered when visitor numbers are high. During the summer, two-hour ranger-led discovery hikes are scheduled as well.

Just down the road from Wupatki is *Sunset Crater Volcano National Monument* (928-526-0502; www.nps.gov/sucr). Sunset Crater, named by Grand Canyon explorer John Wesley Powell for its orange-colored rim, erupted 900 years ago, leaving behind a 1,000-foot-high cone and a bizarre landscape of lava flow and ice caves. Several easy-to-follow hiking trails take visitors around the lava flow, and picnic areas are not too far down the road. Admission is $5 per person, good for seven days at both Wupatki and Sunset Crater National Monuments.To see a volcanic cinder cone and lava flow off the beaten path, head to the 10,141-acre *Strawberry Crater Wilderness.* Explore ancient Indian ruins or take a hike up the established trail on the north side of Strawberry Crater. Views of the San Francisco Peaks, Sunset Crater, and the Painted Desert add to the dramatic views. The Strawberry Crater Wilderness is located 20 miles north of Flagstaff with access on Sunset Crater/ Wupatki Road (FR 545). This 36-mile scenic drive is called the *Volcanoes and Ruins Loop* and exits at US 89. For more information contact the Peaks Ranger Station (928-526-0866; www.fs.fed.us/r3/coconino) at 5075 N. US 89 in Flagstaff.

Flagstaff Area

Fewer than twenty minutes south of US 89 is the alpine community of **Flagstaff,** set at the base of one of Arizona's most stellar mountain ranges. There are two competing theories on the origin of the town's unusual name. One says that more than 125 years ago, a flagpole made from a pine tree was placed near the site to mark the location of an underground spring so that thirsty travelers could find it. Historians generally agree that it was so named following a flag-raising ceremony marking the nation's centennial. Settlers chose a tall pine, trimmed its branches, and attached a flag to the top.

Regardless of how it got its name, the city of 64,000 is now a top getaway destination. The town is located in Coconino County, the second largest county in the United States. Over the years "Flag" (as it's known to Arizonans) has been a logging and ranching community and once was an important stop on the Atlantic & Pacific Railroad. Check out the historic, redbrick Santa Fe train depot on Historic Route 66 in the middle of town, where the **Flagstaff Visitors Center** (928-774-9541 or 800-379-0065; www.flagstaffarizona.org) provides a great starting point for exploration in the area. It is open daily from 8 a.m. to 5 p.m.

In Arizona, Flagstaff is famous for three reasons. It is the home of **Northern Arizona University** (NAU; 928-523-9011; www.nau.edu), which is known for its forestry program; the Babbitt family, lumber barons who moved into the area in the 1880s; and the Lowell Observatory, which is the site of a number of major heavenly findings.

Flagstaff is a city with a lot of charm. Because of the elevation, the forests around here are lush with ponderosa pine (the largest spread of ponderosa pine in the world, in fact, sprouts in this area), aspen, and brilliantly colored wildflowers.

trivia

Flagstaff garnered the honor as the world's first "International Dark-Sky City" by the International Dark-Sky Association.

Surrounded by gorgeous scenery, including the frequently snowcapped 12,000-foot San Francisco Peaks, it has preserved many of its historic sites and much of its architecture and thus retains a small-town feel. Still, it has modern amenities that make it comfortable and convenient for residents and visitors alike. The main street, Milton Road, is lined with restaurants (both national chains and local mom-and-pop places), motels, hotels, and shopping centers; it also passes right by NAU.

Milton Road winds north through town and comes to an abrupt split where you can take a hard left and continue up Mars Hill to the observatory, veer right onto the former Santa Fe Avenue, now named Historic Route 66 (which becomes US 89, heading back toward Sunset Crater), then make a left onto US 180, which heads toward the **Pioneer Museum** (928-774-6272; www .arizonahistoricalsociety.org); open Mon through Sat from 9 a.m. to 5 p.m. Admission is $3 for adults and $2 for children ages twelve to eighteen, and the **Museum of Northern Arizona** (928-774-5213; www.musnaz.org), which is open daily from 9 a.m. to 5 p.m. Admission is $7 for adults and $4 for children ages seven to seventeen. The Pioneer Museum, which is run by the Arizona Historical Society and located in the former 1908 Coconino County Hospital, has an impressive collection of photographs from Flagstaff's early days. This collection includes early twentieth-century photos and equipment from the Kolb brothers, who became famous for capturing the splendor of the Grand Canyon. Also located on the grounds are antique farming machines, an early motorized fire engine, and an original 1880s cabin.

Just up the road, the **Museum of Northern Arizona** first opened in 1928. The exhibits at the museum encompass the biology, geology, anthropology, and fine arts of both northern Arizona and the Four Corners region. The museum has displays ranging from a life-size statue of a Dilophosaurus (a carnivorous dinosaur whose remains are found only in this region), an anthropology exhibit that traces the region's history back 12,000 years, and fine arts made by Zuni, Hopi, and Navajo Indians.

From the Museum of Northern Arizona you can take **Schultz Pass Road**—a scenic drive through the national forest along FR 420. The 26-mile drive offers a relaxing trip with views of the San Francisco Peaks, ponderosa pine forests, and wildlife-watching opportunities. The gravel road is located 2 miles north of Flagstaff off US 180 and is open from April through November.

US 180 also takes you up to the **Arizona Snowbowl** (928-779-1951; www .arizonasnowbowl.com), a prime skiing spot as well as a location for snowboarding and other cold-weather sports. The Snowbowl features thirty-two runs (ranging from dinky bunny hills to some that challenge very experienced skiers). Ski rentals and repairs are available, and you can sign up for beginner or intermediate lessons (also a children's ski school, beginning at age four, runs throughout the season). Lift tickets cost $49 for an all-day pass (from 9 a.m. to 4 p.m.) or $41 (noon to 4 p.m.) on weekends. There are two places where you can park yourself at the end of a long day of schussing—**Hart Prairie Lodge** and **Agassiz Lodge,** both of which offer ski and snowboard rentals, restaurants, and retail shops.

For a more remote high-altitude experience, head to the 18,960-acre **Kachina Peaks Wilderness** encompassing the upper reaches of the San Francisco Peaks, including Humphreys Peak, which is Arizona's highest point at 12,643 feet. Located just 6 miles north of Flagstaff, the wilderness area is accessed by Snowbowl Road, FR 418, and FR 420. To access the lower slopes, take FR 418 and FR 420 from US 89. FR 552 leads to Lockett Meadow and the Inner Basin of this dormant volcano. A multitude of trails offer great mountain scenery and wonderful opportunities for wildlife watching. For more information contact the Peaks Ranger Station (928-526-0866; www.fs.fed.us/r3/coconino) at 5075 N. US 89 in Flagstaff.

Famous Arizonans

Past and present residents

Rex Allen (actor)
Willcox

Charles Barkley (basketball star)
Paradise Valley

Glen Campbell (singer)
Paradise Valley

Lynda Carter (actor)
Phoenix

Alice Cooper (rock star)
Paradise Valley

Clive Cussler (best-selling author)
Paradise Valley

Ted Danson (actor)
Flagstaff

Hugh Downs (news anchor)
Carefree

Joe Garagiola (baseball Hall of Famer/broadcaster)
Paradise Valley

Andy Granatelli (race car driver)
Paradise Valley

Paul Harvey (radio personality)
Carefree

Charles Mingus (jazz musician)
Nogales

Stevie Nicks (singer)
Phoenix

Leslie Nielsen (actor)
Paradise Valley

Nick Nolte (actor)
Phoenix

Marty Robbins (country-western singer)
Glendale

Linda Ronstadt (singer)
Tucson

David Spade (comedian)
Scottsdale

Steven Spielberg (director)
Scottsdale

Tanya Tucker (country singer)
Willcox

Dick Van Dyke (actor)
Cave Creek

Sean Young (actress)
Sedona

The **Lowell Observatory,** located at the top of Mars Hill, was built by astronomer Percival Lowell, a Mars buff who published a book about that planet's canals. It seems silly now, but Lowell erroneously believed there was life on the Angry Red Planet. He was right on the mark, however, when he predicted that a ninth planet—Planet X—would be discovered. In 1930, fourteen years after Lowell's death, astronomy assistant Clyde Tombaugh found the heavenly body, now known as Pluto, while studying photographic plates. Visitors to the observatory can hear the full story at the visitor center (928-774-3358; www.lowell.edu). The observatory is open daily from 9 a.m. to 5 p.m. Mar to Oct, and from noon to 5 p.m. Nov to Feb, with evening programs starting at 5:30. Evening programs include nighttime tours and celestial viewing several nights per week. Seasonal "Night Sky" programs are offered Wed, Fri, and Sat evenings. Admission is $6 for adults and $3 for children ages five to seventeen, with separate admission charges for day and evening programs.

Flagstaff hosts a popular **Winterfest,** voted by the *Events Business News* as one of the "Top 100 Events in North America." Winterfest activities range from wine-tasting events to jazz concerts to sled-dog races. Locations for the events vary, as do costs (some are free, others have a charge). Call the Flagstaff Visitors Center (800-379-0065; www.flagstaffarizona.org) for more information on Winterfest or other annual events.

In the summer Flagstaff's moderate temperature (the average high is eighty degrees) draws many Arizonans who want to escape the heat that builds up in the southeastern and central parts of the state. The surrounding forest area offers premier hiking and camping opportunities. The city even has an urban trails system that allows visitors and residents to access forest areas, canyons, and national monuments. The Flagstaff Visitors Center has specific maps of these trails, which include treks to the summit of Mount Humphrey (the tallest mountain in Arizona) and to many scenic aspen groves and alpine meadows in the Coconino National Forest.

Nature buffs will especially enjoy exploring the wide-open spaces at the **Hart Prairie Preserve** (928-774-8892; www.nature.org). Located 14 miles north of Flagstaff, at 2601 N. Fort Valley Rd., this 245-acre preserve protects such endangered plants as the delicate bloomer stock and the rare Bebb's willow trees. Guided ninety-minute nature walks, held during the summer and fall, will introduce you to the plants and wildlife thriving in the preserve's open mountain meadows.

Nearby, a mile-long lava tube cave offers an opportunity to explore a volcanic vent that was created from a lava flow more than 700,000 years ago. Notice the stone icicles hanging from the ceiling and the ripples in the rock from the path of the molten lava. The temperature stays cool year-round, so be sure to wear warm clothes and sturdy shoes. Also, bring several light sources to explore the mile-long **Lava River Cave.** The cave is located about 14 miles north of Flagstaff. Take US 180 to FR 245 at milepost 230. Turn west and drive 3 miles to FR 171. Turn south and drive 1 mile to where FR 171B ends at Lava River Cave. For more information contact the Peaks Ranger Station (928-526-0866; www.fs.fed.us/r3/coconino) at 5075 N. US 89 in Flagstaff.

All year round, Flagstaff offers the opportunity to hang out in great, funky little restaurants. The **Beaver Street Brewery** (928-779-0079; www.beaver streetbrewery.com) at 11 S. Beaver St., for example, is an actual microbrewery with an eclectic menu that includes everything from salads and sandwiches to wood-fired gourmet pizzas. Killer desserts include a chocolate bread pudding and a huge fruit cobbler.

Downtown, in the older section of Flagstaff (east of Mount Humphrey and north and south of the visitors center), shops, cafes, music venues, and very interesting old churches (including a Gothic cathedral that has gargoyles on its parapets—a most unusual sight in Arizona!) draw visitors year-round. The downtown shops around **Heritage Square** sell everything from outdoor gear to books to local arts and crafts. Along Historic Route 66 is an amazing collection of motels built during the prime years of the "Mother Road." Some look as if they could use a little attention; others are just as shiny as the day they went up.

In the midst of these nostalgic accommodations sits **The Museum Club,** aka "the Zoo" (928-526-9434; www.museumclub.com), at 3404 Historic Route 66. A historic honky-tonk owned by Shanyn and Joe Langes, the huge log-cabin building was built in 1931 by taxidermist Dean Eldredge, who used the structure to display his collection of trophy animals, antique firearms, and other bits of Americana. Five years later the museum was purchased by Doc Williams, a saddle maker who turned the place into a nightclub. Eventually Don Scott, a former member of Bob Wills and the Texas Playboys, bought the club. For years it was the place to play for up-and-coming country talent. Stars like Willie Nelson, Waylon Jennings, and Wanda "Let's Have a Party!" Jackson shook the rafters.

Scott and his wife, Thorna, used to live in an upstairs apartment at the club, and some claim their spirits still haunt the honky-tonk (Don committed suicide in front of the downstairs fireplace, and Thorna died as a result of a fall down the stairs).

In 1978, Martin and Stacie Zanzucchi purchased The Museum Club, which by that time was desperately in need of repairs, and set about the time-consuming and meticulous task of restoring it to its original grandeur. They succeeded so well that the club made *Car and Driver* and *Country America* magazines' lists of the top ten roadhouses in the nation. The Zanzucchis were given the Governor's Award for Historic Preservation; The Museum Club is listed on the National Register of Historic Places. In 2005, the Langeses became the new "Zookeepers" of the club. Today, the famous roadhouse carries on its hip-shaking tradition as the "Best Place to Dance" in town.

Visitors to The Museum Club can study the display of historic photos, buy Historic Route 66 and Museum Club memorabilia (everything from a magnet to an embroidered denim jacket), and listen to live entertainment Tues through Sun nights. The club is open seven days a week. As part of Operation Safe *Rides,* The Museum Club offers free taxis from the club on Fri and Sat nights.

Numerous motels, ski lodges, and bed-and-breakfast inns provide accom-modations in and around Flagstaff. Just about every moderately priced national chain has a presence in Flagstaff, but the **Inn at 410** (800-774-2008; www .inn410.com) at 410 N. Leroux St. is one of the best lodging choices in town. Close to the visitor center, this 1907 Craftsman-style home has six guest suites and three guest rooms. Most of the suites have fireplaces and some offer Jacuzzi tubs. Locals claim that the 410 is the town's top bed-and-breakfast, a fact that was supported by the *Arizona Republic* in Phoenix, which lauded it as "the best bed-and-breakfast in northern Arizona." It has also been praised as one of Arizona's "Best Weekend Adventures" by *Phoenix Magazine.* Rates range from $170 to $300 per night and include a homemade breakfast in the dining room.

For another historic Craftsman-style home, stop by the **Riordan Mansion State Historic Park** (928-779-4395; www.azstateparks.com) at 409 Riordan Rd. Tucked away behind the Target store on Milton Road, this massive, mul-tistory log cabin was built in 1904 for Timothy and Michael Riordan, owners of the Arizona Lumber & Timber Company. The building's architect was none other than Charles Whittlesley, designer of the El Tovar Hotel at the South Rim of the Grand Canyon as well as Old Faithful Lodge at Yellowstone. State Park rangers give guided tours of the mansion. Tours are scheduled every hour on the hour starting at 9 a.m., and there are also self-guided tours of the grounds. The best time to visit this state park is during December when the mansion is decked out in all of its Victorian holiday finery. Tour prices are $6 for adults and $2.50 for children ages seven to thirteen. The last tour is at 4 p.m. Reser-vations are recommended.

Before leaving the Flagstaff area, make sure to stop by **Walnut Canyon National Monument,** which comprises more than 300 rooms built into lime-stone cliffs as part of a prehistoric Sinaguan pueblo. The visitor center (928-526-3367; www.nps.gov/waca) has displays of pottery and artifacts recovered from the area. The monument can be reached by traveling east on I-40 about 7 miles. Admission is $5 for adults and is good for seven days.

South of Flagstaff, Plateau Country extends from the San Francisco Peaks to the rolling highlands, highlighted with scattered prairies and lakes including *Mormon Lake.* Recreational activities include boating, fishing, camping, wildlife watching, hiking, and cross-country skiing. *Plateau Lakes Scenic Drive,* open April through October, follows Forest Highway 3 (Lake Mary Road) about 33 miles to FR 213. Turn west and drive 15 miles on FR 213 to I-17. For more information contact the Peaks Ranger Station (928-526-0866; www.fs.fed. us/r3/coconino) at 5075 N. US 89 in Flagstaff.

During the winter months, the *Mormon Lake Ski Touring Center* offers groomed cross-country skiing trails along the lower slopes of Mormon Mountain. To reach the Mormon Lake Ski Touring Center, drive south from Flagstaff 20 miles on Forest Highway 3 (Lake Mary Road) to the FR 90 intersection. Turn west on FR 90 and drive 8 miles to the Mormon Lake Village. The nearby *Mormon Lake Lodge* (928/354-2227; www.mormonlakelodge.com) has a restaurant, ski rentals, and ski school. For a ski report call the Ski Center at (928) 354-2240.

Many visitors to Flagstaff make Grand Canyon's South Rim their next stop. An excellent way to see this natural wonder is to take I-40 west and drive about 30 miles to the town of *Williams* (928-635-4061 or 800-863-0546; www .williamschamber.com), which is named for William Sherley "Old Bill" Williams, a famous trapper and Arizona pioneer.

This tiny Main Street locale was the last Historic Route 66 town to be bypassed by the completion of I-40 in 1985, and with its old-fashioned street lamps and century-old brick storefronts, it offers visitors a trip back in time. For a bite to eat, drop by *Rod's Steakhouse* (928-635-2671; www.rods-steakhouse .com), a Historic Route 66 (known locally as Bill Williams Avenue) landmark with a steer-shaped sign on the roof. Rod's has steaks, prime rib, and seafood. For a blast to the past, travel a few more blocks west on Historic Route 66 to *Twisters* (928-635-0266). The 1950s soda fountain serves up hamburgers and hot dogs as well as good old-fashioned sundaes, floats, and phosphates. An adjoining gift shop adds to the experience with a wide selection of Historic Route 66 merchandise, classic Coca-Cola memorabilia, and fanciful items celebrating the careers of such celluloid characters as Betty Boop, James Dean, and Marilyn Monroe.

For outdoor adventure, head out of town and check out one of the four nearby lakes—Dogtown, White Horse, Cataract, and *Kaibab Lakes.* The small lakes have some fine fishing and make a great backdrop for camping, hiking, and wildlife watching in Kaibab National Forest. For more information stop by the Williams Ranger District (928-635-8200; www.fs.fed.us/r3/kai) at 800 S. Sixth St.

If camping isn't your style, you can't go wrong with a stay at the *Sheridan House Inn* (928-635-9441 or 888-635-9345; www.grandcanyonbbinn.com) at 460 E. Sheridan Ave. This cozy inn is nestled among two acres of pines on a hillside overlooking town. The bed-and-breakfast offers nice-size bedrooms, a hot tub on the patio, and an entertainment room complete with a pool table and piano. Breakfast is always a grand affair and owners K.C. and Mary Seidner enjoy helping guests plan their Grand Canyon getaways. Rooms range from $150 to $195.

Williams is also the home of the *Grand Canyon Railway* (800-843-8724; www.thetrain.com). Initially built both for passengers and to serve area mines, the railway carried its first passengers to the Grand Canyon in 1901. Over time it transported U.S. presidents as well as other dignitaries and celebrities to see one of the world's most famous attractions.

Unfortunately the train couldn't compete with America's love affair with the automobile, and in 1968 it carried its last passengers. The defunct railroad was purchased in 1989 by Max Biegert, who restored not only the tracks, the engines, and the cars, but also the *Grand Canyon Railway Hotel* (same phone number as the railway), which now serves as the railway's depot as well as a museum and gift shop.

Using historic steam engines and coach cars, the train not only takes passengers through 65 miles of glorious Arizona territory (which is especially spectacular when it's wearing a snowy winter mantle), but it also takes them back in time. While the train chugs along, passengers sit in coach cars that are decorated in original early twentieth-century style. The end car, which has an observation platform, actually uses upholstered chairs and sofas. Entertainers, including a singing brakeman dressed in period attire, perform traditional and original music about life and love on the frontier. If you take this route to the canyon, be prepared for some excitement—it's not unusual for a "train robbery" to take place, staged by bandits on horseback.

Beverages and snacks are served during the trip, which begins in Williams at 9:30 a.m. (be at the depot between 8:30 and 9 a.m.) and arrives at the Grand Canyon's South Rim at 11:45 a.m. Passengers debark at the canyon's historic depot and can tour the area's numerous attractions before the train pulls out at 3:30 p.m. for the trek back to Williams. You will return by 5:45 p.m. There are four classes of service. Prices start at $70 for adults and $40 for children.

Besides being an easy and entertaining way to see the canyon, the train helps to cut down on pollution from the nearly 100,000 cars yearly that— without the railroad—would otherwise all be driven to the scenic wonder.

The railway donates a portion of the ticket price to the Grand Canyon Trust, a conservation organization.

The approximately three-hour layover at the canyon gives you plenty of time to see El Tovar Hotel, Lookout Studio, Bright Angel Lodge, Hopi House, and the other attractions in the immediate area. If you wish to stay longer— especially if you want to hike or take a mule ride in the canyon—you can book a return at a different date and stay at one of the lodges within the park.

Grand Canyon National Park: South Rim

Four million of the 4.4 million visitors heading to **Grand Canyon National Park** (928-638-7888; www.nps.gov/grca) make the **South Rim** their final destination, and most of these people show up during the busy spring and summer season. If nothing but the South Rim will fit your itinerary, try to plan your trip during the slower fall and winter months. Another option is to bypass the main entrance on AZ 64/US 180 from Williams or Flagstaff and enter the east entrance accessed on AZ 64 from Cameron—the home of the **Cameron Trading Post** (928-679-2231 or 800-338-7385; www.camerontradingpost .com), where you can shop for everything from kitschy souvenirs to Native American artifacts.

After entering the east entrance of the Grand Canyon, the 23-mile **Desert View Drive** passes eight overlooks before ending at the visitor center at Canyon View Information Plaza. Coming from the east entrance, the first stop is at the **Desert View and Watchtower.** Designed by Mary Jane Colter (who also was the architect for the Hopi House and Bright Angel Lodge on the South Rim), the Watchtower is a stone reproduction of a Hopi lookout post and is the highest viewpoint on the South Rim. Visitors can climb several flights of stairs to the top of the 70-foot watchtower, where you will find fabulous views of Painted Desert and the Vermilion Cliffs in the distance and an imposing stretch of the Colorado River far below. Other highlights along the Desert View Drive are the remains of an Ancestral Puebloan dwelling at the **Tusayan Ruin and Museum,** the lovely **Buggeln** picnic area, and the **Yavapai Observation Station** at Yavapai Point.

trivia

Explorer John Wesley Powell was a brave soul, venturing into such dangerous territory as the uncharted Colorado River and exploring untold canyons—yet he had only one arm.

The other rim drive at **Hermit Road,** originally built by the Santa Fe Company in 1912, is closed to private auto traffic from March through November and is accessed only by a free shuttle bus. If you go off-season, you will have private access to the historic roadway, which features nine overlooks along the 7-mile drive. Some of the best scenery can be seen at **The Abyss,** which reveals a 3,000-foot cliff to the Tonto Platform and a few isolated sandstone columns. Another favorite stop on Hermit Road is **Mohave Point,** where you can see some of the canyon's most magnificent stone spires and buttes, including the Tower of Set; the Tower of Ra; and Isis, Osiris, and Horus Temples. The road ends at Hermits Rest, the westernmost viewpoint on the South Rim and the trailhead for **Hermit Trail**—one of several trails on the South Rim leading into the inner canyon and the Colorado River below.

trivia

Summertime temperatures on the South Rim range from fifty to eighty degrees Fahrenheit; in the canyon on the Colorado River 5,000 feet below, they can climb higher than one hundred degrees Fahrenheit.

Unlike the North Rim, there are several lodging options available at the South Rim in Grand Canyon Village. **El Tovar** (928-638-2631 or 888-297-2757; www.grandcanyonlodges.com) is the hotel of choice here. This 1905 hotel, named for a Spanish explorer who never personally laid eyes on the canyon, has the elegant ambience of other grand hotels (like the Hotel Del Coronado, just across the bay from San Diego), yet it has an undeniable frontier simplicity and ruggedness that might make you remember the Scout lodges of your childhood. The lobby and common areas are open to sightseeing tourists, and the hotel's dining room serves southwestern cuisine, fresh seafood, and specialty desserts. The restaurant is often booked solid, so reservations are recommended. Another favorite is the **Bright Angel Lodge** (928-638-2631 or 888-297-2757; www.grandcanyonlodges.com), designed by famed architect Mary Jane Colter. The 1935 log-and-stone structure, which sits within a few yards of the canyon rim, offers both motel-style rooms or cabins. The **Bright Angel Dining Room** serves family-style meals all day whereas the **Arizona Room** serves dinner only.

ascenicjaunt

You can take a scenic horseback trail ride up to the East Rim from **Apache Stables** in Tusayan (928-638-2891; www.apachestables.com). The one- to two-hour ride takes you through Kaibab National Forest. One of the best times to make this trek is in the morning when the sun is rising over the canyon and the colors are deep and vibrant.

When you're ready to walk off your meal, check out **Lookout Studio,** which sells everything from fossil specimens (not from the park, which is protected) to books and videos about the area. At the rear of the studio, visitors can step out onto a balcony that offers a great view and a good photo opportunity. Another popular gift shop is the **Hopi House** (928-638-2631), a National Historic Landmark constructed in 1904 to look like an adobe-block Hopi village.

If you'd rather hike than shop, take the **Bright Angel Trail.** One of the most popular trails in the canyon, it is easily reached just west of El Tovar. You should consider yourself warned: It's a lot easier hiking down the steep switchbacks than climbing back up! This hike should only be attempted if you're wearing appropriate hiking shoes and carrying enough water and snacks. To get away from the crowds, you might consider camping out at the bottom. A stay at **Phantom Ranch** is a luxury for hikers looking at hiking to the bottom of the canyon. Originally built in 1922 as a hunting camp, Phantom Ranch offers dormitory beds with shared baths. Breakfast, lunch, and dinner are served up family-style in the mess hall–style restaurant. Reservations, taken up to thirteen months in advance, are a must for services and lodging.

There are three established backcountry campgrounds in the canyon and numerous backcountry campsites. Permits can be requested by mail or fax; applying well in advance is recommended. Call (928) 638-7875 Mon through Fri between 1 and 5 p.m. for information or write to Grand Canyon National Park, Backcountry Information Center, P.O. Box 129, Grand Canyon, AZ 86023. By the way, you can actually post mail from down here—it will be stamped with the postmark "Delivered by Mule from the Bottom of the Canyon."

trivia

Only one Indian tribe occupies the bottom of the Grand Canyon—the Havasupai tribe.

The canyon is well known for its mule trips, which take riders down the steep canyon trails to Phantom Ranch. The **Grand Canyon National Park Lodges Mule Rides** (303-297-2757 or 888-297-2757; www.grandcanyonlodges .com) are offered daily from May through September and range from one- to three-day trips. All riders must weigh less than 200 pounds fully dressed (and, yes, they do weigh everyone!), must be at least 4 feet, 7 inches in height, and, for safety's sake, must be able to speak and understand English. These beasts do walk right along the trail's edge, so the faint of heart may want to find another activity. The treks are hugely popular, so reservations should be made as far in advance as possible.

Travelers who plan ahead may want to consider scheduling one of the excursions offered by the **Grand Canyon Field Institute** (928-638-2485 or 866-471-4435; www.grandcanyon.org/fieldinstitute). Guides from the institute

Lolita's Lepidopterist

During Russian author Vladimir Nabokov's first visit to Arizona in 1941, he and his party stopped at the Grand Canyon. During his visit, Nabokov—who was a serious lepidopterist as well as the author of the controversial classic novel *Lolita*—discovered an unnamed butterfly at the canyon. He called the diminutive brown butterfly *Neonympha dorothea,* after Dorothy Leuthold, the student doing the driving on the trip.

take small groups of people on hiking, backpacking, and educational tours throughout the park. Among the unique jaunts and workshops are *Raptors of Grand Canyon, Rim-to-Rim Geology Backpack,* and *Backcountry Medicine.* Special courses are planned for people interested in geology, human history, ecosystems, wilderness skills (including classes just for women), and photography. Fees and lengths of classes vary, as does the difficulty level of the hikes.

There are so many ways to see the canyon. You can fly over by airplane or helicopter on **Air Grand Canyon** (928-638-2686 or 800-AIR-GRAND; www .airgrandcanyon.com), **Maverick Helicopters** (702-261-0007 or 888-261-4414; www.maverickhelicopter.com), or **Papillon Grand Canyon Helicopters** (702-735-7243 or 888-635-7272; www.papillon.com), or you can tour by bus, using **Fred Harvey Transportation Company** (303-29-PARKS or 888-29-PARKS; www.grandcanyonlodges.com).

Some visitors prefer rafting down the Colorado River to clambering around on the cliffs. About a dozen companies are licensed for canyon river trips. Some offer easygoing, half-day float trips that are perfect for any age or level of fitness. Others do the full-out, go-for-the-gusto, *The River Wild*–style, three-day to three-week white-water expeditions. In any case, you have to book your tour at least six months to one year in advance, or there's a good chance you won't get a slot. Call the park (928-638-7888; www.nps.gov/grca) to find out about trips and companies and for reservations.

Sedona Area and South

One of Arizona's most pleasurable drives for nearly all the senses is the route from the Grand Canyon along US 180 to the switchbacks of US 89A as it winds its way into **Oak Creek Canyon** and Sedona beyond. Especially popular in the fall, when the desert denizens travel north to view the colorful oak and sycamore leaves, the 16-mile gorge is peppered with streams and waterfalls. More than 130 species of birds call the region home, and campgrounds and hiking trails are abundant. Along the way, numerous resorts and cabins are hidden along the banks of the creek, serving up an interesting array of accommodation choices. *Garland's Oak Creek Lodge* (928-282-3343; www.garlands lodge.com; open Apr through mid-Nov) is perhaps the best known and is so popular with its regulars that many have a standing reservation each year. The lodge is closed on Sun and requires a two-night minimum. Cabins range from $235 to $290 a night.

But others are considerably easier to book. The *Canyon Wren, Cabins for Two* (928-282-6900 or 800-437-9736; www.canyonwrencabins.com), at 6425 N. US 89A, is a cluster of four cabins located 6 miles from Sedona and is on the hilly side of the highway away from the creek. Nonsmoking inside and out, the Canyon Wren also caters to couples seeking a tranquil retreat. Continental breakfast is served daily, and each unit comes complete with a small kitchen. Cabins go for $155 to $175 per night with a two-night minimum stay.

Oak Creek Terrace Resort (928-282-3562 or 800-224-2229; www.oak creekterrace.com), at 4548 N. US 89A, is 5 miles from uptown Sedona and features a two-story A-frame cabin that sleeps up to five, two triplexes, eleven motel-style rooms, and two unique bungalows of varying layouts in a creek-side setting. Nearly every unit is complete with fireplace and in-room whirlpool tub; many offer kitchenettes and outdoor barbecues. Room rates start at $99.

Midway up the canyon is *Slide Rock State Park* (928-282-3034; www .azstateparks.com), a state-run facility that, as its name implies, boasts a natural waterslide created by the waters of Oak Creek as they rush over naturally sculpted stone chutes. The area was once an apple orchard and efforts are being made to restore the original century-old buildings and continue apple production. An original apple-packing barn remains, as well as a 1926 homestead that now serves as a ranger station. For visitors, shaded picnic areas are available, and snacks and supplies can be purchased inside Slide Rock Market. Admission is $10 per vehicle.

trivia

Though it is a relatively small community, Sedona is located in both Coconino and Yavapai Counties and is completely surrounded by the Coconino National Forest.

On the other side of Sedona, another state park is undoubtedly more recognizable—even for folks who have never been to Arizona. *Red Rock State Park* (928-282-6907; www.azstateparks.com) has, for years, served as the backdrop for countless TV programs, movies, and commercials. This park is just west of Sedona off US 89A and features hiking trails that range from simple to strenuous. Guided hikes include nature walks, bird hikes, geology hikes, sunset walks, and the ever-popular moonlight hikes. Maps of the 286-acre park are available from the visitor center. Admission is $7 per vehicle. If you continue south on US 89A, in about 5 miles you'll reach the red-rock-ringed community of **Sedona** (928-282-7722 or 800-288-7336; www.visitsedona.com). Named in 1902 for Sedona Schnebly, the wife of founder T. C. Schnebly, this small town is best known as an arts community, a vacation getaway spot, and a haven for people seeking a different spiritual path. In the 1980s, Sedona acquired the reputation of being a New Age center. Allegedly several electromagnetic energy sources (known as vortexes) were found in the area, and a wide variety of psychics and spiritual healers decided to tap into them by making the town their home. One New Age directory lists Sedona organizations like Center for the New Age, Sedona Soul Adventures, the Golden Word, and Mystical Bazaar. **The Center for the New Age** (928-282-2085 or 888-861-6651; www.sedonanewage center.com) at 341 Hwy. 179 has been providing services since 1996. You can get psychic readings, healing massages, and aural photographs at the center or you can sign up for a personalized vortex tour. Four areas have been identified as possessing unusual electromagnetic forces. They are **Cathedral Rock** (off US 89A and Upper Red Rock Loop Road); **Bell Rock** (north of the Village of Oak Creek, off AZ 179); **Airport Mesa** (circling the municipal airport); and **Boynton Canyon Vortex** (Boynton Pass Road, west of Sedona off US 89A and Dry Creek Road). Some believe these outcroppings of red rock (the first two named after their respective shapes, and the latter two named for their locations) emit a palpable energy. Each area is lovely to look at, but quiet, serene Cathedral Rock west of central Sedona near Oak Creek is a personal favorite.

Hollywood filmmakers and music video, television, and television commercial producers have long been lured to Sedona, starting in the 1930s when the Zane Grey feature *Call of the Canyon* was lensed here. The pilgrimage continues today with films like De Niro's *Midnight Run* and the Johnny Depp western *Dead Man*. Glancing around at the intense, vibrant red rocks and the lush vegetation, it's easy to see why so many artists also have been drawn to this setting. Although the **Cowboy Artists of America** (602-677-3123; www .cowboyartistsofamerica.com) was founded here in 1965, artists of every description and from different regions, including the Southwest, have worked here. One of the most famous is painter/sculptor Max Ernst, whose surrealistic works helped to redefine art in the 1950s. Current area artists include Leslie B. De Mille, "shirttail cousin" to the famous film director, as well as a very talented portrait artist and sculptor in his own right, who has done a lot of work for professional golfers.

Many artists have their works on display at ***Tlaquepaque Arts and Crafts Village*** (928-282-4838; www.tlaq.com). Pronounced *T-lockey-pockey,* the center's name is a Native American word meaning "the best of everything." Designed to resemble an actual Mexican village near Guadalajara, the center's shops and galleries surround a courtyard. Each September, ***Fiesta del Tlaquepaque*** is held, and strolling mariachis play while children swing at a piñata and food vendors fill the courtyard with the aroma of southwestern cooking. Tlaquepaque is also the setting for an annual ***Festival of Lights,*** an evening event usually held on the second Saturday in December. Luminarias (more than 6,000) are placed all around the balconies, walkways, and on the fountain, bathing the village in a golden glow. The luminarias are lighted at dusk, but the festival is open from 3 to 8 p.m.

Held next door to Tlaquepaque at ***Los Abrigados*** ("the shelter") ***Resort and Spa*** (928-282-1777 or 800-521-3131; www.ilxresorts.com), a first-class facility set on twenty acres, the annual ***Red Rock Fantasy*** (mid-Nov to mid-Jan) is a big crowd pleaser. The resort, tucked back off the main road with gorgeous views of the surrounding hills, is decorated with more than one million Christmas lights that are lit from 5 to 10 p.m. each night. Displays ranging from salutes to the Phoenix Suns to scenes from *Babes in Toyland* are placed all

Sedona—Arizona's Cinematic Star

Visit Sedona for the first time and you'll likely feel as though you've been there before—and for good reason. Sedona is a star! Here are just a few of the countless productions—vintage and modern—that have used the crimson canyons as their backdrop:

Feature Films

The Karate Kid (Columbia, 1984)

Midnight Run (Universal, 1988)

The Quick and the Dead (Cates, 1987)

Riders of the Purple Sage (Fox, 1931)

Universal Soldier (Carolco, 1992)

Blood on the Moon (RKO, 1948)

Call of the Canyon (Famous Players/ Lasky, 1923)

Gun Fury (Columbia, 1953)

Television

Death Valley Days

Gambler II

Lifestyles of the Rich and Famous

Sesame Street

Commercial products

Coca-Cola, Eddie Bauer, Duracell, Frito-Lay, Kodak, Levis, and almost every foreign and domestic automaker!

around. Visitors pay a nominal admission fee (which is donated to a charity) to tour the displays. The all-suite resort has a health club with workout machines and classes, a tennis court, an outdoor pool and Jacuzzi, and two restaurants. On-site, **Stakes & Sticks** (928-204-7849) is a sports bar and celebrity club that combines elements of an eatery with the essentials of a gentleman's club (cognac, cigars, and a big fireplace).

Besides the previously mentioned spots near Oak Creek, there's lots to do in the great outdoors in Sedona. Southwest of uptown Sedona on US 89A, then north on Dry Creek Road (the route you take to Boynton Canyon, site of one of the vortexes), you can enjoy an easy 2-mile hike to the 40-foot sandstone **Vultee Arch.** The naturally occurring structure is named after a pilot and aircraft designer who crashed near the arch in 1938.

If you tire of hiking, several companies can give you a lift—literally. **Northern Light Balloon Expeditions** (928-282-2274 or 800-230-6222; www .northernlightballoon.com) can take you over the Coconino National Forest for a spectacular view from the basket of a hot-air balloon. Or ramble up twisting Schnebly Road—which affords a great view of Sedona—with **Pink Jeep Tours** (928-282-5000 or 800-873-3662; www.pinkjeep.com). By the way, the Schnebly Road scenic drive can be made on your own using a sturdy, high-clearance or all-terrain vehicle.

One Sedona sight you definitely shouldn't miss is the **Chapel of the Holy Cross** (928-282-4069) at 780 Chapel Rd. This magnificent Modern Gothic cathedral was built in 1956 high in the red rocks by Margurite Brunswig Staude, a sculptor, painter, and jewelry designer who had long envisioned building a contemporary monument to God. Staude chose Lloyd Wright, son of Frank Lloyd Wright, to design the structure, but financial constraints prevented completion of his grandiose design—a 500-hundred-foot monument! Originally slated for Budapest, Hungary, the project was put on hold until Staude moved to Sedona in 1950. No services are held here. Rather, the chapel is open to anyone of any creed to come in and light a candle (for which there is a small donation), study the sculptures (some by Staude, others more than 200 years old), browse in the downstairs gift shop, and marvel at the incredible scenery. The chapel is open daily from 9 a.m. to 5 p.m., except Thanksgiving, Christmas, Good Friday, and Easter.

Besides the wintertime Festival of Lights and Red Rock Fantasy, annual events in Sedona include the **Sedona Annual International Film Festival** (928-282-1177; www.sedonafilmfestival.com) in February; **Jazz on the Rocks Benefit Festival** (928-282-1985; www.sedonajazz.com) in September; and **Sedona Arts Festival** (928-204-9456; www.sedonaartsfestival.org) in October. Jazz on the Rocks, featuring about a half dozen top regional and national acts playing everything from swing to blues, is especially popular. It's held all day outdoors in a grassy amphitheater with Sedona's towering red rocks as a backdrop.

It's not hard to find a comfortable place to stay overnight in Sedona: The area is loaded with quaint bed-and-breakfast inns and has several top-notch resorts.

Despite its small size, Sedona also has a healthy assortment of eateries, from eclectic to European. A personal favorite for decent Mexican dishes and arguably the best red rock views in town is *Oaxaca Restaurant & Cantina* (928-282-4179; www.oaxacarestaurant.com) in uptown Sedona at 321 N. Hwy. 89A. The menu includes everything from huevos rancheros for breakfast to blue corn enchiladas for dinner. The best seats in the house are on the second-story patio. For a more upscale take on Sunday brunch, reserve a table at *L'Auberge Restaurant on Oak Creek* (928-282-1661 or 800-272-6777; www .lauberge.com) at 301 L'Auberge Lane. Open for breakfast, lunch, and dinner, this restaurant exemplifies Sedona's fine-dining scene. For dinner you can sample everything from butter-poached lobster and pan-roasted scallops to Colorado rack of lamb with porcini crust in a French provincial setting.

Those seeking sites off the beaten path have a prime choice of destinations within Red Rock Country. Before you head to any of the following Heritage Sites, make sure you pick up a Red Rock Pass from the *Red Rock Ranger District and Visitor Contact Center* (928-203-7500 or 928-203-2900; www.redrockcountry.org) at 8375 Hwy. 179. The visitor center is open daily from 8 a.m. to 5 p.m. The *Palatki Heritage Site* cliff dwelling and rock art site offers two hiking trails—one leads to the Sinagua dwellings, the other to rock art alcoves. To reach the site from Sedona, take US 89A to mile marker 365 and turn right on FR 525. Call the Palatki Heritage Site at (928) 282-3854 between 9:30 a.m. and 3:30 p.m. to make reservations. While you are here, you might want to take the time to also check out the nearby *Honanki Heritage Site.* The ancient Sinagua Indians lived in both of these cliff dwellings from about A.D. 1100 to A.D. 1300. Reservations are required. Both sites are open to the public seven days a week.

When you're ready to move on from Sedona (and a word of warning: Vortex or not, the town has a very seductive character, so you may be there awhile), you can either continue south on US 89A and head to Tuzigoot National Monument, Jerome, and Prescott (all covered in another section), or you can take AZ 179 south to I-17.

The interstate will steer you toward *Montezuma Well* and *Montezuma Castle National Monument* (928-567-3322; www.nps.gov/moca). Admission is $5 for adults. The well, actually a collapsed limestone cavern 1,750 feet in diameter and fed by underground springs, is a short distance from the main road. Hohokam Indian ruins dot this area. The Hohokam were an ancient Native American tribe that built elaborate communities based upon agriculture. They populated much of the state until around the late fifteenth century, when they seemingly disappeared, a phenomenon that led modern tribes to refer to these ancient ancestors by the name Hohokam, a Native American term often translated as "those who vanished." A few miles south is the "castle," a twenty-room Sinagua cliff dwelling that was built around A.D. 1100. When it was discovered during Arizona's territorial days by white settlers, it was erroneously thought to be the work of the Aztec king.

Just past the intersection of AZ 260 and I-17 is the town of **Camp Verde** (928-567-9294; www.visitcampverde.com) and **Fort Verde State Historic Park** (928-567-3275; www.azstateparks.com). Admission is $3 for age fourteen and older. Like a number of Arizona communities, Camp Verde is a great example of Old West architecture—and outmoded cultural interface: It sprang up as a military outpost to protect miners, ranchers, and homesteaders against Indian raids. The fort was built in 1865, and it was here in 1873 that General George Crook presided over the surrender of Apache Chief Chalipun and 300 warriors. Crook is well known in American history as a tough and savvy commander who used Apache scouts and adapted old-fashioned military tactics to work in the rugged and hostile terrain of Arizona. He also forged a trail connecting Fort Whipple (near Prescott) with Fort Apache in the Apache-Sitgreaves National Forests, a road that is still referred to as **Crook's Trail.** Today the trail passes through Prescott, Coconino, and Apache-Sitgreaves National Forests. Of the 200 miles of trail, 138 miles are maintained. Some portions of the trail are passable by passenger vehicle, while other portions of the trail are suitable for hiking and equestrian use in summer and cross-country skiing in the winter. For more information contact the Apache-Sitgreaves National Forests (928-333-4301; www.fs.fed.us/r3/asnf) or the Prescott National Forest (928-443-8000; www.fs.fed.us/r3/prescott).

The 138-mile trail is used primarily by hikers and horseback riders, with the most popular portion being a 25-mile section east of Camp Verde along the Mogollon Rim, a steep cliff that separates the state's northern plateau from the lower desert. The historic buildings of Fort Verde are now a museum.

Arcosanti (928-632-7135; www.arcosanti.org) sits only a few minutes away, just off I-17 near Cordes Junction at exit 262. Although Arcosanti is visible from the interstate, uninformed motorists may not know what to make of the odd-looking structures perched on the cliffside and simply zip on by unaware of what they've missed. A sort of glorious urban experiment, Arcosanti, established in 1970, is the brainchild of Italian architect Paolo Soleri.

Soleri's theories of "arcology" (a meld of architecture and ecology) prompted him to construct a self-sufficient community that would produce crops and create marketable products.

The buildings of Arcosanti look like nothing you've ever seen before: round and square shapes combining in asymmetrical forms amidst walls of basalt, splashed with color throughout. The effect is sort of "Frank Lloyd Wright through the Looking Glass" (not surprising, given that Soleri was a Frank Lloyd Wright Fellow). In some ways the community will remind you of the styles and decor of the early seventies—a lava lamp would look right at home here—yet it all seems timeless, like a fairy-tale kingdom.

Visitors to Arcosanti, which is open year-round, can tour the ten-acre facility, browse in the gift shop (which sells everything from Soleri's famous ceramic or bronze abstract bells to posters and T-shirts), take part in crafts and building workshops, and attend concerts at the Colly Soleri Music Center, which is named for the architect's late wife. Richie Havens, whose incomparable voice transformed the original Woodstock music festival, is a frequent guest, though the center is a venue for all types of music, including jazz and blues. Some concerts are preceded by dinner and followed by a light show projected on the canyon wall.

Arcosanti also has a bakery and a cafe. Admission to the gift shop and cafe is free, but a $10 donation is requested for the one-hour tour (offered every hour from 10 a.m. to 4 p.m., except at noon).

Places to Stay in Northern Arizona

FLAGSTAFF

Abineau Lodge
10155 Mountainaire Rd.
(928) 525-6212 or
(888) 715-6386
www.abineaulodge.com
Cozy country rooms, charming common areas, a sauna, a decadent breakfast (included), and morning sled-dog serenades. Moderate.

Embassy Suites
706 S. Milton Rd.
(928) 774-4333 or
(866) 774-4333
www.embassysuites.com
Spacious rooms with minikitchens and separate bedrooms. Breakfast only (included). Moderate.

England House Bed & Breakfast
614 W. Santa Fe Ave.
(928) 214-7350 or
(877) 214-7350
www.englandhousebandb
.com

A 1902 stonecutter's house with four rooms with private baths and a two-bedroom suite. Breakfast included. Moderate.

Weatherford Hotel
23 N. Leroux St.
(928) 779-1919
www.weatherfordhotel.com
Built in 1887, this historic hotel offers clean, restored rooms decorated in turn-of-the-twentieth-century style. Some rooms have private baths while others have shared baths. Inexpensive.

GRAND CANYON SOUTH RIM

Kachina Lodge
P.O. Box 699, Desert View Drive
(928) 638-2631 or
(888) 297-2757
(reservations only)
www.grandcanyonlodges
.com
This motel-style lodge has basic rooms; some with partial canyon views ($10 extra). Check in at El Tovar Hotel to the east. Moderate.

Maswik Lodge
P.O. Box 699,
Grand Canyon Village
(928) 638-2631 or
(888) 297-2757
(reservations only)
www.grandcanyonlodges
.com
Accommodations, nestled in the ponderosa pine forest a quarter mile from the rim, range from rustic cabins to more modern rooms. Inexpensive.

Thunderbird Lodge
P.O. Box 699, Desert View Drive
(928) 638-2631 or
(888) 297-2757
(reservations only)
www.grandcanyonlodges
.com
This motel-style lodge has basic rooms; some with partial canyon views ($10 extra). Check in at Bright Angel Lodge to the west. Moderate.

Yavapai Lodge
P.O. Box 699,
Grand Canyon Village
(928) 638-2631 or
(888) 297-2757
(reservations only)
www.grandcanyonlodges
.com
This large motel-style lodge is located near the eastern end of Grand Canyon Village, a quarter mile from the rim. Moderate.

JACOB LAKE

Jacob Lake Inn
Junction of North US 89A and AZ 67
(928) 643-7232
www.jacoblake.com
A rustic lodge with cabins and rooms, restaurant, bakery, soda fountain, service station, and country store. Moderate.

LAKE POWELL

Linda's Lake Powell Condos
P.O. Box 5292
Page, AZ 86040
(928) 353-4591
www.lakepowellresorts
.com
Studio condos with desert or lake views. Located near Wahweap marina. Expensive.

SEDONA

Casa Sedona
55 Hozoni Dr.
(928) 282-2938 or
(800) 525-3756
www.casasedona.com
A 16-room bed-and-breakfast inn offering luxury accommodations, stunning red rock views, gas fireplaces, spa tubs, and refrigerators. Southwestern breakfast and afternoon appetizers included. Moderate to expensive.

Enchantment Resort
525 Boynton Canyon Rd.
(928) 282-2900 or
(800) 826-4180
www.enchantmentresort
.com
A gorgeous resort hidden in scenic Boynton Canyon. Amenities include a full-service spa, three restaurants, tennis courts, a pool, and hiking and biking trails. Expensive.

The Lodge at Sedona
125 Kallof Place
(928) 204-1942 or
(800) 619-4467
www.lodgeatsedona.com
In West Sedona, this secluded bed-and-breakfast, set on two and a half wooded acres, was formerly a private home and now has six rooms and eight suites, each with a distinct theme—from Renaissance to Cherokee. Moderate to expensive.

Sedona Super 8 Motel
2545 W. Hwy. 89A
(928) 282-1533 or
(877) 800-4746
www.sedonasuper8.com
A good, reasonably priced choice on the main road with a pool. Inexpensive.

TUSAYAN

Best Western Grand Canyon Squire Inn
AZ 64
P.O. Box 130
Grand Canyon, AZ 86023

(928) 638-2681 or
(800) 622-6966
www.grandcanyonsquire
.com
Just south of the park's
entrance in Tusayan, this is
the area's only resort hotel,
with 250 deluxe rooms,
heated pool, fitness center,
restaurants, etc. Moderate
to expensive.

The Grand Hotel
AZ 64
P.O. Box 3319
Grand Canyon, AZ 86023
(928) 638-3333 or
(888) 634-7263
www.visitgrandcanyon.com
In the Village of Tusayan
near the park entrance.
Similar in style and appoint-
ments to the park lodges.
Moderate to expensive.

WILLIAMS

**The Canyon Motel and
Railroad RV Park**
1900 E. Rodeo Rd.
(928) 635-9371 or
(800) 482-3955
www.thecanyonmotel.com
Situated on ten acres, this
remodeled 1949 motor
lodge offers rooms in flagstone cottages and reno-
vated, historic cabooses
and railcars. Inexpensive.

Red Garter
137 W. Railroad Ave.
(928) 635-1484 or
(800) 328-1484
www.redgarter.com
This bed-and-breakfast
houses four rooms in a
two-story 1897 brick building that once served as a
bordello and saloon. The
rooms are on the upper
floor and a bakery occupies
the first floor. Closed Dec
through mid-Feb. Inexpen-
sive to moderate.

Places to Eat in Northern Arizona

FLAGSTAFF

**Black Bart's Steakhouse
and Musical Revue**
2760 E. Butler Ave.
(928) 779-3142 or
(800) 574-4718
www.blackbartssteakhouse
.com
Slightly corny, but a lot
of fun, this spot features
food servers who double
as singers—all students
at nearby Northern Ari-
zona University. Open
dinner only. Moderate to
expensive.

WEB SITES FOR NORTHERN ARIZONA

Arizona Department of Tourism
www.arizonaguide.com

Camp Verde Chamber of Commerce
www.visitcampverde.com

Coconino National Forest
www.fs.fed.us/r3/coconino

**Flagstaff Convention and Visitors
Bureau**
www.flagstaffarizona.org

**Glen Canyon National Recreation
Area**
www.nps.gov/glca

Grand Canyon National Park
www.nps.gov/grca

Kaibab National Forest
www.fs.fed.us/r3/kai

Prescott National Forest
www.fs.fed.us/r3/prescott

**Sedona–Oak Creek Chamber of
Commerce**
www.visitsedona.com

**Williams–Grand Canyon Chamber of
Commerce**
www.williamschamber.com

Buster's Restaurant and Bar
1800 S. Milton Rd.
(928) 774-5155
www.busters-restaurant
.com
A steak and seafood res-
taurant rated the "Best
Flagstaff Restaurant" by
the *Arizona Daily News Sun*
for more than a decade.
Moderate.

Salsa Brava
2220 Historic Rte. 66
(928) 779-5293
salsabravaflagstaff.com
Spice things up with the
fresh selections at this
award-winning Mexican
restaurant. The cantina
and fireside patio dining
add extra seasoning to this
local favorite. Inexpensive
to moderate.

Strombolli's Restaurant & Pizzeria
1435 S. Milton Rd.
(928) 773-1960
www.strombollis.com
If you're looking for Italian
food, this Flagstaff landmark is the place to go.
The stone-baked pizzas
and calzones are a favorite
even with locals. Moderate.

SEDONA

Blue Moon Cafe
6101 Hwy. 179, Ste. B
(928) 284-1831
www.bluemooncafe.us
Serves breakfast all day,
plus burgers, sandwiches,
salads, and hand-tossed
pizza. Inexpensive.

Coffee Pot Restaurant
2050 W. Hwy. 89A
(928) 282-6626
Serves a huge selection
of omelets and is known
by locals for the "Best
Breakfast in Sedona."
Inexpensive.

Oak Creek Brewery & Grill
336 Hwy. 179, Ste. D-201
Tlaquepaque Arts & Crafts
Village
(928) 282-3300
www.oakcreekpub.com
Watch your wood-fired
pizza, baby back ribs, rotis-
serie chicken, cedar-plank
salmon, and burgers and
steaks being cooked up in
the grill's exhibition kitchen.
Polish it all off with a mug
of one of the brewery's
award-winning microbrews.
Moderate.

Shugrues Restaurant
671 Hwy. 179
(928) 282-5300
www.shugrues.com/
sedona
This fine-dining establishment serves up such entrees
as whiskey-barbecued duck,
flame-broiled shrimp scampi,
and herb-grilled rib eye gor-
gonzola. Reservations are
recommended. Expensive.

WILLIAMS

Cruisers Cafe 66
233 W. Rte. 66
(928) 635-2445
www.cruisers66.com
This 1950s cafe serves up

a nice selection of burgers,
sandwiches, and salads
on the "Mother Road."
Homemade malts and
microbrews on tap add to
the casual atmosphere.
Inexpensive.

Pancho McGillicuddy's
141 Railroad Ave.
(928) 635-4150
www.panchomcgillicuddys
.com
Dishes up large servings of
Mexican food and features
more than thirty tequilas at
the restaurant bar. Inex-
pensive to moderate.

Pine Country Restaurant
107 N. Grand Canyon
Blvd.
(928) 635-9718,
www.pinecountryrestaurant
.com
Home-style country
cooking in a cozy local
restaurant. Open break-
fast, lunch, and dinner.
Inexpensive.

Red Raven Restaurant
135 W. Rte. 66
(928) 635-4980
www.redravenrestaurant
.com
Casual fine dining empha-
sizing fresh ingredients and
innovative menu offerings
including fish, steak, and
salads. Moderate.

Lake Mead and Grand Canyon West

When it was created in the 1930s by the construction of **Hoover Dam** (702-494-2517 or 866-730-9097; www.usbr.gov/lc/hooverdam), the 110-mile-long Lake Mead was the largest artificial lake in the world. The dam itself was no small achievement either. Built to harness the awesome power of the Colorado River on the mitten tip of the Arizona–Nevada border, the dam is more than 726 feet tall and 1,282 feet long and is linked to a power plant that can generate 1.8 million horsepower. Boy, just imagine if you could tuck that baby under the hood of your car! Besides being an engineering marvel, the dam, with its art deco statues, is a work of art in itself and is the tallest solid concrete arch-gravity dam in the Western Hemisphere. The self-guided **Powerplant Tour** departs every fifteen minutes from 9 a.m. to 5:15 p.m. (4:15 p.m. in winter). Admission is $11 for adults and $6 for children ages four to sixteen. Reservations are recommended. However, the best way to see the dam is on the guided **Hoover Dam Tour,** which gives visitors an up-close look at lesser-known

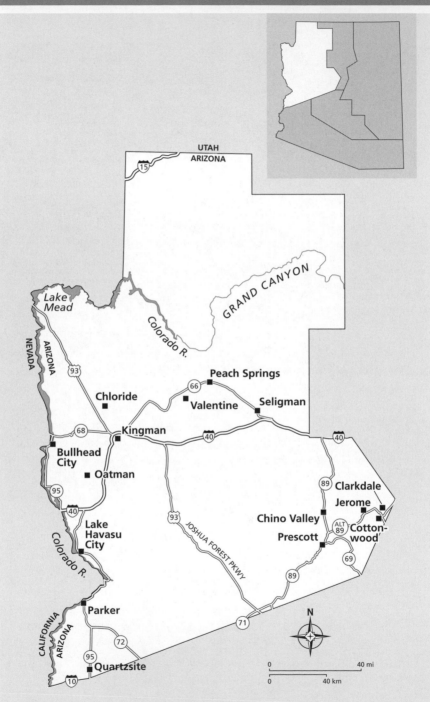

Artistic Leanings

Not only was Hoover Dam considered as an engineering marvel when it was built, but it was also lauded as a modern work of art. Architect Gordon B. Kaufmann, designer of the Los Angeles Times Building, used art deco and modernist ideas in the dam's overall design. This striking design is complemented by Native American geometric designs in the terrazzo floors by artist Allen Tupper True (whose murals are prominent in the Colorado State Capitol in Denver) and the striking 30-foot bronze statues, named the *Winged Figures of the Republic,* sculpted by Oskar J. W. Hansen.

parts of the dam. Hoover Dam Tours start at 9:30 a.m. (Pacific Time) and continue every half hour until 3:30 p.m. Only twenty people (age eight and older) are allowed on this tour on a first-come, first-served basis. Admission is $30. Covered parking (a plus in the scorching summertime) is available for $7 per vehicle. Earlier tours are usually less crowded and January and February are the slowest months, making them the best time to check out the engineering marvel.

If you are looking for some river running below Hoover Dam in **Black Canyon,** sign up for a rafting trip with **Black Canyon/Willow Beach River Adventures** (800-455-3490; www.blackcanyonadventures.com). For those with an added sense of adventure, snag a seat with **Boulder City Outfitters** (702-293-1190 or 800-748-3702; www.bouldercityoutfitters.com), which offers guided kayak tours through Black Canyon.

Rates are $163 per person with a two-person minimum. The 11-mile run to Willow Beach might not appear as challenging as running the Grand Canyon, but there are some rapids, whirlpools, and headwinds that can cause difficulties for inexperienced rafters and kayakers. The scenery is striking with sheer cliff faces, canyon waterfalls, and blue-green water. If you want to strike out on you own, you need to make arrangements with one of the registered outfitters (702-494-2204; www.usbr.gov/lc/hooverdam). They provide permits ($10) and launch and retrieval services.

Just about anything you can do in a body of water, you can do on **Lake Mead.** Swimming is a leisurely pastime in the summer months; Boulder Beach near the Alan Bible Visitor Center is a

trivia

Though Arizona boasts one of the largest per capita boat ownerships in the country, all of Arizona's lakes except one—Stoneman Lake—are man-made. In fact, Lake Mead is the largest man-made lake in the United States.

favorite for sunbathers. With 225 square miles to explore, boating of all kinds rules at Lake Mead. Anglers can cast a line twenty-four hours a day here, year-round. Just be sure to have fishing license for both Arizona and Nevada (details are on the National Park Service Web site, www.nps.gov/lame/planyourvisit/fishing.htm). Once you have your bait set, be ready to land a big one. This lake is known for its record-size fish. Also, be aware that the lake is regularly stocked with rainbow trout and if you plan on catching and keeping one, you have to obtain a trout stamp. Freshwater diving is also a favored activity here, even though the lowered lake levels have closed some of the marked diving sites. Other activities abound, including Jet Skiing, waterskiing, wakeboarding, sailboarding, and snorkeling. If you stay in one of the neighboring towns, you can make this stop a day trip—driving up, renting a Jet Ski, and cruising around the lake for a few hours before heading back to town. If you'd like to spend more than a day at Lake Mead, consider renting a houseboat. There are 550 miles of shoreline, which include hidden coves and tiny backwater inlets that are perfect for lengthy exploration. There are countless areas where you can go ashore and have a picnic lunch while gazing at the surrounding mountains.

The **Alan Bible Visitor Center** (702-293-8990; www.nps.gov/lame), as well as facilities for renting equipment or booking steamboat tours, is on the

reservoir recreation

The construction of Hoover Dam created the 100-mile-long reservoir of Lake Mead, which was named after U.S. Bureau of Reclamation commissioner Elwood Mead. This enormous reservoir drew thousands of visitors to what became the first National Recreation Area in the United States in 1964. Today, nearly two million visitors come to this water-sports wonderland each year.

AUTHOR'S TOP PICKS IN WESTERN ARIZONA

Grand Canyon West	Lake Mead National Recreation Area
Havasu Canyon	London Bridge/English Village
Hualapai River Runners	Historic Route 66
Jerome	Verde Canyon Railroad
Lake Havasu	

Nevada side. However, the **Temple Bar Marina** off US 93 in Arizona (928-767-3211 or 800-752-9669; www.templebarlakemead.com) offers camping and boat rental (including houseboats) and launching facilities, in addition to a cafe, grocery store, motel, and cabins. RV facilities are also available.

About 40 miles south of Lake Mead on US 93, **Dolan Springs** (928-767-4473) sits at the foot of the Cerbat Mountains. Not surprisingly, given the proximity of Lake Mead, Lake Mohave, and the southwest rim of the Grand Canyon, this town is a stopping-off point for many recreation seekers.

A lot of visitors don't realize that just north of Dolan Springs off Pearce Ferry Road on the way to Meadview is one of the largest stands of **Joshua trees** (*Yucca brevifolia*) in the world. (Joshua Tree National Park is actually located in California.) Natives of the dry Mojave Desert, Joshua trees are strange, spiky-topped relatives of the lily family that can reach more than 40 feet in height and live up to 300 years. They were allegedly named by Mormon pioneers who believed that the upraised arms resembled Joshua leading the Israelites. Although there aren't any formal parking lots or picnic areas in this forest, you can easily pull off the road and get out and walk around. If you arrive between February and March, you may see the trees in bloom with their creamy white flowers. The trees don't branch until after they bloom, and, because they rely on perfect conditions to flower, they don't necessarily bloom every year.

If you continue on Pearce Ferry Road (sometimes erroneously labeled on maps as Pierce Ferry Road) north from Dolan Springs to the unpaved Diamond Bar Road, you will be just a hop, skip, and a jump away from Grand Canyon West. The canyon's western end is 4,800 feet above the river and very different from its better-known northern, southern, and eastern boundaries. Sprinkled with high-desert vegetation, the canyon itself seems scaled down, more intimate and peaceful.

Grand Canyon West (702-878-9378 or 877-716-9378; www.destination grandcanyon.com) is part of the one million acres of tribal land owned by the plateau-dwelling Hualapai ("people of the tall pines"). In recent years the Hualapai have successfully developed a booming tourism business on the West Rim—known for its spectacular **Skywalk** ($29.95), a glass walkway suspended 70 feet over the edge of the canyon rim. Unhampered by the tight restrictions in place at Grand Canyon National Park, the Hualapai are able to offer everything from helicopter rides into the canyon to Hummer tours along the rim.

Once you reach the visitor center, you will be required to purchase a tour package from Destination Grand Canyon West. The Hualapai Tribe offers the basic Hualapai Legacy tour package ($29.95 plus an $8 impact fee per person), which includes a Hualapai visitation permit and shuttle transportation. A free shuttle will take you to Eagle Point, where the Indian Village walking tour visits authentic dwellings; Hualapai Ranch, site of western performances, cookouts, and horseback and wagon rides; and Guano Point, where the "High Point Hike" offers panoramic views of the Colorado River. For an extra cost you can add a helicopter trip into the canyon, a boat trip on the Colorado River, an off-road Hummer adventure, a horseback or wagon ride to the canyon rim, or a walk on the Skywalk. Local Hualapai guides add a Native American perspective to a canyon trip that you won't find on North and South Rim tours.

For an overnight stay, the **Hualapai Ranch** (702-878-9378 or 889-878-9378; www.destinationgrandcanyon.com) offers small cabins with front porches perfect for watching the sun set. The cabins are adjacent to a small "western" town, where visitors can pose for snapshots, sign up for guided horseback tours and wagon rides, shop in a western store, watch gunfight reenactments, and visit a petting zoo. There is a dining room open for breakfast, lunch, and dinner. Cabins run $130 a night.

One hundred and twenty miles away, **Peach Springs,** on Historic Route 66, is the tribal capital and the location of the Hualapai Lodge. The **Hualapai Lodge** (928-769-2230 or 888-255-9550; www.destinationgrandcanyon.com) at 900 Historic Rte. 66 offers clean and comfortable rooms and the on-site **Diamond Creek Restaurant,** which is open for breakfast, lunch, and dinner. Be sure to try the Navajo tacos. They are divine. The concierge desk arranges river trips with the **Hualapai River Runners** (928-769-2219 or 888-255-9550; www.destinationgrandcanyon.com) from March through October. The river trips leave the lodge at 8 a.m. and return between 6:30 and 8:30 p.m. Children must be eight or older to take the trip, which runs several rapids and includes a short hike to **Travertine Falls.** River rafting trips run $328 plus tax.

Among the lesser-known, although unquestionably idyllic, settings in the area is an exotic canyon located within the tiny Havasupai Indian Reservation. Secluded and seemingly untouched by time and technology, **Havasu Canyon,** 5 miles wide and 12 miles long, appears to be more Hawaiian than mainland, with its cascading turquoise waterfalls and flowering orchids. No doubt the biggest reason for its enduring tranquility is its remoteness—visitors must either fly, hike, or ride into the canyon.

The Havasupai ("people of the blue-green waters") guard the canyon habitat by limiting the number of visitors allowed access to the village of **Supai** and the renowned canyon waterfalls, reaching as high as 200 feet, cascading over red cliffs into travertine pools below. Over the years, flash floods have devastated the turquoise pools, but the Havasupai persevere through their stewardship and commitment to their homeland. As a result, visitors continue to flock to the Havasu Canyon for the stunning views and the remote location. The only way to access the canyon is the 8-mile-long Hualapai Trail, which drops 2,000 feet from the canyon rim to the Supai and Havasu's main waterfalls—Navajo, Havasu, and Mooney Falls. *Hualapai Trail* leaves from Hualapai Hilltop, 63 miles north on Indian Route 18 from Historic Route 66. You must obtain a reservation to enter the canyon. Each person must pay a $35 entrance fee and a $5 impact fee.

If you'd rather ride, you can rent a horse for the trip down for $150 round-trip, or $75 one way. Riders must be able to mount and dismount by themselves; be at least 4 feet, 7 inches tall; and weigh less than 250 pounds. Reservations must be made at least six weeks in advance with *Havasupai Tourist Enterprise* (928-448-2141 or 928-448-2121 for general information or 928-448-2111 or 928-448-2201 for lodging reservations; www.havasupaitribe .com), which requires a 50 percent deposit. Keep in mind that you will need to secure a room or a camping permit if you're hiking or riding. Another option is to take a helicopter ride into the canyon with *Air West Helicopters* (623-516-2790; www.airwesthelicopters.com). Flights leave from Hualapai Hilltop and cost $85 per person each way. They do not accept reservations, and visitors are transported on a first-come, first-served basis. Tribal members are boarded before tourists.

Minerals and the Mother Road

It doesn't take Bill Nye the Science Guy to figure out how the mining town of *Chloride* (928-565-2204; www.chloridearizona.com), just south of Dolan Springs on US 93, got its name. Silver chloride ore, silver, lead, zinc, and other precious minerals such as turquoise have been found in the area. At one time there were as many as seventy-five mines working in the hills. Today it's not unusual to see rock hounds scrambling around in the foothills of the nearby Cerbat Mountains. Before attempting this yourself, check with the chamber of commerce to get directions and to make sure you won't be stepping on someone else's claim.

If you'd rather look at rocks than dig them, check out southwestern artist *Roy Purcell's murals.* Created in 1966 on a cliff in the Cerbats, the paintings depict images of a snake, an eagle's talon, the phases of the moon, and a princess, all sort of flowing into one another. In 2006 Roy Purcell returned to town and repainted the murals for their fortieth anniversary.

Several sights in Chloride, including the *Old Jail* and the *Santa Fe Train Station* are worth a look. The jail, which may remind you of the drunk tank on the *Andy Griffith Show,* is a two-cell, whitewashed building that's maintained

JANUARY

Great Oatman Bed Race

Oatman

This fun festival includes bed races through the streets, a chamber pot parade, burro biscuit toss, a burro braying contest, and a toilet seat toss. (928) 768-6222; www.oatmangoldroad .org

The Main Event

Quartzsite

This annual "world famous gemboree" and merchandise sale attracts thousands for its wide selection of gems and minerals, trade show, and arts and crafts.
(928) 927-5213; www.maineventqz.com

Tyson Well's Gem and Mineral Show

Quartzsite

Leading the pack of gem and mineral shows, this large event includes incredible displays of gems and minerals from around the world, lapidary work, and artist demonstrations.
(928) 927-6364; www.tysonwells.com

FEBRUARY

Geo-Cache Bash

Lave Havasu City

Look for hidden caches of treasure throughout Cattail Cove State Park. Be sure to bring your GPS (Global Positioning System) to decipher the "treasure" map.
(928) 855-1223; www.azstateparks.com

APRIL

Verde Valley Birding and Nature Festival

Cottonwood

Celebrate nature with workshops and field trips to the area's birding hot spots in the Verde Valley and at Dead Horse Ranch State Park. Other activities include geology trips, butterfly and plant walks, and nature photography exhibits. (928) 282-2202; www.birdyverde.org

MAY

George Phippen Memorial Day Western Art Show and Sale

Prescott

This juried outdoor western art show held at the Courthouse Plaza is one of the best in the state. Other activities include a "Quick Draw" competition, gala benefit, and a miniature masterpiece auction.
(928) 778-1385; www.phippenart museum.org

Greater Cottonwood Antique Aeroplane and Auto Show

Cottonwood

Check out antiques, cycles, street rods, customs, military, kit cars, and vintage and experimental aircraft at the Cottonwood Airport.
(928) 634-7593; www.cottonwood chamberaz.org

Paseo de Casas

Jerome

Take a tour of homes and historic public buildings from Victorians to renovated miner's shacks. Also, be sure to check out the art of Jerome artists and historical photographs at the Jerome Historical Society Archives.
(928) 634-2900; www.azjerome.com

JUNE

Bluegrass Festival

Prescott

Bluegrass rules at this two-day festival held at the Courthouse Plaza.
(928) 445-2000 or (800) 266-7534; www.prescottbluegrassfestival.com

Folk Arts Fair

Prescott

Enjoy a weekend of living history with demonstrations of traditional arts such

as quilting, wood carving, blacksmithing, spinning, weaving, and candle making at the Sharlot Hall Museum. You can also try your hand at churning butter and gold panning before enjoying live music and dancing performances.
(928) 445-3122; www.sharlot.org

Old Miners Day
Chloride
Enjoy this silver mining capital's longest-running event with vaudeville acts, street dance, gunfights, horseshoe-pitching contest, swap meet, parade, live music, and a pie-baking contest.
(928) 565-2204; www.chloridearizona .com

Territorial Days
Prescott
This arts and crafts show at Courthouse Plaza always draws a crowd. Other activities include games for kids, old-time photos, and live entertainment.
(928) 445-2000 or (800) 266-7534; www.prescott.org

JULY

Frontier Days and World's Oldest Rodeo
Prescott
People have been gathering in Prescott since 1888 to watch rodeo games. Enjoy the celebration with rodeo performances, a parade, arts and crafts, fireworks, live entertainment, cowboy church, and a rodeo dance.
(928) 445-3103 or (800) 358-1888; www.worldsoldestrodeo.com

Prescott Indian Market
Prescott
This outdoor market at the Sharlot Hall Museum features traditional and contemporary Indian arts including jewelry, ceramics, sculpture, handwoven baskets, and blankets. Other activities include artist demonstrations, children's

activities and Native American song and dance.
(928) 445-3122; www.sharlot.org

Sidewalk Egg Fry
Oatman
This yearly Independence Day celebration takes place at high noon when contestants attempt to fry an egg solar-style. Other activities include Old West gunfights, games, and arts and crafts.
(928) 768-6222; www.oatmangoldroad .org

AUGUST

Arizona Cowboy Poets Gathering
Prescott
Working cowboys from all over the West converge at the Yavapai College Campus to sing original songs and to recite poetry about their lives and work.
(928) 445-3122; www.azcowboypoets .org

SEPTEMBER

Andy Devine Days and PRCA Rodeo
Kingman
Honoring Kingman's own film and television actor, the city celebrates with a rodeo dance, parade, bluegrass festival, and concert at the Mohave County Fairgrounds.
(928) 753-6106; www.kingmantourism .org

Carrera Regatta
Lake Havasu City
At the Nautical Inn, events include a poker run, boat parade, and awards for the farthest miles traveled.
(909) 735-7000 or (928) 855-2141

Mohave County Fair
Kingman
This "Barn in the U.S.A." county fair touts a lineup of livestock exhibits, arts and crafts, carnival rides, contests, and children's activities.

continued

(928) 753-2636; www.mcfafairgrounds
.org

Verde River Days
Cottonwood
This environmental event showcases
the importance of the Verde River
with environmental exhibits, hands-
on-activities, fishing, canoeing, nature
walks, and live entertainment at Dead
Horse Ranch State Park.
(928) 634-5283; www.azstateparks.com

OCTOBER
Folk Music Festival
Prescott
This family-friendly event features folk
music from around the world being
performed on the grounds of the Sharlot
Hall Museum. Get ready for a good time
listening to everything from bluegrass to
gospel.
(928) 445-3122; www.sharlot.org

London Bridge Days
Lake Havasu City
This weeklong celebration features
a multitude of events, including the

London Days Bridge Parade, Fall Fun
Fair, Lighting of Cupcake Mountain,
Taste of Havasu, Rods and Relics
Run to the Sun, Duck Derby, and the
Symphonic Winds "Halloween Spooks."
(928) 453-3444 or (800) 242-8278;
www.golakehavasu.com

NOVEMBER
Festival of Lights
Lake Havasu City
More than one million lights are on
display at English Village and London
Bridge through New Year's Day.
(928) 453-3444 or (800) 242-8278;
www.golakehavasu.com

DECEMBER
Boat Parade of Lights
Lake Havasu City
This colorful floating parade winds its
way through the Bridgewater Channel
under London Bridge and along Lake
Havasu.
(928) 453-3444 or (800) 424-8278;
www.lhcboatparadeoflights.com

as a museum by the historical society. Every Saturday a local group stages shoot-out reenactments and vaudeville entertainment at the new western village called Cyanide Springs. For tickets and information call the Chloride Chamber of Commerce at (928) 565-2204; www.chloridearizona.com.

The *Mine Shaft Market* (928-565-4888) at 4940 E. Tennessee Ave. sells groceries and goodies like ice cream and soft drinks. In the same building is the visitor center (800-578-3379) where tourists can get Arizona travel information and make reservations for rooms in several national parks, Laughlin, Nevada, and other destinations.

A great way to explore the area west of Flagstaff to the border of Nevada is to follow Historic Route 66. In case you're too young to remember, *Route 66* was built in 1926 as the nation's first transcontinental highway. Beginning in Chicago and ending 2,448 miles later at the Santa Monica pier, it became known as the "Main Street of America." John Steinbeck immortalized it in 1939 as the "Mother Road" in his classic novel of dustbowl-hardened Okies, *The Grapes of Wrath*. Throughout the 1930s, many an Oklahoma farmer followed the rutted tracks of the Mother Road (which hadn't been completely paved yet) out to what he hoped was a better life in the citrus fields of California.

Traveling a vastly improved Historic Route 66 in 1946, singer/songwriter Bobby Troup wrote a song about this highway—"Get Your Kicks on Route 66"—and different versions (sung by everyone from Depeche Mode to Nat King Cole to the Rolling Stones) were hits in the 1940s, 1950s, 1960s, and even later. The early 1960s TV show *Route 66,* about a couple of young guys cruising the Mother Road in a Corvette, introduced the *American Graffiti* generation to Historic Route 66 and created a romanticism about the diners, drive-in theaters, and motels that lined this two-lane road.

trivia

The Beale Wagon Road, surveyed and constructed between 1857 and 1859 by Lt. Edward F. Beale, stretches through New Mexico and Arizona near the 35th parallel. The road, which was one of the major routes to California, made history as the first federally funded interstate highway.

But a death knell was in the air. In 1956 President Eisenhower had signed the Interstate Highway Act, which helped to create safer, multilane super-highways like I-40. The completion in 1985 of I-40 turned much of Historic Route 66 into a memory. Even as the last stretch of I-40 was finished, however, citizens and business owners in the Historic Route 66 towns of northern Arizona began banding together to save the Mother Road by marketing themselves as Historic Route 66 towns to car clubs across the country and lovers of Americana around the world. Today it isn't surprising to drive along Historic Route 66 near Kingman and see a carload of German tourists who've grown up listening to Troup's song or watching dubbed reruns of the TV show pull over to snap pictures of themselves posing in front of Historic Route 66 highway signs.

Driving west from Williams, **Ash Fork** (928-637-0204) will be one of the first places you reach. Ash Fork, named for the area's native trees and the fact that there is a fork in the road going to Prescott, is more than one hundred years old. If you have the time, pull off Historic Route 66 onto First Street (which becomes Double A Ranch Road), follow it across the railroad tracks to Cemetery Road, and turn east. There on a gentle slope you'll find the original **Ash Fork Cemetery,** a collection of splintering wooden crosses and weathered sandstone slabs. The locals say that the first man buried here—Tom Kane—wasn't even a resident. He was a stranger who died as a result of an accidental shooting (so much for frontier hospitality!).

Just north of the cemetery on FR 124, which you can reach by following Double A Ranch Road, you'll come to another big attraction: the *flagstone quarries.* Ash Fork calls itself the "Flagstone Capital of the World," and indeed, these quarries have provided material for countless walls and floors not only all over Arizona, but nationwide via the railroad. The variety of colors and the smooth texture of Arizona flagstone have made it especially popular, and though its appeal peaked in the 1950s, it's still sought after for many types of construction.

Ash Fork also boasts the *first all-steel dam* ever built. This National Historic Engineering landmark was erected in 1898 in Johnson Canyon. The dam is one of two structures near Ash Fork (the other is a stone dam) that were built to create water reservoirs for steam trains. You can reach it (if you have a high-profile, four-wheel-drive vehicle) by taking I-40 east to the County Line Road and turning north. This dirt road bumps along until it reaches a huge cinder pit, where it joins an unmarked access road. Keep driving for about a mile. You should see a large crater that was created during the construction of the dam. You can park here and walk the short distance down to the dam. The mammoth steel plates, which make it look like a massive radiator, are designed to expand and contract with the temperature, and the dam shows few signs of wear after more than century of use.

Located just 5 miles northwest of Ash Fork, you can drive to *Dante's Descent,* which is also known by locals as the Devil's Hole. The natural sinkhole makes an impressive sight, plunging down more than 380 feet.

Seligman, (928-308-8210; www.seligmanarizona.org) just west of Ash Fork, is a sometime stop for Mother Road cruisers (the longest loop of Historic Route 66 left completely intact in Arizona is the 160-mile strip from Seligman to Topock, where this road ends on the Arizona side of the Colorado River).

Ancient Messages in the Rocks

Petroglyphs, left behind by a much earlier civilization, can be seen south of Ash Fork. Head west on I-40 until you reach Crookton Road. Exit heading south, and continue on until you reach Arizona Road. This is a dirt road that shouldn't be traveled during periods of heavy rain. If there's no water on the surface, however, and you drive slowly, you should be able to negotiate it in a conventional vehicle. Continue until you reach the bridge at Partridge Creek. To the right past the bridge, you'll spot a small cliff where the drawings—many of them rectangular symbols but some clearly representing animals—are scratched into the dark rock. The age of these drawings, along with the identity of the Native American tribe who carved them, is unknown.

If you're hungry, tired, or you need to refuel, Seligman has some visitors' services, including restaurants, motels, and gas stations.

As for nearby **Valentine,** it used to be that each year many thousands of Americans sent their Valentine's Day cards here to be canceled with the post office's distinctive stamp. Several years back, however, the community's postal carrier was kidnapped and murdered (a terrible crime anywhere but especially shocking here in this small, peaceful community), and the post office was closed.

In any case, the town is named for a former commissioner for Indian Affairs, not for any romantic notions. Film buffs may be interested to know that Valentine's **Hunt Ranch** (off Buck and Doe Road) is featured prominently in a scene in *Easy Rider.* Peter Fonda's character fixes a flat tire in front of the ranch, while in the background a cowboy shoes a horse.

With such a sweetheart of a name, it may not come as a surprise that Valentine is the heart-warming home for the **Keepers of the Wild Nature Park** (928-769-1800; www.keepersofthewild.org). Located at 13441 E. Rte. 66 (mile marker 87), this wildlife refuge is home to hundreds of exotic animals rescued from neglectful and abusive situations. The 175-acre sanctuary offers educational tours, wildlife viewing opportunities, a gift shop, and a snack shop. The park is open daily (except Tues) from 9 a.m. to 5 p.m. Admission to the park is $16 for adults and $10 for children age twelve and under. Guided **Safari Tours** are offered on a first-come, first-serve basis for an additional $8 per person. Tours leave at 9:30 and 11:30 a.m. and at 1:30 and 3:30 p.m.

Blink! You just missed it. **Hackberry,** the next stop, is that small. Hackberry, named for a regional native tree, was an 1880s mining community located just off the Santa Fe Railroad tracks. With the development of Historic Route 66, Hackberry had a brief new life as a refueling stop for motorists. When Historic Route 66 was diverted to a straighter path in the early 1930s, Hackberry was left stranded behind the Truxton Wash, and the town dried up faster than a sweat bead in the sun.

Farther down the road, just east of Kingman, you'll come to Hualapai Mountain Road. This 15-mile mountain drive will take you through a pine forest perfect for hiking, wildlife viewing, and picnicking at **Hualapai Mountain Park** (928-757-3859, ranger station, or 877-757-0915, cabin reservations; www.mcparks.com). Trail maps for the 16 miles of developed and undeveloped hiking trails are available at the park office. Admission is $5 per person. The nearby **Hualapai Mountain Resort** (928-757-3545; www.hmresort.net), at 4525 Hualapai Mountain Rd., offers three comfortable rooms and three spacious suites. This rustic retreat is light on amenities, but loaded with opportunities to get away from it all. The resort restaurant is open for lunch and dinner

Wed through Sun and offers a delightful breakfast on the weekends. Rooms range from $79 to $159.

Like many frontier towns, **Kingman** (928-753-6106 or 866-427-RT66; www .kingmantourism.org), about 25 miles west and south of Hackberry on Historic Route 66, is named after one of its founders. Lewis Kingman was a surveyor whose work helped to establish the Santa Fe Railway. The town is actually much bigger than its Main Street appearance would suggest, with a population of about 25,000. Because it's within a one-hour drive of Lake Mead, Lake Havasu, Lake Mohave, and other recreational areas, it's a major stopping point for camping and boating aficionados.

Kingman is home to the **Historic Route 66 Association of Arizona** (928-753-5001; www.azrt66.com) located at the **Historic Route 66 Museum** in the restored **Powerhouse Tourist Information and Visitor Center** (120 W. Andy Devine Ave.; www.kingmantourism.org). The Powerhouse—which was constructed as a generating station—was begun in 1907 and was fully operational in 1927. By the mid-1960s, all use of the facility ceased and it sat vacant. Demolition was too costly to be considered, and in 1986 the building was placed on the National Register of Historic Places (in all, sixty Kingman buildings enjoy the same distinction). Following a $1-million renovation, the building reopened in the fall of 1997. Organized to help preserve the vanishing way of life of mom-and-pop grocery stores and motels with names like the "Lariat Inn," the association provides some insight to visitors who want to know more about the Mother Road. In May the Historic Route 66 Association of Arizona holds a **Route 66 Fun Run** (where "Get Your Kicks" songwriter Bobby Troup has been featured), taking riders in every type of vehicle imaginable on a trip down memory lane with a beauty contest, a car show, street cruising, and other activities.

For another look at the history of Mohave County, stop by the **Mohave Museum of History and Arts** (928-753-3195; www.mohavemuseum.org) at 400 W. Beale St. Here you'll discover exhibits on ranching, mining, and pioneer life. Native American artifacts and art (the Mohave, Hualapai, Chemehuevi, Havasupai, and Paiute Indians all had a presence on this corner of the state); displays of military might (there once was a gunnery school in Kingman); and movie memorabilia from actor Andy Devine (Kingman's "favorite son") are all prominently displayed in this often-overlooked, 18,000-square-foot museum. The museum is open Mon through Fri from 9 a.m. to 5 p.m. and Sat from 1 to 5 p.m. Admission is $4 for adults. Admission fees are good for both the Mohave Museum of Art and the Historic Route 66 Museum.

If you're in the mood for more history, head over to the **Bonelli House,** (928-753-1413) at 430 E. Spring St. This two-story territorial-style mansion is named for the wealthy Swiss family that built it in 1915. Today it has been restored as a museum, and the interior has been decorated with much of the same furniture it held nearly one hundred years ago. The home is open Mon through Fri from 11 a.m. to 3 p.m. There is a donation box at the door.

You won't find any bed-and-breakfast inns right in downtown Kingman, but there are a number of motels on the Historic Route 66 strip, such as the 148-unit *Silver Queen Motel* (928-757-4315) at 3285 E. Route 66. If you're hungry, drop into *Mr. D'z Route 66 Diner* (928-718-0066) at 105 E. Route 66.

Wandering into *Oatman* (928-768-6222; www.oatmangoldroad.org) only a few miles from the Nevada border, a visitor might easily imagine that a time warp exists here—the town looks much the same today as it did when it was established near the turn of the twentieth century. A mining town named after a survivor of an infamous Indian attack, Oatman has braved rough economic times, but its gorgeous Mohave County scenery and Old West ambience continue to draw tourists. Oatman is a big rally point for Historic Route 66 cruisers, including motorcycle clubs, so don't be surprised if you pull into town and glimpse a line of Corvettes or Harleys.

Clark Gable and Carole Lombard, two of the town's most famous visitors, arrived in 1939. After a ceremony in Kingman, they spent their wedding night (though some claim it was night number two) in Room 15 of the *Oatman Hotel* (928-768-4408), a two-story adobe building on Main Street. The hotel, built in 1902, is the largest adobe structure in Mohave County. Although you can't rent a room here, you can check out the decorated rooms upstairs. Downstairs you'll find a full bar, a dining room, and an ice-cream parlor.

Visitors to Oatman can see staged gunfights on Main Street every day, get a cold one at the town's two bars, and pet up to a dozen wild burros whenever they wander into town to mooch food. These descendants of pack animals have been damned by some locals as nuisances, but they've also been adopted as mascots.

Andy Devine Country

If you're a fan of old-time western movies, no doubt you're familiar with Kingman's most famous native son, **Andy Devine.** Born in 1905 in Flagstaff as Jeremiah Schwartz, he grew up in Kingman. He began his film career in the mid-1920s as a Hollywood bit player. His shambling, bearlike gait and raspy voice caused him to be cast as the comic relief in numerous westerns, including the John Ford classic *The Man Who Shot Liberty Valance.* Devine also took roles in many vintage TV shows such as *Gunsmoke, Bonanza, The Twilight Zone, Flipper,* and *Love, American Style.* He continued working in colorful character roles until shortly before his death in 1977.

If you have an interest in seeing the Mohave Desert from a different view, saddle up and take a one- or two-hour trail ride with **Oatman Stables** (928-768-3257; www.oatmanstables.com). The stables are open daily from Oct through May. Rates are $30 for one-hour rides and $55 for two-hour rides.

Oatman is the last Arizona town on Historic Route 66. A few miles west Historic Route 66 hooks up with AZ 95, which takes you to either the Nevada or California border.

Just east of the Nevada border on AZ 95 is **Bullhead City** (928-754-4121 or 800-987-7457; www.bullheadchamber.com). To reach it, continue on Historic Route 66 to AZ 95 and then head north. Bullhead City began life more than fifty years ago as a camp for workers building the Davis Dam on the southern end of Lake Mohave. A rock formation here that resembled a bull's head led to the city's name, but it's now submerged in the lake. The dam was completed in 1953. It regulates water delivery to Mexico and generates electrical power that goes to substations in Arizona, California, and Nevada.

Bullhead City languished for years as a sparsely populated bedroom community. It began to grow in the mid-1960s when entrepreneur Don Laughlin began casino and resort development just across the Colorado River in Laughlin, Nevada, creating a need for visitor services on the Arizona side. Bullhead City was finally incorporated in 1984. Today, more than two million people a year visit Laughlin, and many of them launch their vacation from Bullhead City, where there's a $23-million airport that can accommodate planes as big as the Boeing 737. When visiting Bullhead City, stop at the **Colorado River Museum** (928-754-3399) on AZ 95, a half-mile north of the Laughlin Bridge. The museum was opened in 1990. Using photographs and models, the museum has exhibits on local Native American tribes, evidence of European exploration dating back to 1540, steamboat travel on the Colorado River, and the wagon and camel trains that passed through this area. It is open Tues through Sun from 10 a.m. to 4 p.m., from Sept through Jun. Admission is $2.

Lake Mohave can be reached by driving north on AZ 95. Lake Mohave is part of the Lake Mead National Recreation Area (702-293-8990; www.nps .gov/lame). Admission is $5 for five days. The lake has fishing for largemouth and striped bass, catfish, rainbow trout, and bluegill. Fishing licenses and tackle and bait are available at the **Lake Mohave Resort and Marina** (800-752-9669; www.sevencrown.com). The marina also rents houseboats outfitted with air-conditioning, a gas oven/range, freezer, microwave oven, shower and tub, stereo cassette, and other amenities. Smaller boats for skiing or fishing are also for rent. The marina has several different models from which to choose.

If lounging in a casino sounds like more fun than lounging on a lake, there are several casinos only minutes away in Laughlin, Nevada, most of them lining the western bank of the Colorado.

There are no bed-and-breakfast inns in Bullhead City, just hotels and motels, although some of these offer valuable options. A favorite place to stay is the **Lodge on the River** (928-758-8080 or 888-200-7855; www.lodgeonriver .com) at 1717 Hwy. 95. The riverfront suites offer great views and the heated pool makes a great place to relax after a day of water play on the river. Room rates state at $35 and suites start at $65.

For more basic rooms on the waterfront you can check in at **El Rio Waterfront Resort** (928-763-4385; www.elriorv.com) at 1641 Hwy. 95. The resort also doubles as an RV park and includes such amenities as a boat dock, sand beach, swimming pool, fitness center complete with a sauna, and a clubhouse. The resort offers a wide range of rooms including cabins ($109 to $239) and studios ($39 to $145). Rates change dramatically throughout the week, with the weekends and holidays pulling the highest-priced rentals.

For a bite to eat, drop by **Iguana's Mexican River Cantina** (928-763-9109) at 2247 Clearwater Dr. Run for years by a guy locals know simply as "Valdo," Iguana's uses authentic Mexican recipes prepared by chefs from Sonora, Mexico. After a day on the river, join the locals at the popular **Mad Dog Bar & Grill** (928-704-3644) at 2046 Hwy. 95. The half-pound burger and cold brew are the favorites things to order, but this jukebox joint also serves up a menu of salads, sandwiches, and pasta. The bar is the place to be, but the outdoor patio is a nice alternative.

Lake Havasu Area

South of Bullhead City and south of the Historic Route 66 junction with AZ 95 is **Lake Havasu City** (928-453-3444 or 800-242-8278; www.golakehavasu .com). Founded in 1963, it's one of Arizona's youngest municipalities. The lake itself isn't much older, having been created in 1938 when Parker Dam was built on the California border of the Colorado River. **Lake Havasu** attracts a huge number of visitors, especially in the spring when retirees and college students flock there. It used to clear out in the summer, when Lake Havasu City often records the hottest temperature in Arizona—and sometimes in the nation. Today, though, southern Californians and Arizonans alike appear to ignore their thermometers and have turned the area into a popular summer getaway for water sports of all types.

Lake Havasu is a 45-mile-long playground perfect for water sports of all kinds, including waterskiing, Jet Skiing, powerboating, houseboating, swimming, and fishing. *Lake Havasu State Park* (928-855-2784; www.az stateparks.com) is a popular place for surf and sand during the summer with its three boat ramps, swimming beach, picnic areas, nature trail, and forty-seven first-come, first-serve campsites ($15). On the eastern shore, you'll find *Cattail Cove State Park* (928-855-1223; www.azstateparks.com) with sixty-one first-come, first serve campsites ($10-$30), a swimming beach, and boat rentals at Sandpoint Marina and RV Park. Admission to each park is $10 per vehicle. If you don't have a boat of your own, you can rent one at *Arizona Water Sports* (928-453-5558 or 800-393-5558; www.arizonawatersports.com).

trivia

Lake Havasu City's London Bridge is the largest "antique" ever sold to the United States.

Of course, Lake Havasu City offers more than just fun in the sun. As most of the free world knows, the city is home to the *London Bridge,* all 10,276 granite blocks of which were brought over from England in 1968 by city founder Robert McCulloch of McCulloch Chainsaw fame. When the city of London put the bridge up for sale because it was too small to handle its traffic demands, McCulloch bought the bridge in a terrific publicity stunt for a mere $2,460,000. What you may not realize is that the city has gone to great lengths to complete the illusion of an English community. At the base of the bridge is the Tudor-style *English Village.* The shops, the streets, and even the phone booths resemble those in London. Tour guides (who are basically there to give directions) and other village dwellers dress in authentic garb. Stores in the village sell curios and gift items—some British, some not—such as glassware and candles.

The English motif continues in enterprises like the *London Bridge Resort* (928-855-0888 or 800-624-7939; www.londonbridgeresort.com) at 1477 Queen's Bay Rd., the facade of which mimics a stone castle. The resort has boat docks, several pools, a nine-hole executive golf course, tennis courts, a workout room, and other amenities. Like many other properties around the country, the London Bridge Resort is a time-share resort. When available to the public, they rent anywhere from $99 to $399 per night depending on the season. Many other hotels, inns, and resorts are in Lake Havasu City, but no bed-and-breakfast inns. For the budget-minded traveler who would like to stay close to the action, the *Bridgeview Motel* (928-855-5559) at 101 London Bridge Rd. provides the services and facilities typical of a traditional economy motel, within strolling distance of the English Village. Rates range from $50 to $135 per night.

One mile east of the English Village on McCulloch Boulevard, the city continues its re-creation of the United Kingdom with *Shambles Village* at 2126

McCulloch Blvd. No, the name doesn't mean that the place is a wreck. It's a reference to old-fashioned English butcher stalls with the meat hung from the rafters. The shops include art galleries and apparel and gift shops.

For a look at a different point of view, stop by the **Lake Havasu Museum of History** (928-854-4938; www.havasumuseum.com) at 320 London Bridge Rd. This popular museum features displays on the history of the region in a 3,000-square-foot building. Admission is $4.

Another unique way to see the area is on Sea-Doo watercraft. **London Bridge Watercraft Tours** (928-453-8883) at 1519 Queens Bay can take you on a guided tour from the London Bridge up the Colorado River to the **Havasu National Wildlife Refuge** (www.fws.gov/southwest). The marsh-land here supports a variety of birds, including white pelicans, black-crowned night herons, and kingfishers. It's also possible to see bald eagles in the winter. The Sea-Doos (think of them as mini-powerboats) are large enough for two or three people, are easy to operate, and can hit speeds of 40 miles per hour—but hey, let's be careful out there!

The city has a number of major annual events, including Christmas festivi-ties, boat regattas, and the **World Jet-Ski Racing Finals** (www.ijsba.com), held every October. Call the Lake Havasu Tourism Bureau (928-453-3444 or 800-242-8278) for more information about events. Additional information can be found in *Havasu Magazine* (www.havasumagazine.com).

Quartz and Camels

Due south of Lake Havasu City on AZ 95 is the community of **Parker** (928-669-2174; www.parkerareachamberofcommerce.com). Just north of Parker, birders can catch an eyeful at the **Bill Williams River National Wildlife Refuge** (928-667-4144; www.fws.gov/southwest). Look for such migratory waterfowl as vermillion flycatchers, yellow warblers, and summer tanagers. The 6,055-acre refuge is located off AZ 95 between mileposts 160 and 161.

Another prime spot for birders and hikers is the 1,250-acre **'Ahakhav Tribal Preserve** (928-669-2664; www.ahakhav.com) located on the Colo-rado River Indian Tribes Reservation. Nearly 350 migratory and native bird species can be found here. From AZ 95 in Parker, take Mohave Road west about 2 miles. When you reach the PARKER INDIAN RODEO ASSOCIATION sign, continue a half-mile further and turn left at the TRIBAL PRESERVE sign at Rodeo Drive.

A few miles south of Parker is **Poston,** a name that doesn't mean much to most Arizonans but that played a major role in one of the saddest chapters in American history. Beginning in the summer of 1942, and continuing until the end of World War II, nearly 18,000 Japanese-Americans were interned at the Poston camp on the **Colorado River Indian Tribes Reservation** (928-669-9211; www.crit-nsn.gov). This population made the camp the third largest city in Arizona at the time. Though the detainees were able to create the semblance of a real community by building a pavilion and staging theatrical and musical entertainments, they were clearly prisoners within their own country.

trivia

Palm Canyon, southeast of Quartzsite, is the only place in Arizona where native palm trees grow.

In 1992 a monument to the camp's detainees was erected in Poston, which still contains the camp's original gym/theater. The monument is a 9-foot-tall concrete Japanese lantern with plaques that tell the story of the internment. The staff at the **Colorado River Indian Tribes Museum** in Parker can answer some questions about the Poston camp. The museum also has displays of artifacts from vanished tribes like the Anasazi and Hohokam, as well as rugs, baskets, and other crafts made by contemporary tribes like the Mohave, Navajo, and Chemehuevi.

Mention **Quartzsite** (which you can reach by driving south on AZ 95 from Parker to I-10 and heading east on I-10 for a few miles) to Arizonans, and they'll probably respond "Gemboree!" The fact is that this community of about 2,000, just across the border from Blythe, California, is better known for its yearly gem shows than for anything else. It's no wonder, given that the area

Quartzsite Camels

Besides being a rich mining district, **Quartzsite** once had the distinction of being the army's test site for integrating camels into its cavalry. The army had employed Hadji Ali, a Syrian camel driver, to train the troops in the fine points of managing these "ships of the desert." Known as Hi Jolly to his friends, this Middle-Easterner who'd been transplanted to the American Southwest was regarded as a rather colorful character and something of a local hero. Despite Ali's best efforts, the experiment, carried out from the mid-1850s to 1864, was less than a rousing success. One explanation is that the camels couldn't get along with the army's pack mules. In any case, the hapless animals were finally turned loose into the sun-baked surroundings, where they met an untimely death as a result of starvation or trigger-happy pioneers.

Ali died in 1902, and thirty-three years later, Governor Benjamin Moeur dedicated the **Hi Jolly Monument,** a stone pyramid topped with a metal silhouette of a camel. The monument is easily reached off the west-end bypass of I-10.

is laden with minerals and gems of all varieties. In January and February the Quartzsite population swells to bursting with collectors, dealers, and lookie-loos. Some of the gem selling goes on indoors, but much of the dealing is swap-meet style. Most traders will deal with the general public, but some will sell only to wholesalers. You can find some bargains here, but if you know very little about gems and minerals, caveat emptor applies. Some unscrupulous dealers, for example, will sell polished "turquoise" stones that aren't genuine. Rather, they're made by combining turquoise powder and epoxy resin. For more information on Quartzsite gem shows, contact the Quartzsite Chamber of Commerce at (928) 927 5600; www.quartzsitetourism.com.

Non-Ghost Towns

To explore the west central area of the state, take US 89A south and west from Flagstaff. Between Clarkdale and Cottonwood lies *Tuzigoot* (an Apache name meaning "crooked water") *National Monument* (928-634-5564; www .nps.gov/tuzi). This pueblo, built by the long-vanished Sinagua Indians near the Verde River, is more than 500 years old. The Sinaguans, whose culture included farming as well as hunting and gathering, founded settlements throughout northern and central Arizona, often choosing the land near streams and hot springs as sites for building their elaborate dwellings. Besides the ruins, a nearby visitor center displays Sinaguan artifacts and sells books about the area's history. The visitor center is open daily from 8 a.m. to 6 p.m. in the summer, and from 8 a.m. to 5 p.m. in the winter. Admission is $5 per person age sixteen and older for seven days.

Down the road at *Dead Horse Ranch State Park* (928-634-5283; www .azstateparks.com), near Cottonwood, you will find a multitude of outdoor recreational activities. The 423-acre park has access to a 6-mile stretch of the Verde River and is surrounded by the *Coconino National Forest* (928-527-3600; www.fs.fed.us/r3/coconino), making it the perfect base for camping ($12 to $19), mountain biking, hiking, canoeing, picnicking, fishing, and bird-watching. Admission is $6 per vehicle.

Named for the tree that flourishes along area creek banks, *Cottonwood* (928-634-7593; www.cottonwoodchamberaz.org) has a handful of restored 1870s-style shops that sell everything from arts and crafts to clothing to furni-ture. There's also an old-time movie theater that still shows (mostly) first-run films. If you have a few minutes to spend, you may want to pull off the road and browse through some of the shops or head to a wildlife park in the Verde Valley. *Out of Africa Wildlife Park* (928-567-2840; www.outofafricapark .com) at 3505 W. Hwy. 260 showcases big cats and offers a popular attraction, their daily *Tiger Splash* show that involves staffers swimming with white tigers and other ferocious felines. The park is open Wed through Sun from 9:30 a.m. to 5 p.m. Admission is $36 for adults and $20 for children ages three to twelve. The real attraction, however, is in ***Clarkdale,*** a heartbeat away.

Located north of Cottonwood on AZ 260, Clarkdale is home to the ***Verde Canyon Railroad*** (800-320-0718; www.verdecanyonrr.com). This 40-mile railroad was built in 1911 to take mining and other supplies and copper ore from Clarkdale northwest to the town of Drake. Over time it became popular among those who wanted easy access to the wilderness areas of Verde Canyon. The Verde Canyon Railroad's mining days ended in the 1950s, and after years of struggling financially while hauling coal, it was purchased as an excursion train in 1990. The railway uses renovated Metro New York Line coach cars, each of which can accommodate about seventy passengers. There are also open-air cars where passengers from any part of the train can stand and get a good look at the scenery as the trains ramble through the protected Verde Canyon area, a gorgeous stretch that includes a riparian cottonwood forest, desert areas, and towering red rocks.

The trip also is a wildlife lover's delight. Antelope, javelina, black hawks, and blue herons live here. Though it isn't well known to outsiders yet, more than forty bald eagles are nesting in the area. Peak viewing season is from December through March, when the majestic birds inhabit the canyon, usually nesting within a few hundred feet of the river. During the four-hour ride, singer/storytellers dressed in rustic frontier attire keep passengers entertained and help to point out the wildlife.

The railway operates year-round and even has moonlight excursions in the summer. The train operation offers cocktails, hors d'oeuvres, and deli treats. Fares start at $54.95 for adults and $34.95 for children.

Clarkdale is also the site of the ***Flying Eagle Bed and Breakfast*** (928-634-0663; www.flyingeaglecountry.com) at 2700 Windmill Lane. This bed-and-breakfast offers accommodations in a guesthouse or in a sunrise room attached to the main house. Flying Eagle has horseshoe pits, badminton courts, and a hot tub, but the real attraction is the gorgeous view of the valley. The red rocks of Sedona are visible in the background. Rooms start at $115 a night with a two-night minimum.

Due south on US 89A, the former mining community of ***Jerome*** (928-634-2900; www.azjerome.com) is proud to call itself the "largest ghost town in Arizona." The fact is that it isn't a ghost town at all, although it nearly suffered the fate of total abandonment. Built on Cleopatra Hill in the early 1880s, the town thrived with the copper industry. At first the land beneath the town was drilled into and blasted out to form a series of tunnels (almost 90 miles in

Unlucky Day at the First Interstate Bank

While you're in Clarkdale, stop by the **First Interstate Bank.** On a June morning in 1928, two Oklahoma desperadoes made the mistake of choosing this bank for a heist. As they began to drive away with $40,000, one of the robbers fired a round in the direction of Jim Roberts, a 70-year-old town constable who years before had been one of the most dedicated "soldiers" fighting the infamous Pleasant Valley War (a series of bloody range battles between two families of cattlemen and sheepherders) and whom Zane Grey immortalized in *To The Last Man.* Roberts calmly yanked out his nickel-plated Colt .45 SAA and shot the getaway driver in the head. The surviving holdup man bailed out as the car crashed, emptied his gun without effect at the old lawman, and decided he didn't "feel lucky."

all) from which rich copper ore was extracted. Fires drove the workers out of the tunnels, however, in 1918, and surface mining became the new standard operating procedure.

The dynamiting necessitated by this strip mining caused a shake, rattle, and roll greater than anything Jerry Lee Lewis ever dreamed of, and the town discovered to its horror that it had created a massive slide zone. The *City Jail,* known as the "traveling jail," in fact, has slid 225 feet across the highway since a 1920s dynamite explosion dislodged it from its original foundation.

In the early 1950s the mines closed altogether, and Jerome languished. But just as hippies discovered the Haight-Ashbury District in San Francisco in the 1960s, so too did they find the Victorian buildings of Jerome to their liking, and many settled in the area permanently. Today Jerome is a thriving arts community, with renowned sculptors, painters, jewelers, and musicians plying their trades and professions here. About one-third of the community is directly involved in the arts.

Like many Arizona mining towns, Jerome is easy to navigate on foot, though some of the hills are a bit steep and walking shoes are highly recommended. You may want to explore the restaurants, bed-and-breakfast inns, and shops. Many of them are downtown on Main Street. A few of the fun and funky shops on Jerome's steep streets include *Nellie Bly* (928-634-0255, www .nbscopes.com), known for its impressive collection of kaleidoscopes and *Treasures* (928-649-8099), a fabulous gift shop featuring European antiques and collectibles.

Definitely worth seeing (and staying at) is the *Surgeon's House* (928-639-1452 or 800-639-1452; www.surgeonshouse.com), the restored former residence of the Little Daisy Mine's chief surgeon, Arthur Carlson. Furnished with antiques, the Mediterranean-style bed-and-breakfast recalls an earlier time when the pace of life was slower and more elegant. The owner has retained the home's charm while adding modern luxuries such as a hot tub. It can be arranged for a professional masseur to attend to your aches and pains. Spiritual consultations and walking tours of the area's highlights are also available. Rooms start at $120 and include a breakfast buffet and afternoon snacks.

For another lodging option, check into the **Ghost City Inn Bed and Breakfast** (888-634-4678; www.ghostcityinn.com) at 541 Main St., a one-hundred-year-old bed-and-breakfast that has had many incarnations in its time, including a stint as a speakeasy. This Victorian structure, furnished in original style, has modern amenities like air-conditioning and flat-screen televisions. Rooms start at $95.

Like many small communities, Jerome tends to roll up the streets after sunset, so if you plan on arriving in town at night, make arrangements ahead of time for lodging or food. There are several quaint eateries, including the **Flatiron Cafe** (928-634-2733) at 416 Main St., which serves breakfast and lunch and the **Red Rooster Cafe** (928-634-7087), also on Main Street, which is known for its homemade soups and sandwiches. For dinner, try the **Jerome Palace Haunted Hamburger** (928-634-0554) at 410 N. Clark St. for ribs, burgers, and the like.

A Piece of the Old West

Travel southwest on US 89A to the other side of 7,732-foot Mingus Mountain, and you'll arrive at one of Arizona's loveliest towns, affectionately known as "everybody's hometown." But don't call it Presscott. Locals prefer the pronunciation *Press-kit*. ("Just like *biscuit,*" they'll tell you). The town was named after historian William H. Prescott and began its life in the 1860s as a mining and ranching community.

In some respects, **Prescott** (928-445-2000 or 800-266-7534; www.prescott .org) looks like a cross between Flagstaff—because of its high altitude and pine trees—and Bisbee—because of its many Victorian, wood-frame homes. Residents compare it with the sorts of communities you come across in the Midwest. Of course, if you're from the Midwest, maybe that's not so exciting. We Arizonans (including Grammy-nominated jazz pianist Liz Story, who calls the town home) think it's pretty cool.

For visitors the town offers bed-and-breakfast inns, hotels, and motels. Prescott also has accommodations that are listed in the Historic Hotels of America registry. The **Hassayampa Inn** (928-778-9434 or 800-322-1927; www.hassayampainn.com) at 122 E. Gurley St. was built in the late 1920s as a getaway hotel for wealthy residents of Phoenix. The architecture is Pueblo art deco, done in red brick, and includes Arizona's first porte cochere. The inn has been redecorated on a regular basis without taking away the traditional character of its rooms. Near the Courthouse Square and Whiskey Row is *Hotel Vendome* (928-776-0900 or 888-468-3583; www.vendomehotel.com), which is listed on the National Register of Historic Places. It's a grandmother's cottage sort of place with quilts on the beds and a bed-and-breakfast ambience. Legend has it there's a ghost (and a ghostly cat!) in the house, which may be why the brochure says it's a unique lodging experience, not just a place to sleep. Rooms start at $89.

You won't starve in Prescott: Its ninety or so restaurants range from big-name chains to mom-and-pop establishments. *Murphy's* (928-445-4044; www.murphysrestaurants.com) at 201 N. Cortez St. is a former general store that is now transformed into an elegant eatery. Murphy's offers three kinds of fresh fish daily, as well as ribs, lobster tail, and other examples of American and Continental cuisine. The restaurant's lounge affords a view of *Thumb Butte,* where Virgil Earp—before becoming a U.S. marshal for Pima County—once ran a sawmill.

trivia

The pine-forested central Arizona community of Prescott is known as "Arizona's Christmas City."

Prescott was named Arizona's first territorial capital in 1864, a title it relinquished to Tucson in 1867 before regaining it in 1877. The capital was moved—permanently—to Phoenix in 1889. More than 500 Prescott buildings are listed on the National Register of Historic Places.

If you want to find out more about the area's history, the best place to go is the *Sharlot Hall Museum* (928-445-3122; www.sharlot.org) at 415 W. Gurley St. Hall was an early twentieth-century historian, originally from Kansas, who grew up in and around Prescott. Later in life she purchased the former governor's mansion (Prescott was twice the territorial capital) and began a museum of items relating to Arizona history. On the grounds are the Museum Center, housing the archives and research library; the Sharlot Hall Building, a rock and pine log house; the Fremont House of more sophisticated construction; a Victorian-style Bashford House; Fort Misery (which is the oldest log building associated with Arizona); the Transportation Building, exhibiting the vehicle collection; and the Governor's Mansion, built in 1864. In addition there's a ranch house, a schoolhouse, a windmill, and several gardens, including the Pioneer Herb Garden. The museum is open Mon through Sat from 10 a.m. to 5 p.m. and Sun from noon to 4 p.m. Admission is $5 for adults.

Another museum that attracts its share of visitors is the *Phippen Western Art Museum* (928-778-1385; www.phippenartmuseum.org) 4701 Hwy. 89

Chino Valley's Claim to Fame

Although Prescott claims the privilege of being the first Arizona territorial capital, that honor rightly belongs to the little community of **Chino Valley** (928-636-2493; www .chinovalley.org), 15 miles to the north on US 89. In 1863 there was a mining camp in Chino Valley under the command of Lt. Amiel Whipple, and he established the capital at his fort. The most logical choice, Tucson—a much larger town with more amenities—was ruled out because of its large number of southern sympathizers. The territorial capital was moved to Prescott the following year. There are some traveler's services, including gas and lodging, in the area, but because Chino Valley is primarily a bedroom community, there are no real attractions.

North. Named after George Phippen, one of the founders of the *Cowboy Artists of America,* the museum has permanent and traveling exhibitions. Much of the work presented in the museum involves realistic depictions of cowboy life—roundups, campfires, bronc busting—but there are also impressionistic portraits of ranch hands, Native Americans, and other frontier dwellers that give startling insight into the life, work, and soul of the people of the Southwest. The museum also frequently hosts lecturers and special events related to cowboy art. The museum is open Tues through Sat from 10 a.m. to 4 p.m. and Sun from 1 to 4 p.m. Admission is $5 for adults.

Historic **Whiskey Row** is a stretch of Montezuma Street between Gurley and Goodwin. In the "bad old days" of the West, this avenue of saloons and red light establishments was the scene of much debauchery and gunplay, not to mention a horrendous fire in 1900. One of the best places to visit on the Row is the **Palace** (928-541-1996; www.historicpalace.com) at 120 S. Montezuma St. The original Palace burned down in the 1900 fire, but the hand-carved mahogany bar was carried (by hand) out into the street and later incorporated into the rebuilt structure. Like many historic watering holes in Arizona, the Palace is now a restaurant and saloon that occasionally has live country-and-western music.

Although things are quiet now, there were many Indian wars fought here during Arizona's frontier days. **Skull Valley,** just west of Prescott via Montezuma Street, which becomes Iron Springs Road, is named for the grisly aftermath of an 1864 battle between Apaches and Maricopas. The dead warriors were not buried, and white settlers were greeted by the sight of human skulls bleaching in the sun. For years Skull Valley was a stage stop as well as the location of Fort McPherson, established here to protect settlers and overland freighters from Indian attacks. The fort was removed after only a few years of use. A number of historic buildings, however, remain. These include the Santa

Fe Depot, which was built in 1898; a one-room schoolhouse built in 1917; a 1916 general store; and a 1925 gas station. You can see the outside of the old buildings on your own.

Nearby, the *Lynx Lake Recreation Area* (928-443-8001; www.fs.fed.us/ r3/prescott) offers plenty of outdoor recreational opportunities. In addition to bass and crappie, rainbow trout are periodically stocked in the 55-acre lake. Boating is restricted to electric motor-powered watercraft, but is also open to oar, paddle, or sail-powered boats. If you don't have your own, you can rent a boat at the *Lynx Store and Marina* (928-778-0720). Other area activities include hiking, camping ($10), mountain biking, horseback riding, and bird-watching. Check with the *Bradshaw Ranger District* (928-443-8000; www .fs.fed.us/r3/prescott) at 344 S. Cortez St. in Prescott for more information.

Places to Stay in Western Arizona

JEROME

Connor Hotel
164 Main St.
(928) 634-5006 or
(800) 523-3554
www.connorhotel.com
Twelve first-class, Victorian rooms in an 1898 hotel. Note that rooms 1 through 4 are located over the bar and can be noisy on weekend evenings. Moderate.

Jerome Grand Hotel
200 Hill St.
(928) 634-8200 or
(888) 817-6788
www.jeromegrandhotel.net
Thirty rooms/suites in a 1926-era renovated five-story mountainside hotel. Ghost-hunting tours, a restaurant, and a gift shop add to the grand experience. Moderate to expensive.

KINGMAN

Days Inn West
3023 E. Andy Devine Ave.
(928) 753-7500
www.daysinn.com
A reasonably priced choice on the main drag. Includes a free continental breakfast and a heated outdoor pool. Inexpensive.

Historic Hotel Brunswick
315 E. Andy Devine Ave.
(928) 718-1800
www.hotel-brunswick.com
This historic 1909 hotel is located on Historic Route 66—"The Mother Road." Rooms are decorated with period pieces, and this is the only hotel in Kingman with an in-house bar and restaurant. Inexpensive.

LAKE HAVASU CITY

Havasu Springs Resort
2581 State Hwy. 95
(800) 892-2141 or (928) 855-2141
www.havasusprings.com
Four separate hotels at this resort cater to a wide range of needs. The Marina Hotel is closest to the inner harbor, Lakeview Motel offers panoramic views, Vista Suites is geared for families, and the Poolside Motel offers a central location. Moderate.

Nautical Inn Resort
1000 McCulloch Blvd.
(928-855-2141 or
(800) 892-2141
www.nauticalinn.com
One hundred thirty-nine beachfront suites, each with a lake view and balcony or patio. Moderate to expensive.

MEADVIEW

Grand Canyon West Ranch
3750 E. Diamond Bar Ranch Rd.
(702) 736-8787 or
(800) 359-8727
www.grandcanyon westranch.com
This historic, working cattle ranch takes guests on an adventure to the Old West.

WEB SITES FOR WESTERN ARIZONA

Arizona Department of Tourism
www.arizonaguide.com

Bullhead City
www.bullheadchamber.com

Chloride
www.chloridearizona.com

Coconino National Forest
www.fs.fed.us/r3/coconino

Cottonwood
www.cottonwoodchamberaz.org

Grand Canyon West
www.destinationgrandcanyon.com

Havasupai Tourist Enterprise
www.havasupaitribe.com

Hoover Dam
www.usbr.gov/lc/hooverdam

Jerome Chamber of Commerce
www.azjerome.com

Kingman Area Chamber of Commerce
www.kingmantourism.org

Lake Havasu Tourism Bureau
www.golakehavasu.com

Lake Mead National Park
www.nps.gov/lame

Oatman Chamber of Commerce
www.oatmangoldroad.com

Parker
www.parkerareachamberofcommerce
.com

Prescott Chamber of Commerce
www.prescott.org

Prescott National Forest
www.fs.fed.us/r3/prescott

Enjoy the ranch's rustic cabins, home-cooked meals, horseback riding, wagon rides, and a helicopter tour of Grand Canyon West. Moderate.

PARKER

Blue Water Resort and Casino
11300 Resort Dr.
(928) 669-7000 or
(888) 243-3360
www.bluewaterfun.com
Rooms and suites, two restaurants, casino, live entertainment, pool and water park, marina, and sandy beach. Moderate.

PRESCOTT

Prescott Pines Inn
901 White Spar Rd.
(928) 445-7270 or
(800) 541-5374
www.prescottpinesinn.com
This Victorian bed-and-breakfast offers a romantic getaway in the ponderosa pine forest. Breakfast is a delight; it's even served on rose-patterned china. Moderate.

Places to Eat in Western Arizona

JEROME

The Asylum
200 Hill St.
(928) 639-3197
www.theasylum.biz
Located in the Jerome Grand Hotel, this classic restaurant serves lunch and dinner paired with an impressive wine list. Entrees range the gamut and include such

specialties as Sonoran spiced chicken pasta, prickly-pear barbecued pork tenderloin, and roast maple-leaf duck breast. Moderate to expensive.

Mile High Grill

309 Main St.
(928) 634-5094
www.innatjerome.com
This casual grill serves up tasty breakfast and lunch entrees ranging from French toast and chicken-fried steak to salmon salad and blue cheese burgers. Moderate.

KINGMAN

The Cookery

3300 E. Andy Devine Ave.
(928) 757-7311
Casual American cuisine including steaks, sandwiches, and salads. Inexpensive.

Hubb's Bistro

315 E. Andy Devine Ave.
(928) 718-1800
www.hotel-brunswick.com/
bistro-bar

Located in the historic Hotel Brunswick, this fine-dining establishment serves up everything from steaks to seafood. Open for dinner only. Moderate to expensive.

LAKE HAVASU CITY

Chico's Tacos

1641 McCulloch Blvd.
(928) 680-7010
This casual fast-food Mexican joint serves up such standard dishes as tacos, enchiladas, flautas, burritos, and fajitas. Six specialty salsas at the salsa bar spice things up. Inexpensive.

Juicy's River Cafe

25 N. Acoma Blvd.
(928) 855-8429
This cozy cafe is a great place for breakfast. The lunch and dinner menu feature homemade cooking at reasonable prices. Inexpensive to moderate.

Mudshark Brewing Company

210 Swanson Ave.
(928) 453-2981
www.mudsharkbrewingco
.com
Handcrafted beers, gourmet pizza, steak, seafood, and burgers. Inexpensive to moderate.

PRESCOTT

Gurley Street Grill

230 W. Gurley St.
(928) 445-3388
www.cyberfork.com/gurley
This casual eatery serves up a nice selection of ribs, steak, pizza, burgers, and pasta. Specials include roasted chicken potpie, fish and chips, and home-style pot roast. Moderate.

Prescott Brewing Company

130 W. Gurley St.
(928) 771-2795
www.prescottbrewing
company.com
Handcrafted premium beer and pub-style dining in Prescott's only microbrewery. Inexpensive.

EASTERN ARIZONA

→

Indian Country

It's estimated that the ***Navajo Nation*** covers a staggering 27,000 square miles of northeastern Arizona, southeastern Utah, and northwestern New Mexico—making it larger than ten of the fifty United States. With a population of more than 250,000, it's easy to figure out that there are many miles of wide-open territory without a human being in sight. You can see vast expanses of unbroken near-wilderness area, then, suddenly, modern homes or a collection of hogans—traditional, one-room, six-sided Navajo dwellings—pop into view. The solitude of the land is a keen reminder of what this country was like hundreds of years ago.

Therein lies one of the primary attractions of ***Navajoland*** (928-871-6436; www.discovernavajo.com), along with one of the biggest problems for travelers. Few people means plenty of areas with no automotive services, so if your radiator overheats, you break an axle on a rutted road, or you just get very hungry, you can be out of luck.

Here's some advice for anyone planning a trip to the reservation:

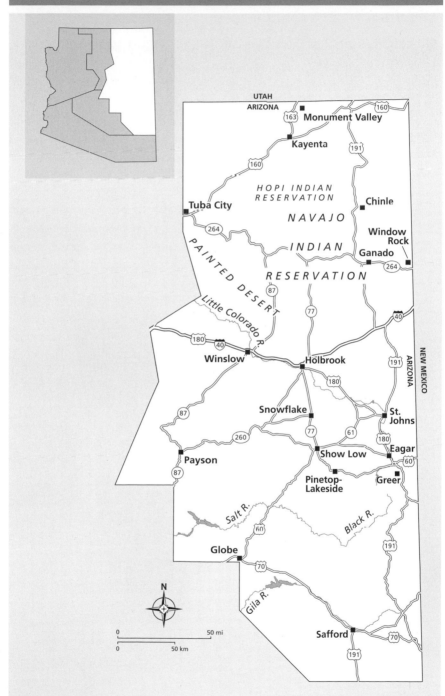

1. Buy a good, detailed map of the area, showing dirt roads, and plan your route well in advance. This will save a lot of aimless driving.
2. Make sure your vehicle is in tip-top physical shape. Check fan belts, hoses, all fluid levels, tires, and so on. If anything seems suspiciously close to being worn-out or broken, have it fixed. If it's a rental vehicle, trade it in for a new one.
3. Calculate distance and gas mileage. There may not be a service station for many, many miles, so make sure you have more than enough fuel to reach your destination and get back. Whenever you come to a gas station, top off your tank.
4. If you want to go somewhere other than the Navajo Reservation visitor center (which is at Window Rock, near the New Mexico border at the junction of I-40 and Indian Route 12), take a vehicle that has adequate ground clearance for rough roads. A truck or four-wheel-drive vehicle is best here. The main roads up to the reservation and to the prime attractions (for example, trading posts) are usually in good shape, but the pathways to Indian ruins and some of the more remote villages are unpaved. These are not all-weather roads, and your $40,000 sporty import—with its touchy race-tuned suspension—will be pounded into an expensive bucket of metric bolts by the time you get where you're going.
5. Travel in good weather. Again, many roads are unpaved and become all but impassable in snow or heavy rain.
6. Bring provisions in a cooler: water, trail mix, and fruit that travels well (like oranges).

And keep this very important fact in mind: When you enter the reservation, you're actually entering another nation's territory. Show respect for its laws, customs, and culture. A good practice is to stop at the visitor center first

AUTHOR'S TOP PICKS IN EASTERN ARIZONA

Canyon de Chelly	Petrified Forest National Park
Gila Box Riparian National Conservation Area	Sunrise Park Resort
	Tonto Natural Bridge State Park
Monument Valley	
Navajo National Monument	

and get the rundown on what you can and can't do on the reservation. You may not be allowed to attend certain ceremonies, and at others you may be required to dress conservatively (no shorts and Hawaiian shirts). Alcohol is usually outlawed on reservation land.

In general, cameras, camcorders, tape recorders, and sketch pads are forbidden in the villages. Visitors who want some record of the colorful, expressive ceremonies or powwows will have to rely on memory to preserve that experience. Occasionally Native American tribes will stage dance or drum competitions (often off the reservations) where cameras and recorders are allowed.

While you're driving, you'll notice that in many well-traveled areas of the reservation roadside vendors sell everything from katsina dolls (which are made to teach children about Hopi katsina spirits) to rugs, baskets, pottery, and jewelry. If your interest is only in fine arts, you should be cautious when buying these arts and crafts. An experienced dealer in Native American art advises as follows: "Most good artists are going to show and sell either directly to their own clients or to galleries." Some work you see is of inferior quality, or it may actually be Mexican in origin. Unless you don't mind this, or you simply want a souvenir, stick with well-established galleries and shops. The visitor center will tell you what and where they are and can also direct you to the homes of artists and craftspeople who sell directly to the public.

Native American craftspeople can spend months or even longer working on a single piece. A lot of time and painstaking work have gone into creating the olla (*oy-yah*, a pot), bracelet, or finely woven rug you're handling. The artist has a good idea of how much it's worth. There are definite established prices, and trying to haggle over money is usually considered an insult.

Though Native American art is often cross-cultural (for example, every tribe has its share of oil painters and sculptors), as a rule of thumb the Navajos are best known for weaving and jewelry; Hopis are revered for their katsina dolls; Zunis are respected for their fetishes and jewelry; and Tohono O'odham (pronounced *Tahano Autum*) and Pima Indians are known for basketry.

In the last few decades, Native American artwork—everything from Pima ollas to Zuni bracelets—has become highly collectible. Blankets and rugs from the 1880s or earlier can sell for hundreds of thousands of dollars. Experts predict that prices for the works of contemporary Native American artists, who often spend as long as a year laboring on a single rug or other piece, will continue to rise. (Recently a woman who had purchased a pot some thirty years ago on a reservation for $50 had it appraised for $5,000.)

Some trading posts are worth a visit if for no other reason than to marvel at their wealth of wonderful arts and crafts as well as their sense of history.

FEBRUARY

Historic Home and Antique Show
Globe/Miami
Transportation to the historic homes is provided by tour guides.
(928) 425-4495 or (800) 804-5623; www.globemiamichamber.com

APRIL

Mining Country Boom Town Spree
Globe/Miami
Enjoy old-fashioned mining competitions, a wild bed race through the streets, an arts and crafts fair, Chihuahua races, and live entertainment at this lively annual event.
(928) 425-4495 or (800) 804-5623; www.globemiamichamber.com

MAY

Native American Art Auctions
Ganado
This biannual auction at the historic Hubbell Trading Post includes authentic Native American art ranging from Navajo rugs to Hopi katsina dolls. The preview for the auction is from 9 to 11 a.m., with the auction starting at noon. The second annual auction is held in Sept.
(928) 755-3475; www.nps.gov/hutr

JUNE

Strawberry Festival
Strawberry
This arts and crafts fair also includes food booths, children's activities, and live entertainment at the Pine-Strawberry Community Center. The festival is held in conjunction with the Annual Strawberry Patchers' Quilt Show.
(928) 474-4515 or (800) 672-9766; www.rimcountrychamber.com

JULY

Native American Art Festival
Pinetop-Lakeside
Held at the Hon-Dah Resort-Casino and Conference Center, this juried Native American art show includes artist demonstrations and Native American music and dance performances.
(928) 367-4290 or (800) 573-4031; www.pinetoplakesidechamber.com

AUGUST

Eagar Daze
Eagar
This local event includes a variety show, horseshoe tournament, junior rodeo, arts and crafts fair, kids' zone, and logging competition.
(928) 333-4128; www.eagar.com

Old West Days Celebration
Hollbrook
Enjoy gunfight reenactments, an arts and crafts fair, a quilt show, a talent contest, bike races, children's activities, and live entertainment at the Navajo County Historic Courthouse.
(928) 524-6558 or (800) 524-2459; www.gotouraz.com/holbrook

Suvoyuki Days
Once known as archaeology days, this annual event features the Hopi Indians through traditional dances, a corn roast, artist demonstrations, cultural exhibits, and a morning run at Homolovi Ruins State Park.
(928) 289-4106; www.azstateparks.com

SEPTEMBER

Gila Valley Cowboy Poetry and Music Gathering
Safford/Thatcher
This weekend event features cowboys from throughout the state performing

poetry readings and musical performances about life on the range. (928) 428-2511 or (888) 837-1841

White Mountain Apache Tribal Fair and Rodeo

Whiteriver

More than eighty years old, this annual event features all-Indian rodeos, concerts, carnival, exhibits, and competitions.
(928) 338-4346; www.wmat.nsn.us

Navajo County Fair

For more than seventy-five years, folks have been gathering for this county fair. Highlights include a rodeo, Junior pageants, a livestock show, a carnival and midway, and a demolition derby at the Navajo County Fairgrounds.
(928) 524-4757; www.navajocountyfair .org

Navajo Nation Fair

Window Rock

More than sixty years old, this fair features arts and crafts, contests, exhibits, concerts, horse racing, powwow, rodeo, and traditional song and dance.
(928) 871-6647; www.navajonationfair .com

Fall Artisan's Festival

Pinetop-Lakeside

More than 150 artists display their wares at this arts and crafts fair. The festival is held in conjunction with an antiques show, quilt show, 10K run, and the "Run to the Pines" car show.
(928) 367-4290 or (800) 573-4031; www.pinetoplakesidechamber.com

OCTOBER

Apache Jii Day

Globe/Miami

All-Indian celebration, crafts, paintings, baskets, quilts, dolls and clothing, and entertainment by various tribes.
(928) 524-6558 or (800) 804-5623; www.globemiamichamber.com

NOVEMBER

Cowboy Christmas Arts and Crafts Show

Safford
(928) 428-2511 or (888) 837-1841

Christmas Parade

Winslow

More than sixty years old, this event features the longest-running hometown Christmas parade in Northern Arizona.
(928) 289-2434 or (928) 289-2435; www.winslowarizona.org

DECEMBER

Festival of Lights

Globe/Miami

Besh-Ba-Gowah Archaeological Park, luminarias, Christmas program and bonfire.
(928) 524-6558 or (800) 804-5623

Parade of Lights Festival

Holbrook

Arizona's oldest Electric Light Parade works it way down Historic Route 66 starting at 6 p.m. Day activities include a holiday arts and crafts fair, visits with Santa Claus, and live entertainment at the Navajo County Historic Courthouse.
(928) 524-6558 or (800) 524-2459; www.gotouraz.com/holbrook

Native American Art

Having once made the mistake of not buying a piece of Indian pottery that by now would have doubled or tripled in value, I've decided it's high time I learned. Now living in Arizona I understand and appreciate so much of what the Indian cultures of our country are all about. For one thing, their love of the land is saving the open spaces of the West. Their reverence for the earth is also reflected in their pottery, made from the rich clay of the Arizona mesas. Utilitarian in origin, native pottery is an art form that dates back 2,000 years. Each tribe has its own way of decorating and coloring their grain and water pots—Hopi Tewa pottery is distinguished by the intricacy of their designs; Zuni use an owl motif, and the Acomas prefer figures of both animals and birds. The Navajos are known for their weaving, which is a 300-year-old craft passed from mothers to daughters, possibly with a grandmother also providing both instruction and tribal lore as part of the learning process. There are more than thirty styles of Navajo rugs, each named for the various regions of their vast reservation (nearly five million acres in total size). Geometric shapes and representations of their deities are the distinguishing features. Katsina dolls are a Hopi tradition given as gifts and teaching tools to their children. Carved from the root of a cottonwood tree, they represent dancers and spiritual beings who carry the prayers of the living to the deities who control events of everyday life. Women are particularly fond of buying Native American jewelry when they visit Arizona. The Navajos and the Zunis are the tribes associated with necklaces, bracelets, rings, belts, and cluster work. Among the Navajo motifs are squash-blossom necklaces and crescent-shape pendants. Zunis are known for their combination of silver and stones. Zunis also produce fetishes, which are either polished stones that appear in the shape of a bear or carvings of wildlife (for example, a snake) that are thought to contain a spirit.

One of the best places to look or buy is the **Hubbell Trading Post** (928-755-3475; www.nps.gov/hutr), about a mile west of the tiny town of **Ganado** off AZ 264 west of Window Rock. Founded in 1878 by John Lorenzo Hubbell, this establishment has been frequented by celebrities, visiting dignitaries, and U.S. presidents. If you can't find the katsina doll, basket, or blanket you want here, it probably doesn't exist. Next door to the trading post at the visitor center, you can take a guided tour of the Hubbell home ($2 for those age seventeen and older) and see exhibits on Hubbell and the history of trading posts on the western frontier. Quite often Native American artisans use the area around the visitor center as a work space, and for a tip of a few dollars they'll pose for pictures. Every year the trading post hosts the popular **Native American Art Auctions** in May and September.

The best place to start an exploration of the Navajo Reservation is the pueblo-style complex that houses the **Cameron Trading Post, Motel, and Restaurant** (928-679-2231 or 800-338-7385; www.camerontradingpost.com), which was established in 1916. The hotel features two-story or three-story rooms decorated in a rustic southwestern style. The restaurant has specialties like Navajo stew and fry bread, as well as traditional burgers and sandwiches. More spectacular than the food, however, is the view from the dining room of the Little Colorado River. The trading post offers a vast assortment of katsinas, rugs, baskets, sand paintings, and pottery. Additionally, an attached gallery has high-end items, including ceremonial headdresses. Prices in the trading post and gallery are reasonable, and you can be assured of the authenticity.

Motorists unfamiliar with this vast land should understand that though many towns appear on the typical road map, services like food, water, and gasoline can be dozens of miles apart. Heading northeast to **Kayenta** and Monument Valley or southeast towards Window Rock, the town of **Tuba City,** near the intersection of US 160 and AZ 264, is a good place to stop, fill up, and stock up on supplies.

The capital of the Navajo Nation is **Window Rock,** located on AZ 264 just a few miles west of the New Mexico border. There are several interesting attractions near Window Rock. About 3 miles west on AZ 264 you'll see the **St. Michaels Historical Museum** (928-871-4171). This stone building was a home for Franciscan friars during the

> ## trivia
>
> Near **Tuba City,** the desert is crisscrossed by Dilophosaurus tracks, evidence that the plant-eating dinosaur the size of a horse roamed this countryside until it was annihilated by the Tyrannosaurus rex.

1890s. The friars came to Arizona to spread the gospel and establish schools for Native Americans. They were instrumental in helping to create a written language for the Navajos, and there are displays in the museum of some of the original Franciscan translations. There are also photographs and exhibits depicting the friars' daily lives. The museum is open daily from 9 a.m. to 4 p.m.

Next door is the wood and brick building that houses a statue called *The Redemption of Mankind, The American Pietà*. Ludwig Schumacher, born in Germany as the son of a Nazi, rejected his father's beliefs for a life of pacifism. He immigrated to America in the mid-1980s and settled in Arizona. A craftsman by trade and a sculptor by temperament, he found a section of a juniper tree that he wanted to carve into a representation of Michelangelo's *Pietà*. Unlike the original, Schumacher's is a vertical statue, standing 16 feet tall. It depicts Jesus being taken off the cross to where Mary waits.

If you take AZ 264 east, you'll quickly arrive back at Window Rock. The **Navajo Tribal Museum and Gift Shop** (928-871-6673; www.navajonationmuseum.org) and the **Navajo Arts & Crafts Enterprise** (928-871-4090;

www.gonavajo.com) are located downtown next to the **Quality Inn Navajo Nation Capital** (928-871-4108 or 877-424-6423; www.qualityinnwindowrock .com) at 48 W. AZ 264. Rates start at $89. The museum houses intricate exhibits featuring life-size mannequins involved in tribal ceremonies and everyday activities. The arts and crafts enterprise is a Navajo organization that dates back to 1941. The purpose of this guild is to assure the quality, innovativeness, and authenticity of the crafts of its artisans. The guild also purchases arts and crafts from the Hopi, Zuni, and Santo Domingo tribes, so the selections here are very good. If you like Native American jewelry, make sure you see the Zuni pieces—especially the bracelets, which are for men as well as women.

At the one and only street light in Window Rock, take Indian Route 12 north to **Tségháhodzání** (the Navajo name for "the rock with the hole in it"). This red sandstone landmark that gave the town its name is several stories tall, with a 130-foot hole in the center. There are picnic areas nearby, as well as the hogan-shaped **Navajo Nation Council Chambers** where the tribe's eighty-eight council members meet four times per year. The chambers are open for self-guided tours (928-871-6417). Nearby, you can visit the **Window Rock Tribal Park and Veterans' Memorial** (928-871-6647; www.navajo nationparks.org), which is open daily from 8 a.m. to 5 p.m. The park features a monument to the Navajo Code Talkers—a group of Navajo soldiers who created a code during WW II that was never broken. Other symbolic structures within the park include a circular path pacing to the four cardinal directions, angled steel pillars engraved with the names of Navajo war veterans, and a healing sanctuary featuring a sandstone fountain.

One of the most spectacular sites on the reservation is **Canyon de Chelly** (928-674-5500; www.nps.gov/cach). Canyon de Chelly (Shay) is the scene of the final defeat of Navajo warriors who were holding out against troops commanded by General James Henry Carleton. In January 1864, in the final battle, twenty-three warriors died and more than 200 Navajos surrendered. You can reach Canyon de Chelly by taking Indian Route 12 north along red rock cliffs and past lush orchards. When you reach the junction for Indian Route 7, take Indian Route 7 (the back road, some parts gravel) northwest to the town of **Chinle** at the entrance of Canyon de Chelly. For an alternative route on which all the roads are paved, head west on AZ 264, then north on AZ 191 to Chinle. This route is about 80 miles. Follow the highway signs to the visitor center. The center has a museum that traces the history of Native Americans in the canyon. It also has an art gallery, demonstrations of Indian arts and crafts, and an information desk. Navajo guides can also be hired here.

At the visitor center you can also get a map that will show you the route of the rim drives. You can take these roads unescorted, though you will miss

Exploring Canyon de Chelly

When you arrive at the entrance to **Canyon de Chelly,** the canyon walls are only about 30 feet high, but they eventually soar to 1,000 feet above the sandy floor. While in Canyon de Chelly, don't miss **Spider Rock Overlook. Spider Rock** is an 800-foot-tall chunk of sandstone about which there are many legends. In one Navajo version of a Bogey Man story, Navajo children are told by their parents that if they don't behave, Spider Woman—a demigod who also supposedly taught the Navajos how to weave—will take them away and leave them on top of the rock to die. Also be sure to see the **White House Ruin.** These remains of an 800-year-old Anasazi village were named for the white plaster used on one of the pueblo's walls. **Antelope House** is another set of Anasazi ruins that's worth a look. This more-than-90-room pueblo is located near a rock crevice where, in the 1920s, a mummy was recovered by archaeologists. The Anasazi sometimes wrapped their dead in ceremonial garments and placed them in hidden crevices where the weather and scavenger animals couldn't get to them. Mummies were found in the appropriately named **Mummy Cave,** also the site of a large set of ruins in the section of Canyon de Chelly known as **Canyon del Muerto** ("the canyon of the dead," so named because of burial sites uncovered here by archaeologists in the 1880s).

the most spectacular sights. If you want to experience Canyon de Chelly more fully, you must hire a Navajo guide and obtain a National Park permit to enter the canyon. Guides charge $15 an hour. If you opt for a horseback tour, there is an additional $15 an hour fee for horse rentals. Cameras are permitted on these trips, and usually the guides will pose for a picture provided you don't want to sell it to a photo stock agency or some such thing. Some guides will be willing to take you to villages where you can see jewelers and rug weavers at work and watch scenes of contemporary Navajo life. In some of these locations, you may be asked to leave your camera or sketch pad in the Jeep.

The steep 2.5-mile round-trip trail to *White House Ruin* is the only place where visitors can enter Canyon de Chelly without a Navajo guide. With sixty rooms in the lower section and another twenty tucked away in the cliff, this Anasazi structure housed as many as one hundred people at a time during the years between A.D. 1060 and A.D. 1275. The trailhead begins at the White House Overlook on the South Rim Drive. Guided hikes are available for $15 an hour.

West of Canyon de Chelly, off US 160, 20 miles south of Kayenta, lies the *Navajo National Monument* (928-672-2700; www.nps.gov/nava). The 360 acres protected by the Navajo National Monument contain the ruins of three of the most intact Anasazi cliff dwellings. Stop at the visitor center 9 miles north of US 160 on AZ 564. Like most visitor centers on the reservation, there is an exhibit hall, an arts and crafts shop, and presentations on Navajo history. Best of all, the center is next to a moderately strenuous 5-mile round-trip hiking trail that takes you to a view of the **Betatakin Ruins.** Betatakin, situated about 700 feet below the rim of the canyon, has about 135 rooms that were built sometime between A.D. 1250 and A.D. 1300. You'll need binoculars or a spotting scope to see much detail, but even from a distance they are impressive.

If you're feeling adventurous and want a truly off-the-beaten-path experience on the Navajo reservation, sign up for a hike to **Keet Seel** (928-672-2366), a 160-room, well-preserved Anasazi settlement. After trekking the 8.5 miles to the remote cliff dwelling, you can climb up ladders with a ranger to walk the streets of this ancient civilization. People began settling in Keet Seel in A.D. 950, nearly 300 years before construction began in Betatakin. In A.D. 1250, a new group of settlers arrived and a steady influx kept the village growing until it contained more than 150 rooms—making it the largest of its kind in the state. The diversity of Keet Seel residents is reflected in the building styles used to construct the four distinctly different kivas, three common streets, and a retaining wall stretching 180 feet along the eastern half of the village.

Betatakin and Keet Seel tours are conducted daily from Memorial Day weekend through Labor Day weekend. Free tickets for the guided Betatakin hike are handed out at 8:15 a.m. and 10 a.m. daily on a first-come, first-serve basis with a limit of twenty-five hikers for each tour. Free permits are available for the Keet Seel tour with a limit of twenty people a day. Orientation is at 8:15 a.m. and 4 p.m. Reservations can be made up to two months in advance for Keet Seel. The Navajo Nation is on daylight saving time and is one hour ahead

Exploring Canyon Mysteries

The sandstone walls of the extensive *Tsegi Canyon* system cradle the remains of an ancient civilization that inhabited lands that are now part of the vast Navajo Nation. The Anasazi, a word meaning the "ancient ones" or "ancestors of the aliens" in the Navajo tongue, inhabited the vivid landscape found in southeastern Arizona for nearly a thousand years before finally mysteriously abandoning their far-flung dwellings.

Deep within the sandstone canyons, three cliff dwellings are protected by Navajo National Monument—Inscription House, Betatakin, and Keet Seel. Visitors can take a 5-mile round-trip hike led daily by Navajo guides to the base of a looming cave measuring 450 feet high and 370 feet wide. Nestled inside are the crumbling ruins of Betatakin. An 18-mile round-trip hike into a tributary canyon of the system leads to Keet Seel, one of the largest and best preserved cliff dwellings in the state. However, the location of Inscription House is kept secret in hopes of preserving the crumbling vestige of the small dwelling.

Monuments of Time

Pulitzer-prize winner N. Scott Momaday described *Monument Valley:* "You see the monoliths that stand away in space, and you imagine that you have come upon eternity. They do not appear to exist in time. You think: I see that time comes to an end on this side of the rock, and on the other side there is nothing forever."

This desert highland, situated at 5,564 feet, began to form twenty-five million years ago as a vast inland sea. When the waters receded, all that remained were expansive beds of red sandstone, which the wind used to sculpt the massive monuments—grain by grain, year by year.

Hogans nestle along the road and farther out into the valley, where the Navajo people live and play as they have since they first came to this region in the late fifteenth century. Since that time, the Navajo were only parted from its stark beauty after their forced removal to New Mexico between 1864 and 1868. Ninety years later, the Navajo Tribal Council designated the 29,816-acre *Monument Valley National Navajo Tribal Park* to preserve the lifestyle of the Navajos residing within its boundaries.

of other Arizona locations during the summer months. Guided hikes to both ruins are occasionally available in the winter months, depending on weather conditions, scheduling, and staffing. Check with the visitor center (928-672-2700) for more information.

While on the hikes, beware of rockfall hazards, watch for flash floods and stay on trails to avoid quicksand. Livestock pollute the stream so all water must be carried in. Take a minimum of two liters of water per person for the Betatakin hike and four quarts for the Keet Seel hike. The trails run primarily through Navajoland, and all hikers must stay on designated paths.

Don't leave the Navajo reservation until you've seen *Monument Valley* (435-727-5870; www.navajonationparks.org), where numerous westerns have been filmed. You can reach Monument Valley Navajo National Tribal Park by driving north on US 163. Though it straddles the Utah–Arizona border, most of the park is actually within Arizona. The nearly 30,000-acre valley spills across the landscape like a watercolor set of purples, reds, and golds. Jutting up at irregular intervals are tremendous mountains of sand-sculpted rock. The valley is unquestionably one of Arizona's most widely photographed sites, with its soaring sandstone monoliths and cliff formations that bear curious names like the Three Sisters and the Mittens. Many of the accommodations, such as *Goulding's Trading Post, Lodge and Museum* (435-727-3231; www.gouldings .com), are located north of the Arizona border. The museum features the role Monument Valley played in director John Ford's memorable movies, including

Stagecoach, The Searchers, and *She Wore a Yellow Ribbon,* all starring actor John Wayne. **Goulding's Lodge** offers great views of Monument Valley, the **Stagecoach Dining Room,** and an indoor pool. Rooms range from $73 to $180 depending on the season. The **Monument Valley National Navajo Tribal Park Headquarters and Visitor Center** (435-727-5870; www.navajonation parks.org) is also in Utah, about 5 miles past the state line off US 163. Watch for the crossroads on US 163, and take the one that goes to the right. The visitor center offers dramatic views of Monument Valley. You can purchase a permit at the visitor center to take your vehicle on a 17-mile loop drive through the valley, but the road is poorly maintained and bumpy. You'll have a much better time if you hire a guide at the visitor center to take you by Jeep or horseback on a tour of the full valley. Admission to the park is $5 for age ten and older.

One place that nearly everyone visits on the Navajo Reservation is **Four Corners National Monument** (928-871-6647; www.navajonationparks.org), the only place in the nation where four states (Arizona, Utah, Colorado, and New Mexico) converge. There's a marker at this point, and few Arizona vacations are complete without a photo of the travelers straddling this landmark. Four Corners is easily reached by taking US 160 northeast. Admission is $3 per person.

There isn't an endless array of motels and eateries on the reservation, but of the few, most are well known and time-tested. In **Kayenta the Best Western Wetherill Inn** (928-697-3231), located on US 163, has fifty-four rooms, no restaurant, but a small gift shop and an indoor pool. Rates start at $116. About 10 miles away is the **Anasazi Inn at Tsegi Canyon** (928-697-3793; www .anasaziinn.com), which is only a few minutes away from the Navajo National Monument and has great views. Rooms start at $80. There's a twenty-four-hour restaurant and a gift shop but no pool. In Chinle the **Thunderbird Lodge Motel** (928-674-5841 or 800-679-2473; www.tbirdlodge.com) has a cafeteria that's open until 8 p.m. and a gift shop. Rates start at $109. Half-day inner

Inscription Rock

One place you're sure to want to visit on the Hopi Reservation is Inscription Rock. Take AZ 264 east until it ends at the Keams Canyon Trading Post. After a 2-mile hike along Keams Canyon, you'll come to a dam. Nearby is a sandstone wall, called *Inscription Rock,* that bears the 1864 signature of Kit Carson. Carson, a buffalo hunter and sometime army scout, was the man General James Carleton ordered to deliver an ultimatum to the Navajos—that they must relocate to the Bosque Redondo reservation by the Pecos River or be destroyed.

canyon tours, which leave at 9 a.m. and 2 p.m., can be booked in the gift shop for $65 per person.

For restaurants try *Amigo Cafe* (928-697-8448), off US 163 just north of US 160; it serves Mexican, American, and Navajo cuisine.

Tucked entirely within the Navajo Reservation is the comparatively tiny 1.5-million-acre *Hopi Reservation* (928-734-2441), home to about 8,000 people. This rocky terrain has been inhabited by the Hopi and their ancestors for hundreds of years. In fact the village of *Oraibi* on the third mesa (plateau) is the oldest continuously inhabited town in the United States, having been settled around A.D. 1100.

The reservation's villages are grouped on three separate mesas, with the *Hopi Cultural Center Restaurant and Inn* (928-734-2401; www.hopi culturalcenter.com) accessible from the second mesa off AZ 264. At the center you will find the *Hopi Museum,* which features Hopi history spanning hundreds of years. Modern Hopi art sits side by side with ancient artifacts. The museum is open from 8 a.m. to 5 p.m. on weekdays and 8 a.m. to 3 p.m. on weekends. Just keep in mind that life runs a little differently here and the museum might very well be closed during regular hours, so it's best to call ahead before making the trip. Admission is $3 for adults and $1 for children ages two to thirteen. The rooms are clean and casual and the restaurant dishes up everything from American favorites to traditional Hopi dishes. Room rates start at $105. The motel's front desk staff is an excellent source for information about any tribal dances and ceremonies that the public may view. Though friendly, the Hopi closely guard their privacy and religious rituals. Some areas of the Hopi Reservation are open to tourists, whereas others are not. And although the Hopi do invite visitors to observe many of their colorful ceremonies, the use of cameras, video or audio recorders, and sketch pads is strictly forbidden. Hopi dances traditionally begin in December, with ceremonies stopping in July, but call ahead if you'd like to plan your visit to coincide with these events.

Wild West Country

Just south of the Navajo reservation, near the junction of AZ 77 and I-40, is the town of *Holbrook* (928-524-6558 or 800-524-2459; www.gotouraz.com/ holbrook). More than one hundred years ago, Holbrook was known as "the town too tough for women and children." Cowboys shot it out in saloons like the Bucket of Blood, and some of the killings associated with the Pleasant Valley War took place here. To get a look at what the town used to be like, drop by the 1898 *Navajo County Courthouse* (928-524-6558 or 800-524-2459) at

100 E. Arizona St. (The Holbrook Chamber of Commerce is also located in the courthouse building.) You can tour the sheriff's office and the jail and see exhibits depicting everything from the area's geologic history to an old-time barbershop. It's open Mon through Fri from 8 a.m. to 5 p.m. and Sat and Sun from 8 a.m. to 4 p.m. For a special treat, stop by the courthouse on the weekends during June and July and enjoy Native American dance performances from 6:30 to 8:30 p.m.

Once a year (usually in Jan) the town offers visitors a chance to obtain a very unusual souvenir: a letter delivered by the *Pony Express.* In commemoration of the area's history and as a kickoff to other festivities, a team of riders known as the *Hashknife Pony Express Riders* (www.hashknifepony express.com) sets off from the Holbrook Post Office on a three-day trek to Scottsdale through the White Mountains. They carry thousands of letters with them, and each is canceled with a special mark that designates it as a Pony Express delivery. The riders' arrival in Scottsdale heralds the official kickoff of the city's annual Parada del Sol celebration. For more details about having a letter sent in this manner, contact Holbrook Postmaster, Pony Express Ride, Holbrook, AZ 86025.

For restaurants in Holbrook try the *Wayside Cafe* (928-524-3167) at 1150 W. Hopi Dr. (Historic Route 66). It serves Mexican and American food Monday through Friday. *Romo's Cafe* (928-524-2153) at 121 W. Hopi Dr. has been serving up Mexican favorites since the 1960s. Romo's Cafe is open 10 a.m. to 8 p.m. daily. Holbrook does not have any bed-and-breakfast inns but it does have more than 1,000 motel rooms, ranging from simple mom-and-pop–style lodging to more elaborate chain accommodations. The *Best Western Arizonian* (no, we don't normally spell it that way) *Inn* (928-524-2611 or 877-280-7300) at 2508 E. Navajo Blvd. has a pool and serves up a complimentary breakfast and dinner (included in the room rate) in the dining room. Rates start at $112. A favorite place to stay for families is the Historic Route 66 icon *Wigwam Motel* (928-524-3048; www .wigwam-motel-arizona.com) at 811 W. Hopi Dr. Room rates start at $52. Reservations are highly recommended.

The *Petrified Forest National Park* and *Painted Desert* (928-524-6228; www.nps.gov/pefo) are a short drive north from town on I-40. The Painted Desert, north of the freeway, provides vistas of green desert vegetation with mountains of red and purplish hues. If you're wearing polarized

trivia

Arizona has its own "Triassic Park," actually the *Petrified Forest National Park,* where the remains of Triassic reptiles have been unearthed and ancient trees turned to stone 225 million years ago.

sunglasses, the effect can be quite striking. Conversely, if you're not wearing sunglasses, or if they're of the nonpolarized variety that don't block stray light, the scenery will look washed out and you'll wonder why you bothered to stop. If you plan to take pictures here, the same rule applies. If you can, use a polarizing filter on your lens or wait until the sun is at an angle, just after sunrise or just before sunset.

Across the road, the **Petrified Forest** is a marvel of the unique properties of nature. Littered across the landscape are giant chunks of what were once logs, part of a conifer forest that thrived millions of years ago. Long before humans walked the earth, the forest was covered by water, and sediments settled on the trees. Gradually, as the trees decayed, all that was left was hardened stone in the shape of the original tree. Because these fossils haven't been polished, you often have to look really hard to see the array of colors lurking in the stone. Admission to the park is $10 for seven days.

Before heading off to see the sights, stop at the visitor center and grab a descriptive brochure. You'll probably want to see **Agate Bridge,** where a petrified log fell over a canyon. One story has it that more than one hundred years ago, on a ten-dollar bet, a cowboy rode his horse over that bridge—not a feat I'd care to duplicate! Another place to stop is **Newspaper Rock,** where ancient Indian tribes chiseled in all the news that was fit to chip.

By the way, it's illegal to remove any pieces of wood from the park, and, really, the stuff is so nice in the gift shops you'd be foolish to risk the fine. Stop by **Jim Gray's Petrified Wood Co.** (928-524-1842; www.petrified woodco.com) gift shop on US 180 at AZ 77, and you'll see many crafts made from petrified wood, as well as polished chunks of the material. Admission to the museum is free, and it's open from 8 a.m. to 6:45 p.m. every day with extended summer hours.

The Winslow area has long been inhabited. Hopi archaeological remains in the nearby **Homolovi State Park** (928-289-4106; www.azstateparks.com or www.homolovi.com) date back many hundreds of years. The park, located off I-40 via AZ 87, sprawls over 4,000 acres at 4,900 feet and has campsites ($12) and hiking trails, some of which will take visitors to petroglyphs and an old Mormon cemetery. Two of the Hopi-Anasazi sites are open to the public. Several other sites are still being excavated. In the past, the park has held "dig days" when visitors were allowed to observe the research. Write to the park officials at HCR63–Box 5, Winslow, AZ 86047 to see about such special events. Hopi artists give art demonstrations each Sat from 9 a.m. to 4 p.m. Admission is $5 per vehicle.

Winslow (928-289-2434; www.winslowarizona.org) itself, founded in 1881, has quite a history. Named for Gen. Edward F. Winslow, president of the St. Louis & San Francisco Railroad, the community was raised on the three Rs: ranching, railroading, and Route 66. The **Old Trails Historical Museum** (928-289-5861) at 212 N. Kinsley Ave. has displays of all three stages of the area's history, as well as artifacts from the region's Native American history. The museum is open Tues through Sat from 10 a.m. to 4 p.m.

Not all the sites being excavated are as old as the Anasazi ruins at Homolovi. The remnants of **Brigham City,** a rock fort founded in 1876 by Mormon settlers near the banks of the Little Colorado River, are a "restoration in progress." To take a peek at the site, take exit 253 off I-40 and drive west on North Road to La Prade Lane.

Aircraft aficionados may want to make the drive along Second Street to AZ 87 and out Airport Road to the **Winslow-Lindbergh Regional Airport** (928-289-0100), which is named after the famous pilot Charles Lindbergh. This airport is unique because it has the longest runways in North America. In addition, it was designed by Charles Lindbergh (on his honeymoon, no less!) and built by Howard Hughes. The airport saw extensive military use during World War II, and today you still may be able to see old planes there because it's a slurry base for converted bombers used in fighting forest fires.

trivia

In its heyday, Winslow's historic **La Posada Hotel** housed such celebrity guests as Clark Gable and Carole Lombard, Douglas Fairbanks and Mary Pickford, Charles and Anne Morrow Lindbergh, Gary Cooper, Jimmy Durante, John Wayne, Howard Hughes, Will Rogers, Harry Truman, and Franklin Roosevelt, as well as Japanese royalty.

No visit to Winslow is complete without a stroll over to the park to see the two-story mural at **Standin' on the Corner Park** (www.standinonthe corner.com). The Glenn Frey/Jackson Browne song "Take It Easy"—recorded first by the Eagles on their debut album and later by Browne—recounts an incident that occurred on the corner of Second (actually Historic Route 66) and Kinsley. In September, the town holds the **Standin' on the Corner Park Festival,** which includes a "Miss Flatbed Ford" contest in honor of the famous song's lyrics. This park utilizes the space created by a fire that leveled the old Winslow Drugstore. The park is designed to resemble a 1944 photograph of the corner, depicting a long, lean cowpuncher lounging against a lamppost and speaking to a shorter cattle driver. T-shirts of this scene are available for sale.

Winslow has attracted filmmakers as well as musicians. Oliver Stone came to town to film part of *Natural Born Killers.* The kickoff scenes were shot in the **Red Sands Bar,** which has been closed for years but was refurbished as the roadside Valentine Diner just for the film. The building is located on Second Street across the street from the La Posada Hotel.

One of the most exciting projects in Winslow in years was the renovation and reopening of the historic **La Posada Hotel** (928-289-4366; www.laposada .org), a Fred Harvey hotel located by the Santa Fe Railroad tracks at 303 E. Second St. The hotel, a National Historic Landmark, is a 60,000-square-foot Spanish Mission–style palace designed by famed architect Mary Jane Colter and built in 1929 at a cost of more than $1 million dollars; it was frequented by many celebrities. During World War II, as many as 3,000 troops were fed in the dining hall each day. It closed in 1957 as the result of declining rail travel. In 1997 Allan Affeldt and his wife, Tina Mion, purchased the building and restored it to its former glory. Today it is filled with an intriguing mix of Mission-style antiques, Mexican furniture and artwork, and comtemporary sculpture and art. The hotel has a dining room, gardens, an art gallery, trading post, and museum. Room rates range from $99 to $169.

Winslow has many chain restaurants as well as cafes, such as the **Brown Mug** (928-289-9973) at 308 E. Second St. This Mexican restaurant is open every day but Sunday. Open for more than fifty years, the **Casa Blanca Cafe** (928-289-4191), located at 1201 E. Second St., serves Mexican and American fare daily.

You won't find any bed-and-breakfast inns in Winslow, but the dozen-and-a-half motels range from simple to sophisticated. For basic rooms at a good price try the **Adobe Inn** (928-289-4638) at 1701 N. Park Dr. Rooms start at $72.

Apache and Mormon Country

The **Apache-Sitgreaves National Forests** (928-333-4301; www.fs.fed.us/r3/ asnf) is an impressive stand of vegetation (about two million acres) that ranges from about 3,500 feet in elevation to more than 11,000 feet above sea level. Flora and fauna from many diverse environments can be seen here. Three dozen campgrounds, several hundred thousand acres of wilderness or primitive area blocked to vehicles, and nearly 900 miles of trails are here for those who love hiking and camping.

Many small towns, including Heber, Show Low, Pinetop-Lakeside, and Alpine, lie within the forest boundaries, and quite a few others are within an hour's drive or less. Widely used by vacationers during ski season, this area is also a cool (well, mostly) summer retreat. Bluegrass festivals and other activities help to draw visitors from all over the country.

Incidentally, it's within this stand of forest that Travis Walton, who lived in the Heber area, claimed to have been abducted by a UFO on November

Mogollon Rim Overlook

If you visit the forest, be sure to take the *Mogollon Rim Overlook Trail,* which is accessible from AZ 260. This easy, 1-mile hike through pine forest affords magnificent canyon views where you'll be tempted to sit, listen to the wind, and observe the squirrels. The squirrels seem to like watching people, too—just don't move too fast.

5, 1975 (an intriguing refutation of his story is presented in Philip J. Klass's *UFO Abductions: A Dangerous Game).* Walton's story was told in *The National Enquirer* and in the 1993 film *Fire in the Sky,* which was filmed around the area.

Settled in 1878, *Snowflake* (928-536-4331) was one of the first Mormon communities founded in Arizona. Believe it or not, it wasn't named after an ice crystal—rather, it was built by Erastus Snow and William J. Flake. Flake was responsible for the actual acquisition of the land. He bought the land from rancher James Stinson, only to discover it also had been given to the Santa Fe Railway, and then to the Hashknife Ranch. Like many Mormon settlers in Arizona, Flake met with hostility regarding his religious beliefs and, in 1884, he was arrested for polygamy and spent some months in the gruesome Yuma Territorial Prison.

The town follows Brigham Young's City of Zion design—wide boulevards and neatly squared-off city blocks. Today in the downtown area, many of the original homes—ranging in style from Greek revival to Victorian to bungalow—look exactly as they did more than one hundred years ago. You can take a self-guided tour of the exterior of the historic homes year-round. You can also arrange for an interior tour of several of the homes Tue through Sat from 10 a.m. to 4 p.m. To schedule a tour, call the *Stinson Pioneer Museum* at 928-536-4881. The museum, which is located at 102 N. First St. East, offers exhibits of artifacts and photos from Snowflake's frontier days. Every July the community celebrates its heritage with *Pioneer Days,* when there are guided house tours by costumed Snowflake residents, parades, theatrical productions, and other activities.

For a relaxing base to explore the area, check into the *Osmer D. Heritage Inn Bed & Breakfast* (928-536-3322 or 866-486-5947; www.heritage-inn .net) at 161 N. Main St. Choose from eleven charming rooms decorated with country provincial flair. Guests are treated to a full gourmet breakfast, evening snacks, and an exercise room complete with an indoor hot tub. Rooms range from $95 to $150. Reservations are highly recommended.

Situated along AZ 61, **St. Johns** (928-337-2000; www.stjohnschamber
.com), the Apache County seat, prides itself on having a major **Equestrian
Center** (928-337-4517) located next to the airport. The center has facilities
for cross-country competition, dressage, and other events; however, no riding rentals for visitors are offered here. Call to find out if any horse shows
are scheduled during your visit to the White Mountains. The **Apache County
Museum** (928-337-4737) is also located here at 180 W. Cleveland Ave. Artifacts
of the area's history and prehistory—including a 24,000-year-old set of woolly
mammoth tusks— are on display. The museum is open Mon through Fri from
8 a.m. to 4 p.m. Guided tours are available upon request.

For a cool summer treat, enjoy water sports at one of the largest lakes
in northeastern Arizona at **Lyman Lake State Park.** Located 11 miles south
of St. Johns on US 191 near St. Johns, this state park is a great place for
boating, fishing, waterskiing, camping ($12 to $16 for tent sites and $19 to
$25 for electric sites), and hiking. The park also rents yurts ($35 to $50) and
cabins ($50 to $75). The annual **Fourth of July Fireworks** brightens up the
1,200-acre state park. Day use fees are $5 per vehicle. (928-337-4441; www
.azstateparks.com)

You can certainly be forgiven if you think the communities in the White
Mountain region blend together. It's easy to forget which town is on what
side of which lake. In simple terms, **Show Low** (928-537-2326 or 888-SHOW-
LOW; www.showlowchamberofcommerce.com) was named after an 1875 card
game that supposedly established the town's ownership. It is west on US 60
and just south of **Fool Hollow Lake Recreation Area** (928-537-3680; www
.azstateparks.com). The 800-acre recreation area is located in the Apache-
Sitgreaves National Forest and offers year-round fishing and boating on the
150-acre lake. Other outdoor activities include camping ($15 for tent sites and
$25 for electric sites), hiking, and wildlife watching. Entrance fees in the sum-
mer are $6 per vehicle. In winter, from Oct 16 through Mar 14, the admission
fee is reduced to $3 per vehicle.

The town of **Pinetop-Lakeside** (928-367-4290 or 800-573-4031; www.pine
toplakesidechamber.com) is south of Show Low along AZ 260. Sunrise Park
Resort lies to the southeast along AZ 273.

The entire **White Mountains Apache Reservation** (928-338-1230; www
.wmat.nsn.us) area is loaded with recreational opportunities: lakes, streams,
nature trails, golf courses, and even **Hon-Dah** (Apache for "welcome") **Resort
Casino** (928-369-0299 or 800-929-8744; www.hon-dah.com) on AZ 260 just
south of Pinetop-Lakeside. Many of these enterprises are owned by the White
Mountain Apache Tribe, which has done a phenomenal job developing visitor
services while maintaining the natural look of the terrain.

trivia

Eastern Arizona is home to much of what is considered to be the world's largest stand of virgin ponderosa pine.

One of their finest accomplishments is the **Sunrise Park Resort** (928-735-7669 or 800-772-SNOW; www .sunriseskipark.com), Arizona's largest ski resort. Three mountains—Sunrise Peak (10,700 feet), Apache Peak (11,000 feet), and Cyclone Circle (10,700 feet)— comprise the skiable terrain, which is laced with sixty-five trails and served by modern, high-speed quad, triple, and double chairlifts.

Day lodges on each of the peaks provide food and full rental facilities for skis and snowboards. Additionally the one-hundred-room **Sunrise Park Lodge** (928-735-7669 or 800-772-7669; www.sunriseskipark.com) provides accommodations, whirlpool spas, and saunas just 3 miles from the base of the mountain. The season starts in early December and, weather permitting, runs through late March or longer. Because the resort has extensive snowmaking equipment, it isn't totally dependent on Mother Nature; on a sunny, warm day in Phoenix, you can hop in your car and in four hours or so be in the snow. The lodge includes two restaurants, a gift shop, an indoor pool and hot tub, and a game room. Rates start at $69.

About 30 miles south of Hon-Dah Resort Casino on AZ 73 is **Fort Apache Historic Park** (928-338-1230; www.wmat.nsn.us). This historic piece of frontier and military history operated from 1870 to 1922. Its primary mission was to keep the peace between white settlers and northern tribes of Apaches. General George Crook used the fort as a base of operations during his expeditions against Geronimo and Cochise. Today the fort doubles as a museum, with many of its buildings intact, including officers' quarters, horse barns, and a cemetery. Among the exhibits on display at the **Fort Apache Museum,** which is located in the **White Mountain Apache Cultural Center** (928-338-4625; www.wmat.nsn.us) are some on the history of the White Mountain Apache Tribe in Arizona. The museum is open Mon through Sat from 8 a.m. to 5 p.m. and Sun from 11 a.m. to 3 p.m. Admission is $5 for adults and $3 for ages seven to seventeen.

You'll find many little cafes and family restaurants in the White Mountains.

There's little evidence of it now, but more than one hundred years ago **Springerville** (928-333-2656; www.springerville.com) was one of the toughest towns in the Arizona territory. Because the dense foliage of what is now the Apache-Sitgreaves National Forests provided so many excellent hiding places and made tracking difficult, a countless number of stolen horses and cattle ended up here. Even the tattered remnants of the Clanton gang, after an infamous shoot-out in Tombstone, decided to avail themselves of this area's greater tolerance of lawless activity.

The town's name is actually the result of the hard-luck nature of its early days. Henry Springer, a merchant, went broke attempting to help out some ranchers, and as an ironic twist the town founders decided to name it after him.

Springerville's history as a pioneer outpost is honored by being one of twelve sites in the nation to have a ***Madonna of the Trail Statue.*** These statues, made of algonite stone that incorporates Missouri granite to achieve a glowing hue, were placed on points along the National Old Trails Road by the Daughters of the American Revolution in the late 1920s. The statue depicts a sturdy, stoic pioneer woman in homespun clothes, cradling one child in her left arm and holding a rifle in her right, while another child clings to her skirts. To find the statue, drive down Main Street to the post office; the Madonna is directly across the street.

About 2 miles north of town is ***Casa Malpais*** ("house of the badlands") ***Pueblo Archaeological Park*** (928-333-5375). This ancestral Puebloan ruin and National Historic Landmark site was first reported by an archaeologist in 1883. Stone walls, pottery, and other features of the site indicate that it was occupied for nearly one hundred years before being abandoned in the fourteenth century. Some areas related to the site remain off-limits to the public, but there's still plenty to see, including a museum on Main Street in Springerville. The park is open Mon through Sat from 8 a.m. to 4 p.m. Guided tours are offered daily at 9 and 11 a.m. and at 2 p.m., weather permitting. Admission for the tours is $8 for adults and $5 for children. For more information write to Casa Malapais Pueblo, 418 E. Main St., Springerville, AZ 85938.

The tiny towns of ***Greer*** and ***Alpine*** (fewer than 1,000 residents total) have some visitors services, including quaint lodges and cabins, but most

Round Valley Ensphere

There's another unusual, albeit modern, structure you may want to take a look at: the $11 million **Round Valley Ensphere.** Located 2 miles south of Springerville in the nearby town of **Eagar** (928-333-4128; www.eagar.com), this dome looks a bit like something out of *The Jetsons* and boasts the distinction of being the first domed high school stadium in the country. Built in 1992, the dome is 440 feet in diameter and covers a total floor area of 189,000 square feet. Besides a football field, the dome can accommodate up to seven removable basketball courts. It also has tennis courts and 5,000 seats.

shops and restaurants in the area are in Springerville. For a quick meal, try **Booga Reds** (928-333-2640) at 512 E. Main St., which offers homemade Mexican and American food from 6 a.m. to 9 p.m. daily. (The name, by the way, is a nickname given to the owner by an old cowboy.)

Motels, guest ranches, and cabins are spread throughout the White Mountains area, including the **Oakwood Inn B&B** (928-537-3030 or 800-959-8098; www.oakwoodinnbandb.com) at 6558 Wagonwheel Lane in Pinetop-Lakeside. Room rates range from $110 to $150 and include a full country breakfast. Another great place to kick up your feet is at the **Tal Wi-Wi** ("where the sun rises first") **Lodge** (928-339-4319 or 800-476-2695; www.talwiwilodge.com) in Alpine. The Tal Wi-Wi Lodge, incidentally, features some suites that have fireplaces and hot tubs. There is also an on-site restaurant and saloon. Rates range from $75 to $105.

Payson and Tonto

If you take AZ 260 west from Show Low, you'll travel a scenic route through the Apache-Sitgreaves National Forests, across the Mogollon Rim and down into the **Tonto National Forest** (602-225-5200; www.fs.fed.us/r3/tonto). There are many small towns along the way in which you can stop for gas and travel supplies. The area also features scads of national forest campgrounds and developed hiking trails. Within a few hours you'll reach **Payson** (928-474-4515 or 800-672-9766; www.paysonrimcountry.com), only about 90 miles from the major metropolitan area of Phoenix, yet close to immense stands of ponderosa pine and numerous lakes and streams. As you might expect, this small community of about 15,000 is a recreational stop for people on their way to the White Mountains, as well as a vacation spot for world-weary warriors from the Phoenix area.

Nature trails, campgrounds, and various frequent festivals keep this area active. In August, Payson is the location of **The World's Oldest Continuous Rodeo.** In September, the **Old Time Fiddlers' Contest** (www.paysonfiddlers .com) brings the region's finest pickers and fiddlers to the pine country. In October a regional fine arts festival is held here, and in December, Payson kicks off the holiday countdown by lighting Christmas trees at the Swiss Village. The **Swiss Village Shopping Plaza** is at the southern tip of town. It is a small collection of gift shops, restaurants, and a hotel, the **Best Western Payson Inn** (928-474-3241 or 800-247-9477; www.bestwesternpaysoninn .com). The hotel, located at 801 N. Beeline Hwy. 87, has an outdoor pool and hot tub, an exercise room, and some rooms with fireplaces, microwaves, and refrigerators. Rates start at $99. Though rather touristy, the shops have some interesting handmade items (check out the **Payson Candle Factory,** 928-474-2152, where you can watch candles being dipped and carved), and the Alpine-style village is an unusual sight in the midst of an Arizona forest. Those seeking an even more off-beat shopping experience can stop at one of the quirky antique shops, such as **Granny's Attic Antique Store** (928-474-3962) at 800 E. Hwy. 260.

Just north of here up AZ 87 is the **Tonto Natural Bridge State Park** (928-476-4202; www.azstateparks.com), a limestone formation that's believed to be the largest such formation (400 feet long) in the world. The state park is open on select weekends only; call ahead for the schedule. Admission is $4 for adults and $1 for children ages seven to thirteen. A bit farther north are the tiny mountain towns of **Pine** and **Strawberry** (928-474-4515 or 800-672-9766; www.rimcountrychamber.com). The **Strawberry Schoolhouse,** built in 1884, is the oldest standing one-room schoolhouse in the state. It held its last classes in 1907, and today it's a historic state monument that's open for tours on the weekends.

Globe (928-425-4495 or 800-804-5623; www.globemiamichamber.com), a town of about 7,500, is a mining community with strong links to Arizona's past. You can reach Globe by driving south on AZ 87 to AZ 188, which soon becomes AZ 88 beyond the **Tonto National Monument** (928-467-2241; www.nps.gov/tont). This often-overlooked national monument preserves prehistoric cliff dwellings lived in by the Salado Indians more than 700 years ago. The Lower Cliff Dwelling can be viewed on the observation deck at the visitor center or by a half-mile hike along the Lower Cliff Dwelling Trail. The Upper Cliff Dwelling can only be reached by a guided hike along the 3-mile round-trip Upper Cliff Dwelling trail, which is only open from November through April. Reservations are required. While you are here you might want to check with the park rangers on special activities including full-moon hikes, living-history demonstrations, and off-site hikes. Admission to the park is $3 for adults and is good for seven days.

Continue south on this scenic route through the pines of Tonto National Forest, and you'll soon enter Globe. From the Phoenix area, it's an easy jaunt east on US 60. In the downtown area, more than two dozen historic buildings date from just before the turn of the twentieth century until the late 1920s. They range in style from territorial adobe to Queen Anne Victorian. You can drop by the **Gila County Historical Museum** (928-425-7385)—the former Globe-Miami Mine Rescue Station, built in 1920—at 1330 North Broad St., on US 60 next to the chamber of commerce, to look at exhibits of how the community grew and changed. The museum is open Mon through Fri from 10 a.m. to 4 p.m. and Sat from 11 a.m. to 3 p.m. Also worth a look is the town's

Cobre ("copper") *Valley Center for the Arts* (928-425-0884), in the building that used to be the Gila County Courthouse. It has been lovingly restored as a venue for the Copper Cities Community Players and also houses visual arts studios. You can take a self-guided tour and browse in the gift shop, which sells everything from hand-painted furniture to stationery. The center is open Mon through Fri from 10 a.m. to 5 p.m., Sat from 10 a.m. to 4 p.m., and Sun from noon to 4 p.m. Follow Broad Street through Globe for about 1.5 miles, and you'll see a clearly marked road leading to *Besh-Ba-Gowah* ("metal house") *Archaeological Park* (928-425-0320 or 800-804-5623). This Salado pueblo settlement was built around A.D. 1225 on top of what was once a Hohokam pit house. The site has been restored to allow visitors a self-guided tour. You can climb around in the ancient settlement using ladders to follow the same paths original occupants took to get to the roof or down to the first floor. An on-site museum houses artifacts retrieved from the excavation, including the world's largest single-site collection of Salado pottery. Admission is $3 for adults. It's open daily from 9 a.m to 5 p.m.

After you've worked up an appetite crawling in and out of the pueblo, try a home-style meal at *Judy's Cook House* (928-425-5366) at 2280 E. Hwy. 60 in Globe. Refreshed, you can prowl Globe's half-dozen or so antiques or gift shops, such as *Past Time Antiques* (928-425-2220) at 150 W. Mesquite St.

As for accommodations, several bed-and-breakfast inns in Globe provide rest for the weary. *Cedar Hill B&B* (928-425-7530; www.cedarhillaz.com) at 175 E. Cedar St. is an early-twentieth-century wooden home built by one of the area's most influential families. Antiques (including a queen-size brass bed) have been used in furnishing the three guest rooms, and amenities like cable TV in the living room help you feel comfortably at home. Rates start at $60 per night. A relatively new—but very old—find is the *Noftsger Hill Inn* (928-425-2260 or 877-780-2479; www.noftsgerhillinn.com), a bed-and-breakfast that has guests sleeping in the actual classrooms and janitor's closet of the old Noftsger Hill School at 425 North St. Owners Rosalie and Dom Ayala purchased the property from the previous owners in 2001 and have six rooms currently available—all furnished in "comfortable antiques." Rates are $90 to $125 per night.

Arguably the best reason to visit the *Safford* (928-428-2511 or 888-837-1841; www.visitgrahamcounty.com) area is to drive up the 35-mile *Swift Trail* to the summit of *Mount Graham* (928-428-4150; www.fs.fed.us/r3/coronado), a 10,713-foot peak in the Pinaleño Mountains known as a "sky island," as its lofty green peak appears to be a lush island hovering in the clouds. This mountain has had an interesting history over the years. More than one hundred years ago when there was a fort nearby, injured soldiers were taken up Mount

Graham to recuperate in the pine-scented air. For a number of decades there have been cabins, Christmas tree farms, and campgrounds on the mountain. As an aside, on your way up Swift Trail you'll pass **Safford Federal Prison Camp** on your left, where Watergate conspirator John Ehrlichman was imprisoned for a while.

More recently the University of Arizona and the Vatican have each built telescopes on the peak. The University of Arizona has an international reputation for its astronomical research, which has been based at several locations in southeastern Arizona. The Vatican's involvement in celestial research dates back to the time of Galileo. Together the university and the Catholic Church were able to create telescopes on Mount Graham whose data augment each other's. The Mount Graham telescopes have thrilled astronomers because the scopes are on the cutting edge of technology, but they have angered some environmentalists, who feel the vehicular traffic created by the telescope projects threatens the already endangered Mount Graham red squirrel. University of Arizona biologists are monitoring the squirrels for potential negative impact. To date, there are no signs that the observatory construction has negatively affected the squirrels.

The telescopes aren't visible from the ground, and indeed they are all but invisible in the forest (on a visit to the site, I couldn't detect them until I was only a few hundred yards away). They also are off-limits to anyone without an official U.S. Forest Service permit, which keeps unwanted traffic off the final dirt road to the top where the squirrels live.

Although you can't drive up Swift Trail to where the scopes are, there are many beautiful areas on the mountain where you can pull off and have a picnic. There are also several scenic overlooks where you can see gorgeous, sweeping vistas of the valley all the way down to Safford. If hiking is on your agenda, there are nine major trails on Mount Graham. One of the best is the moderately difficult 14-mile Round the Top Mountain Trail, which meanders through shady pine forest and also offers some good views of the countryside. Check with the Coronado National Forest Safford Ranger District (928-428-4150; www.fs.fed.us/r3/coronado) at 711 Fourteenth Ave., Ste. D, for detailed hiking maps. Whenever you visit Mount Graham, bring a jacket, because it's chilly even in the summer.

Other favorite activities in Graham County include hunting for fire agates at the **Black Hills Rockhound Area** (928-348-4400; www.blm.gov) located 18 miles north of Safford on AZ 191. To check out the living treasures in the area, head to the 23,000-acre **Gila Box Riparian National Conservation Area** (928-348-4400; www.blm.gov), where bird-watchers can keep an eye out for the more than 200 species of birds that inhabit the region. This riparian area features four waterways (the Gila and San Francisco Rivers and Bonita and Eagle Creeks), cliff dwellings, sandy beaches, hiking trails, and shady woodlands. Favored activities in the area include kayaking, canoeing, fishing, wildlife watching, swimming, and camping ($5). The Gila Box Riparian National Conservation Area is located 20 miles northeast of Safford. For an adventurous backcountry drive, take the 21-mile-long **Black Hills Back Country Byway,** which travels between Safford and Clifton. Along the way, you'll travel through desert grasslands and the Gila Box Riparian National Conservation Area. Activities include rockhounding, wildlife watching, birding, hiking, and cultural sites. Access to the backcountry road is from US 191. The southern end of the road is at milepost 139 and the northern end is at milepost 160. The rugged, dirt road is only for high clearance and four-wheel-drive vehicles. For driving directions or more information on the Gila Box Riparian National Conservation Area or the Black Hills Back Country Byway, contact the Bureau of Land Management's Safford Field Office (928-348-4400; www.blm.gov) at 711 Fourteenth Ave.

About a half-hour drive to the south, along AZ 266 off AZ 191, is the town of **Bonita** (no chamber of commerce). Like a lot of Arizona towns, this one can claim a rather wild and woolly heritage. Bonita's old, two-story general store is no longer open; it was formerly known as George Atkins' Saloon. Right out front on August 17, 1877, Francis P. Cahill, a strapping Irish laborer, picked a fight with a youngster known as Henry Antrim. He called Antrim a pimp. Skinny, buck-toothed Antrim—a known horse thief and ne'er-do-well—was no match for Cahill. When the big man rushed him, the eighteen-year-old kid pulled a pistol and gut-shot his tormentor. Cahill died the following day, and the boy who went on to be called William H. "Billy the Kid" Bonney chalked up his first kill. Some stories dispute this and insist that Billy began killing in another state at the age of twelve, but it seems likely that those tales are the sort of tabloid fabrications that were rampant in Victorian times (some things don't change).

From Bonita it's a quick drive north to **Fort Grant,** the site of an even more infamous frontier tragedy. In March 1871, about a half-mile outside what was then Camp Grant, lived a settlement of several hundred Apaches—mostly women and children—who were under the care of the camp's commander, Lt. Royal Whitman. Though the camp seemed peaceful and Whitman had reason to be optimistic about future relations between the Apaches and the U.S. government, a group of men from Tucson, including some civic leaders, held the opposite view. On April 28 they rode out from Tucson with a force of about one hundred Papagos and Mexicans to attack the Apache camp in retribution for previous Indian raids, which actually had nothing to do with the Camp Grant Apaches.

On the morning of April 30, the raiders leveled the peaceful Indian camp, slaughtering all the inhabitants. In the aftermath Whitman and his troops buried the dead and tried to assure other Apaches in the area that the U.S. Army had not played a part in the massacre. President Grant ordered the Arizona territorial governor to find the men responsible for the carnage. The leaders of the raid were brought to trial in Tucson, but all were acquitted. Today Fort Grant is a penitentiary, and there are no visitor services.

For more information on the original Camp Grant story, check the ***Graham County Historical Museum*** (928-348-0470) archives located in the old high school in Thatcher at 3430 W. Hwy. 70. The museum, which has exhibits detailing the frontier history of Graham County, is open Mon, Tues, and Sat from 10 a.m. to 4 p.m.

Places to Stay in Eastern Arizona

GREER

Greer Lodge Resort and Cabins
44 N. Main St.
(928) 735-7216
www.greerlodgeaz.com
This mountain resort offers lodge rooms and cabin rentals, a full-service spa, two restaurants, a gift shop, and three private lakes. Moderate to expensive.

Hidden Meadow Ranch
620 County Rd. 1325
(928) 333-1000 or
(866) 333-4080
www.hiddenmeadow.com
The twelve lovely guest cabins at this gem of a ranch, are decorated by theme, ranging from the pet-friendly Squash Blossom to the elegant Elkhorn. The all-inclusive ranch features a dining room (three meals a day included), a private pond, horseback riding, and a mercantile. Expensive.

HOLBROOK

Motel 6
2514 E. Navajo Blvd.
(928) 524-6101
www.motel6.com
These basic motel-style rooms come with microwaves and refrigerators. Additional amenities include an outdoor swimming pool and a coin-operated laundry. Inexpensive.

KAYENTA

Holiday Inn
Junction U.S. Hwy. 160 and U.S. Hwy. 163
(928) 697-3221 or
(888) 465-4329
www.holidayinn.com
This modern facility is conveniently located near Monument Valley. Amenities include an outdoor swimming pool, coin-operated laundry, and fitness center. Remember: Navajoland is alcohol-free! Moderate.

PAYSON

Days Inn & Suites
301-A South Beeline Hwy.
(928) 474-9800 or
(800) 329-7466
www.daysinn.com
Comfortable rooms at this popular chain hotel include refrigerators, microwaves, and fireplaces (some). Other amenities include an indoor pool and hot tub, a guest laundry, and a deluxe continental breakfast. Moderate.

Mountain Meadows Cabins
25 miles east of Payson off AZ 260 in Christopher Creek
HC2 Box 162 E
Payson, AZ 85541

WEB SITES FOR EASTERN ARIZONA

Apache-Sitgreaves National Forests
www.fs.fed.us/r3/asnf

Arizona Department of Tourism
www.arizonaguide.com

Coronado National Forest
www.fs.fed.us/r3/coronado

Eagar Chamber of Commerce
www.eagar.com

Globe-Miami Chamber of Commerce
www.globemiamichamber.com

Graham County Chamber of Commerce
www.visitgrahamcounty.com

Holbrook Chamber of Commerce
www.gotouraz.com/holbrook

Navajo Nation Tourism Office
www.discovernavajo.com

Payson Department of Tourism
www.paysonrimcountry.com

Petrified Forest National Park
www.nps.gov/pefo

Pinetop-Lakeside Chamber of Commerce
www.pinetoplakesidechamber.com

Rim Country Regional Chamber of Commerce
www.rimcountrychamber.com

Show Low Chamber of Commerce
www.showlowchamberofcommerce.com

Springerville Chamber of Commerce
www.springerville.com

St. Johns Chamber of Commerce
www.stjohnschamber.com

Tonto National Forest
www.fs.fed.us/r3/tonto

White Mountain Apache Reservation
www.wmat.nsn.us

Winslow Chamber of Commerce
www.winslowarizona.org

---

(928) 478-4415
www.mountainmeadows
cabins.com
The six cozy cabins at this retreat are for adults only. Cabins come complete with kitchens, fireplaces, and porches. There is a two-night minimum stay on weekends. Moderate.

PINETOP-LAKESIDE

Rainbow's End Resort
On Pine Lake Road off Rainbow Lake Drive
Route 2

Box 1330
Pinetop-Lakeside, AZ 85929
(928) 368-9004
Relax at the charming accommodations on Rainbow Lake. Inexpensive to moderate.

Woodland Inn and Suites
458 E. White Mountain Blvd.
(928) 367-3636 or
(888) 746-3867
www.woodlandsuites.com
This pet-friendly motel offers a breakfast bar in the

mornings and an afternoon snack. You can also relax in the indoor hot tub. Inexpensive to moderate.

SAFFORD

Olney House Bed and Breakfast
1104 Central Ave.
(928) 428-5118 or
(800) 814-5118
www.olneyhouse.com
Originally built in 1890, this historic house offers two rooms, a bridal suite, and two cottages. Each

morning a full breakfast is served in the lovely Victorian dining room. Inexpensive.

SHOW LOW

Days Inn
480 West Deuce of Clubs
(928) 537-4356 or
(800) 329-7466
www.daysinn.com
This full-service hotel has 122 rooms with refrigerators and microwaves. A complimentary breakfast is served Mon through Fri. Other amenities include a heated outdoor swimming pool and hot tub, a coin-operated laundry, and an on-site restaurant and lounge. Moderate.

THATCHER

Black Rock Ranch Wilderness Retreat
Black Rock Road
P.O. Box 543
Thatcher, AZ 85552
(928) 428-6481
www.blackrockranch.com
This working cattle ranch offers five rustic cabins, a dining room, wildlife watching, and western adventures on this 130-year-old property bordered by the Coronado National Forest. Open mid-Sept though mid-June. Moderate.

TUBA CITY

Quality Inn
10 N. Main St.
(928) 283-4545 or
(800) 644-8383
www.qualityinn.com

This pet-friendly hotel is centrally located on the Navajo Reservation and is less than two hours away from Grand Canyon National Park, Monument Valley, and the Navajo National Monument. Moderate.

WINSLOW

America's Best Value Inn
2035 W. Hwy. 66
(928) 289-1010
This hotel has an indoor pool and hot tub and is close to I-40, several restaurants, and gas stations. Inexpensive.

Super 8 Motel
1916 W. Third St.
(928) 289-4606
www.super8.com
Basic rooms with a free continental breakfast. Inexpensive.

Places to Eat in Eastern Arizona

HOLBROOK

Jerry's
2600 Navajo Blvd.
(928) 524-2364
A family-style diner serving American food. Inexpensive.

PAYSON

El Rancho Mexican Restaurant
200 S. Beeline Hwy.
(928) 474-3111
www.elranchorestaurant.net
Tacos, enchiladas, burritos, and other Mexican favorites are served up at this family-friendly restaurant. Inexpensive.

Gerardo's Italian Bistro
512 N. Beeline Hwy.
(928) 468-6500
Casual Italian dining in a relaxing atmosphere. Inexpensive to moderate.

Macky's Grill
1111 S. Beeline Hwy.
(928) 474-7411
This casual Payson restaurant serves American food for lunch and dinner and offers a full children's menu. Inexpensive to moderate.

PINETOP-LAKESIDE

Chalet Restaurant and Bar
348 W. White Mountain Blvd.
(928) 367-1514
www.thechaletrestaurant.com
Seafood, ribs, and the only sushi bar in Navajo County. Open Tue through Sat for dinner only. Moderate.

Charlie Clark's Steak House
1701 White Mountain Blvd.
(928) 367-4900 or
(888) 333-0259
www.charlieclarks.com

This local favorite has been serving up everything from salad to steak since 1938. Patio dining is offered during the summer months. Moderate.

Christmas Tree Restaurant

455 N. Woodland Rd.
(928) 367-3107
Enjoy fine dining among the pines at this curiously named eatery—a longtime favorite of the late humorist Erma Bombeck. Open for dinner only. Closed Mon and Tues. Moderate.

SAFFORD

El Coronado

409 Main St.
(928) 428-7755
Mexican specialties and American favorites are the mainstays at this casual eatery. Inexpensive.

Manor House Restaurant and Rock'n Horse Saloon

415 East Hwy. 70
(928) 428-7148
This bustling restaurant serves up a full menu of seafood, steaks, pasta, Mexican entrees, and pizza. Inexpensive to moderate.

WINSLOW

Turquoise Room

303 E. 2nd St. (Route 66)
(928) 289-2888
www.theturquoiseroom.net
Located in the historic La Posada Hotel, this fine-dining establishment serves a stylish southwestern-inspired menu of dishes such as pork carnitas, Churro lamb cassoulet, and elk medallions. Open for breakfast, lunch, and dinner. Moderate to expensive.

CENTRAL ARIZONA →

The Valley of the Sun and Phoenix

The **Valley of the Sun** cuts a diagonal swath from Wickenburg in the northwest to Florence in the southeast with Arizona's primary gateway, **Sky Harbor International Airport,** located almost exactly in the center and encircled by the major interstates and highways that provide access in every direction, to every region of the state. Covering approximately 2,000 square miles of the **Sonoran Desert,** the Phoenix metro-plex is made up of twenty-two separate cities and towns, the best-known of which are Phoenix (the core city), Scottsdale (best known for its resorts and art galleries), and Tempe (home of Arizona State University and excellent coffee shops). Gaining in popularity and in recognition are Mesa and Apache Junction in the east valley, Florence and Casa Grande to the south, and Glendale (known for its antiques shops and as the home for the NFL Arizona Cardinals and the NHL Phoenix Coyotes) and Wickenburg (which bills itself as the "Dude Ranch Capital of the World") in the west valley.

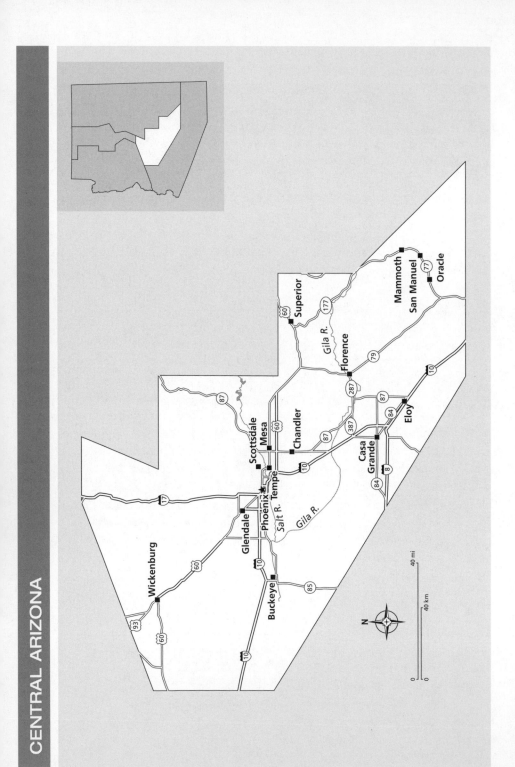

For information about the Valley of the Sun, your best starting point is the ***Greater Phoenix Convention and Visitors Bureau*** (602-254-6500 or 877-225-5749, www.phoenixcvb.com) in Phoenix. When you get to town, the CVB has a downtown walk-in information center (602-452-6282 or 877-Call-PHX) that is open Mon through Fri from 8 a.m. to 5 p.m. at 125 N. Second St., Ste. 120.

If you were born to be wild and you're looking for a unique way to see the Valley (or even the rest of Arizona), you may want to contact ***Street Eagle Motorcycle Rentals*** (480-391-9959 or 800-717-7970; www.street eagle.com) at 9419 E. San Salvador Dr., Ste. 106, Scottsdale. The company rents Harley-Davidson, Honda Gold Wing, BMW, and Yamaha motorcycles, as well as Honda and Harley-Davidson trikes. Pick your speed and climb on and get the thrill of an open-air ride. Employees can either offer you advice on where to ride or arrange a guided tour for groups of five or more riders.

Phoenix is the fifth largest city in the nation, with more than 1.5 million residents within city limits and about 3.8 million total in the greater Phoenix area. Towns spread out along I-10 and I-17 like strands of a giant spiderweb, covering the Valley of the Sun with attractions that are sure to ensnare travelers. The Valley is made up of a myriad of pseudo-, micro-, and full-scale communities, and it can be quite daunting to find your way around if you don't have a detailed map. To the west of Phoenix are the suburban communities of Sun City West, Surprise, El Mirage, Youngtown, Sun City, Peoria, Glendale, Buckeye, Wickenburg, Litchfield Park, Goodyear, and Avondale. To the east are Paradise Valley, Scottsdale, Tempe, Mesa, and Apache Junction. Farther south are Guadalupe, Ahwatukee, Chandler, Gilbert, Sun Lakes, Higley, Queen Creek, and Casa Grande. And that's just a partial list!

AUTHOR'S TOP PICKS IN CENTRAL ARIZONA

Arizona Science Center	Historic Heritage Square
Boyce Thompson Arboretum State Park	Old Town Glendale
	The Phoenix Zoo
Chase Field	
	Rawhide Wild West Town
Desert Botanical Garden	
	Taliesin West
Heard Museum	

JANUARY

West Valley Native American Invitational Arts Festival
Litchfield Park
Enjoy the work of more than fifty Native American artisans at this popular annual event.
(623) 935-6384

Arizona National Horse Show
Scottsdale
One of Arizona's largest horse shows, this annual event includes a quarter horse show, 4-H/FFA horse show, and a saddlebred show at WestWorld in North Scottsdale.
(602) 258-8568; www.anls.org

FBR Open
Various locations
"The Greatest Show on Grass" tees off one of the PGA Tour's top events featuring some of the finest golfers in the world.
(602) 870-0163; www.phoenixopen.com

FEBRUARY

Gold Rush Days
Wickenburg
A senior rodeo (age fifty and older) includes gold panning, carnival, western dances, arts and crafts, barbecue, gem show, and mucking and drilling.
(928) 684-5479; www.wickenburg chamber.com

Arizona's Renaissance Festival
Apache Junction
This traveling festival (Feb and Mar) is situated at a permanent site, built to resemble a sixteenth-century European village. Visitors can shop at in the village market with over 200 authentic shops including an apothecary, blacksmith, toy-maker, potter, and glassblower. The festivities are highlighted by daily jousting matches and rousting meals

at the various food stands loaded with turkey legs, cold beer, and roasted nuts.
(520) 463-2700; www.royalfaires.com/ arizona

Lost Dutchman Days
Apache Junction
The southwest Phoenix Valley rodeo includes gold panning, a parade, a carnival, a rodeo pageant, and the Budweiser Clydesdales.
(480) 982-3141; www.lostdutchman days.org

O'Odham Tash
Casa Grande
The largest all–Native American rodeo, held on Presidents' Day weekend, includes arts and crafts, a parade, and Native American dances.
(520) 836-4723 or (800) 916-1515; www.casagrandechamber.org

Native American World Championship Hoop Dance Championship
Phoenix
The Heard Museum hosts top Native American dancers from the United States and Canada in a national hoop dancing competition.
(602) 252-8848; www.heard.org

Arizona Scottish Highland Games
Mesa
This exciting festival, sponsored by the Caledonian Society of Arizona and honoring Scottish heritage, features piping and drumming, a dance competition, and clan/society registration.
(602) 431-0095; www.arizonascots.com

Scottsdale All-Arabian Horse Show
Scottsdale
Two thousand of the world's most beautiful Arabians, Half-Arabians, and

National Show Horses compete in this annual equestrian display.
(480) 515-1500; www.scottsdaleshow.com

MARCH

Jaycees Rodeo of Rodeos
Phoenix
This nearly eighty-year-old rodeo opens annually at WestWorld and includes a traditional rodeo, dances, and a live concert.
(602) 254-6500

Heard Museum Guild Annual Indian Fair and Market
Phoenix
This annual fair features more than 300 of the nation's top Native American artists.
(602) 252-8848; www.heard.org

Arts Festival
Scottsdale
The festival is rated among the top in the country and includes 200 selected artists from over 1,000 applicants. The event includes live music from local performers as well as fresh food and wines from the area.
(480) 994-ARTS or (800) 877-1117

Old Town Tempe Spring Festival of the Arts
Tempe
This is the second-largest arts and entertainment festival in the Southwest.
(480) 355-6075; www.tempefestivalofthearts.com

APRIL

Gaslight Antique Walk
Glendale
Seventy-five stores, specialty shops, and restaurants stay open from 6 to 9 p.m. on the third Thurs of the month.
(623) 930-2960

Culinary Festival
Scottsdale
Sample the best in food and drinks from around the area at this grand picnic and Le Tour Culinaire in the heart of downtown Scottsdale.
(800) 877-1117; www.scottsdaleculinaryfestival.org

MAY

Summer Concerts in the Park
Scottsdale
This free concert series features local bands from the Phoenix Valley. The concerts are held at the McCormick Ranch Park. The train runs at night and refreshments are available for purchase.
(480) 312-2312; www.therailroadpark.com

JUNE

Grand Canyon State Summer Games
Phoenix
Athletes of all ages and abilities compete in an Olympic-style event, featuring twenty-two different sports. Elite athletes have only one category available to them for competition.
(480) 517-9700; www.gcsg.org

JULY

Summer Spectacular Art Walk
Scottsdale
A meandering trail through the streets of downtown Scottsdale leads to some of the best galleries in the city. Patrons can cool off during the hot summer nights as they pop in and out of shops hosting the work of local artists.
(800) 877-1117; www.scottsdalegalleries.com

Downtown Cooldown
Tempe
The event features twenty tons of snow and numerous games for kids and families to beat the summer heat.
(480) 921-2300

continued

AUGUST

Bring in the Clowns
Scottsdale
The largest clown gathering in the Southwest brings together families and performers alike. Kids get faces painted for free and the clowns march through the western town in a grand parade.
(480) 502-1880; www.rawhide.com

SEPTEMBER

"Bye Bye Buzzards" Day
Superior
At Boyce Thompson Arboretum State Park, a local flock of turkey vultures are due back to their roosts in the eucalyptus grove. A bird-watching tour follows buzzard viewing.
(520) 689-2811; www.azstateparks.com

Fiesta Septiembre
Wickenburg
The festival at the Desert Caballeros Western Museum features arts and crafts, folklorico dancers, mariachi bands, mercado, and a salsa contest.
(928) 684-5479 or (928) 684-0977; www.wickenburgchamber.com

OCTOBER

Cowboy Artists of America Sale and Exhibition
Phoenix
This exhibition specializes in American Southwest and cowboy imagery in various mediums at the Phoenix Art Museum.
(602) 257-1222; www.phxart.org

NOVEMBER

Fountain Festival of Arts and Crafts
Fountain Hills
Over 200,000 visitors attend this festival featuring more than 450 visiting artists.
(480) 837-1654; www
.fountainhillschamber.com

Feeling of Fall Festival
Superior
The Boyce Thompson Arboretum celebrates the sights and smells of fall. Enjoy Arizona apple cider, apple pie, and doughnuts, live music, and special events for kids.
(520) 689-2811; www.azstatepark.com

Arizona Temple Christmas Lighting
Mesa
Enjoy the 500,000-plus lights in the garden and a lighted reflection pool.
(480) 964-7164; www.ldschurchtemples .com

Thunderbird Balloon Classic
Scottsdale
Experience the liftoff of over 1,300 balloons with adjoining continuous entertainment.
(800) 877-1117; www.thunderbird balloonandairclassic.com

Fantasy of Lights
Tempe
Downtown Tempe celebrates the holidays with the city tree lighting, fireworks, and live entertainment.
(480) 921-9300

DECEMBER

Fiesta Bowl Block Party
Tempe
Thirty-plus musical groups gather on five different stages for an unforgettable New Year's Eve.
(800) 635-5748; www.fiestabowl.org

Cowboy Christmas, Cowboy Poets Gathering
Wickenburg
The Desert Caballeros Western Museum hosts a night of poetry, ballads, stories, singing, and storytelling.
(928) 684-2272; www.westernmuseum .org

Gliding over the desert in a hot-air balloon is an interesting way to travel off the beaten path; so is doing it yourself with a parasail or sailplane (aka glider). Flying adventures are available in several corners of the Valley. For glider flights *Arizona Soaring/Estrella Sailport* (520-568-2318; www .azsoaring.com) is located south of the city at 22548 N. Sailport Way in Maricopa, a short drive off I-10. They offer rides and instruction seven days a week from 11 a.m. on weekdays, and from 9 a.m. on weekends. Rides start at $105. Northwest of the city is *Turf Soaring School* (602-439-3621; www.turfsoaring .com) at the Pleasant Valley Airport in Peoria. They are open every day from 9 a.m. to 5 p.m. Hot-air balloon rides are available from *Unicorn Balloon Company* (480-991-3666 or 800-755-0935; www.unicornballoon.com), which launches near Scottsdale Airport, and *Hot Air Expeditions Inc.* (480-502-6999 or 800-831-7610; www.hotairexpeditions.com), which launches from a site in North Phoenix. *Adventures Out West* (480-991-3666 or 800-755-0935; www.adventuresoutwest.com) runs out of the same office with the Unicorn Balloon Company and offers combination Jeep-balloon trips (one with a western breakfast option). Balloon flights run $185 for adults and $155 for age twelve and under. Combination trips start at $205 per person. Early morning is the traditional time to balloon, and Hot Air Expeditions (HAE) makes it an occasion available year-round with a champagne breakfast catered by Vincent Guerithault, chef of a well-known Phoenix restaurant, Vincent's on Camelback. HAE also does a sunset trip during the winter months (Nov through Mar) with champagne and hors d'oeuvres catered by Chef Vincent (who does a mean chocolate truffle, by the way). Flights are $175 or $195 if you require pickup service at your hotel.

Jeep tours are another great way to see the desert. Two companies operating in the Valley of the Sun are *Arizona Desert Mountain Jeep Tours* (480-860-1777 or 800-567-3619; www.azdesertmountain.com), which offers a choice of five three-and-a-half-hour itineraries and operates twice a day, seven days a week; and *Desert Storm Hummer Tours* (480-922-0020; www.dshummer .com), which gives you four hours in one of those double-wides that are billed as the most powerful four-by-four vehicles on earth. Day tours leave at 8 a.m. and 1 p.m.; evening tours are seasonal. Jeep tours start at $75 and Hummer tours start at $95.

Phoenix emerged from the ashes of Hohokam settlements, prospector claims, and military camps around 1850. It was long an agricultural center, diverting water from the Salt River to irrigate many acres of farmland. In true colorful western fashion, the man most credited with envisioning the irrigation potential of the Valley was Jack Swilling, a drug-addicted Confederate deserter. Probably the biggest contrast between the Valley of the Sun and other areas in central and southern Arizona is that Phoenix and its environs are much greener, with sizable lawns, countless public parks, and many nonnative trees.

All this greenery provides some much-needed summer shade. Many areas of the Southwest are hot during the summer, but Phoenix has the reputation as a true hot spot, with 100-plus-degree temperatures the norm throughout the summer. As miserable as that may sound, particularly to those from the north, the area's nearly nonexistent humidity—coupled with the zillions of swimming pools that dot the landscape—makes it relatively bearable even in the dead of summer. Even locals will talk about soaring highs of 120 and 125, but thankfully, those days are as rare as snow in the desert.

Sports fans may want to begin their exploration of the Valley at the *US Airways Center*—the home of the National Basketball Association's Phoenix Suns, as well as the Women's National Basketball Association's Phoenix Mercury, and the American Football League's Arizona Rattlers. US Airways Center is also one of the best places in the Valley to see musical performers, ice shows, rodeos, and whatever. US Airways Center (602-379-7800; www.usairwayscenter.com) can be found at 201 E. Jefferson St. The exit is well marked from I-17 North, and once you find Jefferson Street, just keep your eyes peeled for the giant basketball mural. The arena is the modern, gray brick building on the opposite side of the street. Several businesses within the arena cater to fans and tourists. On the first level, the *Team Shop* (602-514-8321) sells posters, key chains, wearables, and other items related to the Suns and other Phoenix-area teams. The *Lexus Club and B Lounge* (602-379-7719) on the second level is open during events. Down the street, *Chase Field* (877-994-0471; www.azchasefield.com), at 401 E. Jefferson St., opened in 1998 as the home field for the world-champion Arizona Diamondbacks. Even when the Arizona Diamondbacks aren't playing, this massive, $350-million, retractable-roofed stadium is worth seeing—perhaps over lunch at *T.G.I. Friday's Front Row* (602-462-3503; www.tgifridaysfrontrow.com), a casual eatery built right into the stands that's open daily. Here, too, you can shop for sports memorabilia at *Team Shop* (602-462-6700). As an aside,

It's a Cool 100° Outside

According to the National Climatic Data Center's summer heat stress index comparison, Phoenix's low humidity results in more comfortable summer weather than most would imagine. Although the outdoor temperatures average 100.5 degrees Fahrenheit, it feels like it's only 96. Compare that with Dallas, where the average high may be only 93, yet high humidity makes it feel more like 109.

Chase Field Fun Facts

The park's retractable roof has six operable telescoping panels that, when open, provide 5.25 acres of open sky.

The roof is driven by two 200-horsepower electric motors that consume between $1.20 and $2.00 worth of electricity to open or close the roof.

The park has 650 television sets, 81 concession stands, and 580 bathroom stalls.

Using as much cooling power as 2,285 average homes, the 8,000-ton air-conditioning system takes about four hours to lower the temperature inside the stadium from 110 to 72 degrees.

About 17,000 tons of structural steel were used to build the park.

Chase Field is the first ballpark ever to be built with its own swimming pool off right field. Only in Phoenix!

Just north of US Airways Center is **Majerle's** (*Mar-leez*) **Sports Grill** (602-253-0118; www.majerles.com) at 24 N. Second St. This is the place that Suns' former star "Thunder Dan" Majerle built with his phenomenal three-point shooting ability. Besides being a great pub and restaurant (with menu items named after the players and probably the best french fries available anywhere), the grill is packed tighter than an overstuffed gym bag during Suns' games, when you can watch the action on a projection TV. Hours here are from 11 a.m. to 2 a.m. daily. Another popular spot that has sprung up within walking distance of the sports and entertainment venues is **Sliders American Grill** (602-462-3800; www.azsliders.com) at 201 S. Fourth St.

Alice Cooper'stown Phoenix (602-253-7337; www.alicecooperstown .com) at 101 E. Jefferson St. was opened by the legendary hometown boy and rock star known as Alice Cooper. Basically a sports and music bar, Cooper'stown is located near the US Airways Center and Chase Field. Since it opened in 1998 it has been a hot spot for celebrity sightings and is known as a place to see and be seen. The menu features barbecue and waitstaff sport the Alice Cooper trademark teardrop.

A themed eatery at 3 S. Second St., where the trademark Fender guitar shape heralds your arrival, is the **Hard Rock Cafe** (602-261-7625; www .hardrock.com). The restaurant displays mucho memorabilia, including instruments and costumes donated by musicians. Outdoor seating is available, illuminated by an unusual flame-spouting fountain.

Your best bet to sample the variety of nightlife Phoenix offers is the classy downtown complex called **The Arizona Center** (602-271-4000; www

.arizonacenter.com). Located between Third and Fifth Streets north of Van Buren Street, it's a complete dining, shopping, and entertainment complex. There's the *AMC Arizona Center 24 Theatres,* a twenty-four-plex movie theater (888-AMC-4FUN) that shows first-run features in their full digital sound splendor and offers reduced ticket prices for the early shows. You'll find familiar formats at *Uno's Chicago Grill* (602-253-3355; www.unos.com) and *Hooters* (602-495-1234; www.hooters.com). You'll also find local favorites: *Mi Amigo Mexican Grill* (602-256-7355; www.miamigos.com), *Sam's Cafe* (602-252-3545; www.canyoncafe.com), and *1130 The Restaurant* (602-368-3046; www.1130therestaurant.com) for everything from steaks to seafood. For something quicker and cheaper, stop by one of the smaller eateries where you can get everything from gourmet coffee at *Starbucks* (602-258-8472; www.starbucks.com) to ice cream concoctions at *Cold Stone Creamery* (602-252-5572; www.coldstonecreamery.com).

For concert lovers, *Cricket Pavilion* (602-254-7200; www.cricket-pavilion.com) at 2121 N. 83rd Ave. offers about three dozen events per year, including most of the top pop/rock and country acts that tour Arizona. The Pavilion, which seats about 20,000 under the stars, has provisions for video screens and adjacent areas for booths that sell everything from bottled water to concert tees to margaritas. During major events such as Jimmy Buffett's annual visit, the Pavilion turns into Party Town, with a forest of colorfully decorated Parrotheads—which is what Buffett fans call themselves—bopping to the tunes.

The Valley is a great place to hear up-and-coming musical acts, and as you might expect, there are a lot of hip clubs. Your best bet for finding the hot new spots in town is to look for one of three local freebie publications distributed from street stands and in local restaurants and shops. *The Rep* and *Get Out* are published by the local newspapers; another source is *New Times* (602-271-0040; www.newtimes.com), a fairly hefty read that does a good job covering the Valley's nightlife.

They may have built this city on sports and rock-and-roll, but art and architecture also offer significant appeal. Several key buildings were designed, built, or influenced by master architect Frank Lloyd Wright; some of them are private residences, but four are public buildings that can be toured. The most impressive is *Taliesin* (Welsh for "shining brow") *West* (480-860-2700; www.franklloydwright.org) at 12621 Frank Lloyd Wright Blvd., Scottsdale. Built against the foothills of the McDowell Mountains just outside of Scottsdale, this winter retreat was begun in 1937 by Wright, who made many changes to it over time (the original structure used canvas flaps instead of glass windows). Today, it's the headquarters of the Frank Lloyd Wright Foundation, which operates a school of architecture and maintains an archive of the master's

A Musical Spawning Ground

Phoenix is well known as a stepping stone to the recording mecca of Los Angeles. Over the years this city has given the world the Tubes, jazz/pop vocalist Rickie Lee Jones, and Francine Reed (a gospel/blues vocalist who recorded with Lyle Lovett). The Valley's most memorable contribution to the music industry is probably glam/heavy-metal/shock-rock god Alice Cooper. Alice (aka Vincent Furnier) attended Cortez High School (8828 North 31st Ave.), if any of you rock fans want to see where this self-styled bad boy got his start. Together with his band, the Earwigs, he first recorded in the Valley on the Santa Cruz label. Away from the stage, he lives a quiet life north of Phoenix in beautiful Paradise Valley. He plays golf and has, on occasion, dispensed advice to local bands. At one time he owned a Native American art gallery in Scottsdale.

designs. Taliesin West has a gift shop and offers tours that range from a one-hour overview to an in-depth, behind-the-scenes study. Special events at the site include desert walks and nighttime city-light gazing.

Wright also had an influence on one of Phoenix's best-known resorts, the **Arizona Biltmore Resort and Spa** (602-955-6600 or 800-950-0086; www .arizonabiltmore.com) at 2400 E. Missouri Ave., which at one time was run by the Wrigley chewing gum family. Though most believe that the resort was designed by Wright, it was actually at the hand of his former apprentice, Albert Chase McArthur. The story goes that McArthur invited the famous architect to oversee construction of the hotel, which he did quietly for a few months before completely removing himself from the project. Nevertheless, Wright's touch can be seen in the block structure of the resort as well as in its distinctive spire. You have to be a guest to get a guided tour, but you're welcome to look around the lobby and other public areas.

If you're still looking for the "Wright stuff," drop by **Grady Gammage Memorial Auditorium** (480-965-3434; www.asugammage.com) on Apache Boulevard and Gammage Parkway in Tempe. This structure, on the grounds of Arizona State University, was actually begun after Wright's death and was completed in 1964. The circular building has been extensively praised for its physical beauty as well as its acoustics. Tours are conducted during the academic year from September through May, and the center regularly hosts touring Broadway groups that perform such hits as *Cats, Wicked,* and *Rent* to sold-out crowds.

Last on a tour of Wright structures would be The **First Christian Church** (602-246-9206) at 6750 N. Seventh Ave., Phoenix, which could perhaps win an award as the Frank Lloyd Wright building completed most posthumously.

DASH around Downtown Phoenix—It's Free!

Whether your reason is tired feet or summer heat, the **DASH (Downtown Area Shuttle)** (602-253-5000; www.valleymetro.org) is the easy way to see downtown Phoenix. These orange and purple minibuses run every twelve minutes from 6:30 a.m. to 8 p.m., Mon through Fri. They take you past—or near—all the major downtown hotels, restaurants, theaters, and sights, including Heritage Square, the Arizona Science Center and Phoenix Museum of History, Chase Field, and the Arizona Center. The DASH government loop runs from the Arizona State Capitol to Phoenix City Hall every twelve minutes from 6:30 a.m. to 6:30 p.m. Mon through Fri. Best of all, DASH is free. Look for a stop where you see the signs with a dashing jackrabbit.

Though this slant-roofed structure with its repeated triangular motif was drafted in 1950, construction didn't take place until 1970. In any case, the design is breathtaking. Tours are available by special arrangement.

Architecturally, **Downtown Phoenix** has a lot to admire. The copper-domed 1900 historic **State Capitol** building (602-542-4675; www.lib.az.us/museum) at 1700 W. Washington St. is now a historical museum. (The actual government offices now occupy the modern, nine-story tower that rises behind the historic dome.) You can wander about at your own pace, or take one of the guided tours to peer into exhibits on the state's political past. The State Capitol building is open Mon through Fri from 9 a.m. to 4 p.m., with guided tours at 10 a.m. and 2 p.m. Also worth a look in the downtown area are Heritage Square, St. Mary's Basilica, and the Old County/City Hall complex.

The **Historic Heritage Square** complex (602-262-5029; www.rosson housemuseum.org) at Seventh and Monroe Streets is a group of historic houses from the original Phoenix town site. Now the buildings house museums, boutiques, a bistro, and a gift shop/tearoom surrounding a cool, green courtyard. The **Arizona Doll and Toy Museum** (602-253-9337) is located here, as are the Phoenix Museum of History, the Arizona Science Center, and the **Victorian Rosson** and **Silva Houses.** For lunch or afternoon tea you can drop by the **Teeter House** (602-252-4682; www.theteeterhouse.com) or for dinner, **Pizzeria Bianco** (602-258-8300; www.pizzeriabianco.com). Hours vary on the various attractions, and some are closed during the summer, so call ahead to avoid disappointment.

The **Arizona Science Center** (602-716-2000; www.azscience.org) at 600 E. Washington St. is the kind of place where Carl Sagan would have felt right at home. Now located in a $47-million building just east of the Phoenix

Convention Center, the facility is a hands-on (and in some cases, whole-body-on) learning complex that encompasses Arizona's largest planetarium, a wide-screen theater, and 350 interactive exhibits that beg to be touched and explored. The center is open from 10 a.m. to 5 p.m. daily. General admission is $12 for adults and $10 for children ages three to seventeen. There are separate fees for the planetarium and the IMAX shows.

Next door is the **Phoenix Museum of History** (602-253-2734; www .pmoh.org) at 105 N. Fifth St., between Washington and Monroe Streets, where interactive exhibits highlight territorial and early statehood days in Arizona and emphasize the multicultural heritage of the state. The museum is open Tues through Sat from 10 a.m. to 5 p.m. Admission is $6 for adults and $3 for children ages seven to twelve.

St. Mary's Basilica (602-354-2100) at 231 N. Third St. is a soaring edifice that seems out of place, yet is oddly natural amid all the modern downtown structures. Built in 1881, it is the oldest Catholic church in the city and a popular place for weddings and other major events. If there aren't any services taking place when you visit, you can walk around inside and marvel at the various forms of architecture that were used in constructing this Phoenix landmark (call for hours). It also, interestingly enough, has its own gift shop selling religious articles and mementos.

The **Herberger Theater Center** (602-254-7399; www.herbergertheater .org) at 222 E. Monroe St. is an understated earth-tone structure that provides space for eight performing arts groups—including the very popular (and

The Old County Courthouse

No tour of the downtown area is complete without a look at the **Old County Courthouse** on Washington Street between First and Third Avenues. The county structure, thought to be the largest terra-cotta–surfaced structure in the state, is a grand old courthouse built in the late 1920s. On the second floor is the courtroom where the famous Miranda trial took place. The 1963 case, involving Ernesto Miranda, who was arrested for a rape that occurred near Bethany Home Road and Seventeenth Street in Phoenix, threw a harsh spotlight on police interrogation tactics and resulted in the Miranda Rights ruling ("You have the right to remain silent. If you give up the right to remain silent . . . ").

Ironically, the building also played a key role in one of Clint Eastwood's cop films. In *The Gauntlet,* Eastwood plays a Phoenix policeman who has to provide protection for a witness. In the film's climax, Eastwood drives a bus through downtown Phoenix and runs it up the steps of the Old County Courthouse. The structures in the county/city complex are public buildings; as such they are open to visitors, but no tours are offered.

deservedly so) Arizona Theatre Company, which uses professional actors from stage and screen to perform original and time-tested works in Phoenix and Tucson. The company's season usually runs October through May.

Along Washington Street en route to the State Capitol you'll find a small off-the-beaten-path museum worth considering. The *Arizona Mining & Mineral Museum* (602-771-1600 or 800-446-4259; www.admmr.state.az.us) at the corner of West Washington Street and Fifteenth Avenue, which honors the industry that built Arizona and made it the number-one mining state in the country for nonfuel production. You'll see turquoise, smithsonite, wulfenite, malachite, azurite, and pyrite; you'll also see some gold. The museum is open Mon through Fri from 8 a.m. to 5 p.m. and Sat 11 a.m. to 4 p.m. Admission is $2 for adults.

If you're hungry after a downtown tour, a great place to eat is *Tom's Tavern* (602-257-1688; www.tomstavernphoenix.com), centrally located on the corner of Washington Street and First Avenue. Seating is indoors and out (with misters in the summertime), and the politically driven menu offers sandwiches named after local office holders, past and present.

Another choice in the neighborhood is at *Seamus McCaffrey's Irish Pub & Restaurant* (602-253-6081; www.seamusmccaffreys.com) at 18 W. Monroe St.

While you're downtown, be sure to get a look at the Spanish Colonial–style *Orpheum Theatre* (602-262-7272 for tickets) at 203 W. Adams St. Built in 1929, the theater was used for films and vaudeville performances. Mae West and W. C. Fields both graced this stage. Following an exhaustive, meticulous $14-million restoration project, the Orpheum reopened in early 1997. Broadway road shows play here.

America's Heroes: Phoenix's Firefighting Museum

Among the many unusual places to visit in Phoenix is the largest firefighter museum in the world. The *Hall of Flame* (602-275-3473; www.hallofflame.org) at 6101 E. Van Buren St. has almost one hundred antique and classic fire engines as well as firefighting artifacts of all types. The fire engines date as far back as 1725 and are as new as 1961. One of the carriages was used to fight the 1871 Chicago Fire. Photos, artwork, badge and arm patch displays, and even a fire safety exhibit for kids round out the items of interest here. Admission is $6.00 for adults, $4.00 for children ages six to seventeen, and $1.50 for ages three to five. It's open Mon through Sat from 9 a.m. to 5 p.m. and Sun from noon to 4 p.m.

Finding an Address in Phoenix

The Greater Phoenix area is built in the western tradition of squares. It's exactly 1 mile from one main road to the next, often with a semi-main thoroughfare at the halfway point. The only things that stand in the way of this perfect patterning are the buttes and mountains that pop up here and there in the Valley of the Sun. Finding an address east to west is fairly simple. The numbering begins at Central Avenue and moves logically and predictably either west through the avenues or east through the streets, so you know that 2400 East Camelback is at Twenty-Fourth Street or 4300 West Indian School is at Forty-Third Avenue. North-South addresses are not as simple—numbering begins at Washington Street downtown, but you have to know that Camelback Road is 5000 North. Similarly, when you get into other towns in the Phoenix metro area, you'll find they too have a First Street or a Fifth Avenue and in some cases—Scottsdale or Tempe for example—it's the roads running north–south that are named and some of the east-west streets that are numbered. Go figure! And be sure you know which city you're in, because numbering starts again—and goes town by town—when you get into what's called the East Valley (see below). Here's a bit of help with some of the more well-traveled thoroughfares in the Greater Phoenix area:

Street or Road Name	Numbers Begin At
Washington	0 North/South (1000 North in Tempe)
Van Buren	300 North
Roosevelt	1000 North
McDowell	1600 North
Thomas	2900 North
Osborn	3400 North
Indian School	4100 North
Camelback	5000 North
Lincoln	6600 North
Glendale	7000 North
Northern	8000 North
Shea	10600 North
Thunderbird	13800 North
Bell/Frank Lloyd Wright	17000 North
Pinnacle Peak	23400 North
Southern	6000 South (3300 South in Tempe; 1200 South in Mesa)
Elliot	10800 South (7600 South in Tempe; 3000 South in Chandler)
Ray	14000 South (1000 South in Chandler; 1600 in Gilbert)

Before leaving central Phoenix, the *Heard Museum* (602-252-8848 or 602-252-8344; www.heard.org) is an Arizona "must-see" located at 2301 N. Central Ave. near Monte Vista Road. Long known for its vast collection of Native American art, this museum features the craftsmanship and design abilities of the Native people of the Southwest. Barry Goldwater's collection of hand-carved katsina dolls is there; so is the doll collection of the Fred Harvey Corporation. Also fascinating to see and study are baskets, jewelry, pottery, and textiles. The artist-in-residence program gives you a chance to meet and hear artists discuss their work; plus, you can see replicas of traditional Indian dwellings including a Navajo hogan, an Apache wickiup, and a Hopi corn-grinding room. The museum is open Mon through Sat from 9:30 a.m. to 5 p.m. and Sun from 11 a.m. to 5 p.m. Admission is $10 for adults and $5 for children age six and older. There are free guided tours offered at noon, 2, and 3 p.m. daily.

trivia

Arizona is known as the Copper State. It produces more than 65 percent of the nation's domestic supply.

There's a twofer waiting to be discovered at Phoenix's *Papago Park,* and they're side-by-side on Galvin Parkway east of downtown. The *Phoenix Zoo* (602-273-1341; www.phoenixzoo .org) at 455 N. Galvin Parkway is the only zoo in the country that is 100 percent privately funded; it's spacious, neat, and amusing, which is why it's also regarded as one of America's finest. Designed as a series of habitats, it includes an African veldt, a South American rain forest, and a traditional Arizona farm. Docents and teen volunteers make the exhibits come alive, and a Disney-style tram covers the entire complex. Two worthwhile special events during the year are "Boo at the Zoo," when children visit wearing Halloween costumes, and during the holidays, "Zoo Lights," a must-do. It's a monthlong celebration (late Nov to early Jan) when the trees and the cacti are lit every evening until 10 p.m., and mimes, magicians, and carolers appear in the central courtyard or on the pathways. The zoo is open 364 days of the year (closed only Dec 25); hours are from 9 a.m. to 5 p.m., except in summer to early fall (June 1 through Sept 30) when hours are 7 a.m. to 4 p.m. weekends and holidays, and 7 a.m. to 2 p.m. on weekdays. Next along the road is *Desert Botanical Garden* (480-941-1225; www .dbg.org) at 1201 N. Galvin Parkway, home to one of the world's largest and most diverse collections of desert plants as well as fine examples of Native American housing styles. It's a great place to learn more about cacti and their nasty habits before you set off on a desert hike; it's also an eye-opener to the beauty and delicacy of desert wildflowers, bushes, and small trees. Events here during the year include spring and fall plant sales, Music in the Garden, and Jazz in the Garden, and like its neighbor the zoo, the garden holds a winter holiday celebration of lights called *Las Noches de las Luminarias* each year. The Botanical Garden is open every day except July 4, Thanksgiving, and Dec 25; hours are from 7 a.m. to 8 p.m. June through Sept, and from 8 a.m. to 8 p.m. Oct through May. Admission is $15.00 for adults, $7.50 for students ages thirteen to eighteen, and $5.00 for children ages three to twelve.

North on Central Avenue from downtown is the *Phoenix Art Museum* (602-257-1222; www.phxart.org) at 1625 N. Central Ave. at McDowell Road, which houses a wide-ranging collection of artworks, including American, European, Spanish Colonial, Latin American, and Asian paintings and sculptures. Of particular interest to visitors may be the museum's collection of western American works featuring the works of southwestern artists. Children will enjoy both the ArtWorks Gallery—a hands-on, "brains-on" activity room for children—and the Thorne Miniature Rooms, which show how people lived during historic periods in the United States and Europe. Admission is $10 for adults and $4 for ages six to seventeen. Guided tours are held daily at noon, 1, and 6 p.m. The museum is closed Mon and Tues.

The *Phoenix Public Library* (602-262-4636; www.phoenixpubliclibrary .org) at 1221 N. Central Ave. is an exceptional research and reading resource. The building also is of architectural interest. You can also see exhibits there relating to city life in Phoenix. One not-to-be-missed example of cooperation among residents is the library's centennial quilt, which hangs in the central area of the first floor near the children's book section.

One of the Valley's most unusual attractions is the *Mystery Castle* (602-268-1581) at 800 E. Mineral Rd. near South Mountain Park in Phoenix. This eighteen-room stone structure, which also incorporates wire rims from a Stutz Bearcat, was put together completely by hand. The mystery comes from the fact that the builder never told his family about the work. He had always promised his daughter that he would build her a castle, and one day he left their home in Seattle and came to Phoenix to undertake the project. She only found out about the castle when his will was read, and she lives there to this day. The castle has thirteen fireplaces, lots of antiques, and the general sense of being smack dab in the midst of somebody's dream. You can tour this unique home Thurs through Sun from 11 a.m. to 4 p.m., Oct through May only. The cost is $5 for adults and $3 for children ages five to fifteen.

The *Pioneer Arizona Living History Village* (623-465-1052; www .pioneer-arizona.com) at 3901 W. Pioneer Rd. on I-17, 1 mile north of Carefree Highway, is a group of more than two dozen buildings, some authentic, and some reproductions that are used by reenactors to re-create the image of the frontier West. Visitors can see metalworking, dressmaking, carpentry, and other activities going on just as they were more than one hundred years ago. Open Wed through Sun from 9 a.m. to 5 p.m., Oct to May, and Wed through Sun from 8 a.m. to 2 p.m., from June to Sept. Admission is $7 for adults and $5 for ages six to eighteen.

The *Pueblo Grande Museum and Archaeological Park* (602-495-0901 or 877-706-4408; www.pueblogrande.com) at 4619 E. Washington St. is an actual Hohokam village that was abandoned around A.D. 1450. The museum's exhibit rooms have permanent displays of artifacts and also serve as a venue for workshops such as pottery making and archaeology. Hikes to nearby ancient petroglyph sites are also a featured event. For almost thirty years the museum also has held an annual Indian market (usually in December), where more than 500 artists sell their works. The market also features traditional music and dancing, food, and beverages. The museum is open Mon through Sat from 9 a.m. to 4:45 p.m., and Sun from 1 to 4:45 p.m. The museum is closed Sun and Mon, May through Sept. Admission is $6 for adults and $3 for ages six to seventeen.

If you're in the mood to shop during your trip to Phoenix, you're in luck—the Valley is flush with shopping centers. One of the first, and still one of the most popular, is the west side *Metrocenter* (602-997-2641; www.metrocenter mall.com) at 9617 Metro Parkway (at I-17 off Peoria Avenue). A sprawling complex of more than 200 shops and restaurants, it also boasts a multiplex theater, an indoor arcade, and an outdoor amusement park. The whole complex is surrounded by hotels and eateries.

Another cool place to shop is the *Biltmore Fashion Park* (602-955-8401; www.shopbiltmore.com) at Camelback and Twenty-Fourth Streets. The shops here aren't joined by enclosed corridors, but the inner court is shaded, so it's pretty comfortable year-round. There are boutique-style shops, nationally known retailers such as Macy's and Saks Fifth Avenue, plus Williams Sonoma, Ann Taylor, Escada, Ralph Lauren, and Border's Books and Music, among others.

Scottsdale and Its Neighbors

Scottsdale, as a community, began in 1888 when army chaplain Winfield Scott purchased land to grow citrus and other crops. Over the years the town has emerged as a world-renowned resort destination, offering great shopping, public parks, nationally recognized museums, frontier-type attractions, and galleries galore.

In fact Scottsdale is loaded with galleries. In at least three separate areas—Main Street Arts and Antique District, Marshall Way, and Fifth

Cosanti and Cause Bells

In addition to the architectural work of Frank Lloyd Wright that is so much a part of the Phoenix-Scottsdale landscape, you'll also want to try to see the more fantastical and futuristic work of Italian architect Paolo Soleri. *Cosanti* (480-948-6145 or 800-752-3187; www.cosanti.com) at 6433 E. Doubletree Ranch Rd., Scottsdale, is an example of his concept of blending desert landscaping with earth-formed concrete structures. Everywhere you walk among the courtyards, terraces, and gardens, there are bronze and ceramic wind bells tinkling. Designed by Soleri and his artisans, these Cause Bells, as they are known, represent national and global issues. You can watch them being made; you also can buy them to provide funding for the various organizations that work on solving world problems. Cosanti is open Mon through Sat from 9 a.m. to 5 p.m. and Sun from 11 a.m. to 5 p.m. The foundry is open to the public in the morning—it's best to call first. Donations accepted.

Avenue Shopping Area (in which there are more than 200 specialty shops)—you can stroll for hours and get a close-up look at everything from traditional Native American arts and crafts to nineteenth-century fine art. You can easily walk or take Scottsdale's local transportation—a trolley—to these various areas, but you may want to take your car, because you'll no doubt buy something!

Faust Gallery (480-946-6345; www.faustgallery.com) at 7103 E. Main St. represents emerging and established Native American artists, with katsinas, pottery, paintings, and other works. *American Fine Art Editions, Inc.* (480-990-1200 or 800-466-8276; www.americanfineartgallery.com) at 3908 N. Scottsdale Rd., represents the contemporary art scene very well with an eclectic collection of original work by internationally acclaimed twentieth-century artists (Neiman, Wyeth, Picasso). The *Borgata at Scottsdale* (602-953-6538; www.borgata.com) at 6166 N. Scottsdale Rd. is a Mediterranean-style complex of more than thirty shops and eateries, with cobblestone paths, fountains, towers, and all the ingredients of a fairy-tale setting (albeit one that takes plastic!). If all the shopping makes you hungry, wander into *J. Alexander's* (480-991-2504; www.jalexanders.com), a contemporary American restaurant serving up a divine selection of steaks, baby back ribs, seafood, salads, and sandwiches.

If you're staying at a hotel or resort way north in Scottsdale, you'll be glad to know there are art museums within

trivia

The Phoenix/Scottsdale area is home to more Mobil Five-Star and AAA Five-Diamond resorts than any other destination in the United States.

A Carefree Life

About twenty minutes north of Fountain Hills are the twin communities of **Cave Creek** and **Carefree.** Cave Creek was a mining community one hundred years ago, and over time it has become a diverse town of a little more than 3,000 residents. Nearby Carefree is a bedroom community that began development in the 1950s and today serves as home to famous faces such as news anchor Hugh Downs and actress P. J. Soles (*Halloween, Carrie, Rock 'n' Roll High School*). Carefree also is the location of the largest, most accurate sundial in the Western Hemisphere. This impressive timepiece, which sweeps out of the earth like a giant scimitar, can be found off Cave Creek Road and Sunshine Way.

reach, including the **Heard Museum North** (623-344-2200; www.heard.org/ north) at 32633 N. Scottsdale Rd. This community extension of the Heard Museum moved to its new location at The Summit at Scottsdale in the summer of 2007. This state-of-the-art facility features two exhibition galleries, a museum gift shop, and a garden cafe. The museum is open Mon through Sat from 10 a.m. to 5 p.m. and Sun from 11 a.m. to 5 p.m. Guided tours are offered at 1 and 3 p.m. on Sat and Sun. Admission is $5 for adults and $2 for children six and older.

If your wandering takes you north to Carefree, you can check out the shops and galleries at **el Pedregal Festival Marketplace** (480-488-1072; www.elpedregal.com) on Scottsdale Road and Carefree Highway. Shops include everything from upscale fashion boutiques such as **Stefan Mann** (480-488-3371; www.stefanmann.com), which specializes in exotic leathers, to glamorous art galleries including **Zuva Gallery** (480-488-6000; www.zuva gallery.com), which offers a dazzling array of contemporary African art. The colorful marketplace also has several restaurants and a full schedule of events, and it is within walking distance to The Boulders Resort.

About 12 miles east of Scottsdale is the community of **Fountain Hills** (480-837-1654; www.fountainhillschamber.com). Fountain Hills can be reached by taking Shea Boulevard east through the desert foothills until it runs into Fountain Hills. Besides being home to the **Tallest Fountain in the World** (560 feet, as verified in the *Guinness Book of World Records*), this picturesque town has a number of local sights that are worth a look. If you want to try for your own record, hit the jackpot at **Fort McDowell Casino** (800-THE-FORT; www.fmcasino.com), where visitors challenge Lady Luck twenty-four hours a day, seven days a week; there's a free shuttle, if you need it. **Saguaro Lake,** an artificial reservoir on the Salt River, offers a number of boating, waterskiing, and swimming opportunities, as well as the ***Desert Belle*** steamboat paddle wheeler (480-984-2425 or 877-749-2848; www.saguarolake.net) that does regular tours and dinner cruises. The ***Saguaro Lake Marina*** (480-986-5546; www .saguarolakemarina.com) has boat rentals, a general store, and the ***Lakeshore Restaurant*** (480-984-5311). You can reach Saguaro Lake by taking AZ 87 north until you reach Bush Highway. Head south on Bush Highway, and it will take you to the lake.

While you're in Fountain Hills, drop by for a bite at ***Que Bueno*** (480-837-2418) at 13207 N. LaMontana Dr. This Mexican restaurant has won plaudits for its homemade salsa and features savory desserts like chocolate chimichangas.

The West Valley

On the western side of the Valley—accessible by heading west out of downtown Phoenix on I-10—is the tri-city area of Avondale, Goodyear, and ***Litchfield Park*** (623-932-2260; www.southwestvalleychamber.org). Litchfield Park sprang to life as a company town in 1916 when Goodyear Tire and Rubber executive Paul Litchfield purchased the land to use as a cotton farm back in the days when cotton cords were utilized in automotive tires. Today the town is best known as the location of The ***Wigwam Golf Resort and Spa*** (623-935-3811 or 800-327-0396; www.wigwamresort.com) at 300 Wigwam Blvd. This four-star resort is composed of charming adobe casitas that were initially built for Goodyear officials. The Wigwam is especially favored by golfers because it features three eighteen-hole golf courses. Two of these, the Gold Course and the Blue Course, were designed by well-known golf-course architect Robert Trent Jones Sr. The Gold Course, which has earned several accolades and awards, is a whopping 7,100 yards long. Because of the Wigwam's off-the-beaten-path location, it also offers guests amenities such as horseback riding and trap and skeet shooting.

trivia

There are more than 200 golf courses in Greater Phoenix— making it one of the top five golf destinations in the world!

Not surprisingly for an area that was raised by the rubber giant, nearby ***Avondale*** is home to ***Phoenix International Raceway*** (623-463-5400 or 866-408-RACE; www.phoenixintlraceway.com), the location of the world's fastest paved 1-mile oval track. The raceway attracts huge crowds; famous drivers such as Mario Andretti, Emerson Fittipaldi, and Al Unser Jr.; and brings hundreds of millions of dollars into the tri-city coffers.

Wickenburg and Northwest of Metropolitan Phoenix

At the junction of US 93 and US 60, ***Wickenburg*** (928-684-5479 or 800-942-5242; www.wickenburgchamber.com) is a frontier town that's been a popular getaway destination for decades. Within a half-dozen or so miles there are five guest ranches that offer dudes and dudettes a close-up glimpse of the cowboy way of life. Because of this concentration of lodges serving the "City Slicker" set, Wickenburg has earned the title of "The Dude Ranch Capital of the World."

Prospector/farmer Henry Wickenburg, a native of Prussia, founded the town in 1863 after discovering the largest gold-producing strike in the history of the state. He called his mine the ***Vulture Gold Mine*** (602-859-2743). If you're interested in viewing the remains of Wickenburg's mining camp, it's about a dozen miles from town. Drive about 2.5 miles west of Wickenburg on US 60, turn left onto Vulture Mine Road, and continue for 12 miles. The pavement will end, and you'll be on a dirt road that can be a bit bumpy (don't attempt this drive during or immediately after a rainstorm). When you pull off the road, you'll see Vulture Peak, a tall hill with a crease in the middle of its summit. Vulture Mine is just to the southwest of the peak.

The remains of the wood and adobe buildings that once made up the Vulture camp can still be explored. Though the mine mostly dried up around the turn of the twentieth century, some limited excavation is still being carried on in the area. Be careful to confine your explorations to buildings and hillsides that aren't marked as private property. Hours are from 8 a.m. to 4 p.m. daily, except July and Aug when the property is open only on weekends.

Mining is no longer a major portion of Wickenburg's economy. The lovely scenery—which ranges from creosote bush and cacti to oak and pine trees—draws visitors. Ranching and agriculture have helped to keep the city's coffers well stocked.

The Code of the West

If you're fascinated by the "Code of the West" (as is nearly anybody who grew up watching *The Rifleman* and *Wanted: Dead or Alive*), head for the Circle K store in Wickenburg near Tegner and Wickenburg Way. Behind the store is a 200-year-old mesquite tree, known as the "jail tree," which was used from 1863 to 1890 as a place to chain miscreants before the town had a jail.

If you drive in from the west off US 60, you can continue on the roadway that becomes Wickenburg Way, center of many of the area's hotels and restaurants. US 89/93 also leads into the town; once in the town limits, it's called Tegner Street. Either way, it's easy to get around, and most of Wickenburg's attractions are in the downtown center grid.

There's a lot of history in this town, including many buildings that date from the turn of the twentieth century or earlier. One of the most interesting is the **Hassayampa Building** near Apache and Frontier Streets. Originally built as a hotel for railroad passengers, it had nine separate fireplaces and a huge kitchen. Today it's office and shop space. Other locations worth stopping by to have a look at include **Hyder's Livery Stable** across the street from the Hassayampa Building. The stable, with its distinctive rock wall, is much classier than the simple barn-like buildings you generally see in western towns. When it ceased being a stable in the 1920s, it was turned into a garage and auto dealership. The **Upton House** on Washington Street, west of Apache Street, was built from locally produced bricks. It was once occupied by one of the wealthiest families in the area.

> ## trivia
>
> *Hassayampa* is actually an Apache word that means "river that runs upside down." Oddly, the preserve is one of the few locations where the river does not run underground.

Nearby on Frontier Street and Wickenburg Way is the **Desert Caballeros Western Museum and Park** (928-684-2272; www.westernmuseum.org) at 21 N. Frontier St. The museum displays modern artwork from members of the *Cowboy Artists of America* in addition to pieces by American masters like Frederic Remington. There are also period rooms depicting Wickenburg's early years. The small park adjacent to the museum features a life-size statue by Joe Beeler of a cowboy kneeling beside his horse. The museum and museum store are open year-round, Mon through Sat from 10 a.m. to 5 p.m. and Sun from noon to 4 p.m. In the summer, from May through Aug, the museum is closed on Mon. Admission is $7.50 adults.

Wickenburg is better known for its current hospitality than for its earlier law enforcement policies. Its guest ranches range from a cozy, historic hacienda to an elaborate resort that has its own golf course. **Kay El Bar Ranch** (928-684-7593 or 800-684-7583; www.kayelbar.com) is a traditional adobe guest ranch with a pool and horseback riding; it is open mid-October to May 1. **Flying E Ranch** (928-684-2690 or 888-684-2650; www.flyingeranch.com) is an actual working cattle ranch that also has a tennis court, horse stables, pool, spa, and sauna; its season is November to April. **Williams Family Ranch**

(928-308-0589; www.williamsfamilyranch.com) is another working cattle ranch offering cowboy adventures September through May. **Rancho de los Caballeros** (928-684-5484 or 800-684-5030; www.sunc.com) caters not only to horse lovers but also to tennis buffs and golfers; it is open from October to May.

In keeping with Wickenburg's frontier history, area restaurants include steakhouses and several establishments serving Mexican fare, but you also can find Chinese cuisine, fish and chips, and several cafes that have home-cooked specialties. The **Horseshoe Cafe** (928-684-7377) at 207 E. Wickenburg Way has American cuisine and is open daily from 5 a.m. to 1 p.m. Another cool hangout is **Screamers** (928-684-9056) at 1141 W. Wickenburg Way, a 1950s-style diner named after the owner's daughters—I swear I'm not making this up! Screamers features a variety of dishes, including chicken, fish, hamburgers (even a Hawaiian Burger), hotdogs, and more. They're open Mon through Sat from 6 a.m. to 8 p.m. and Sun from 10:30 a.m. to 8 p.m.

A must-see attraction is the **Hassayampa River Preserve** (928-684-2772; www.nature.org), about 4 miles southeast of town on US 60 at mile marker 114. The 730-acre preserve, managed by the Nature Conservancy, is a refuge area for birds like the zone-tailed hawk and the yellow-tailed cuckoo. It's not unusual to see the white posteriors of mule deer as they frolic through the brush. You may also see tracks made by raccoons, bobcats, and javelinas. The preserve's office is in a restored 1860s ranch house. Guided nature walks are offered daily at 8:30 from Oct through Apr. The preserve is open Wed through Sun from 8 a.m. to 5 p.m., mid-Sept through mid-May, and Fri, Sat, and Sun from 7 to 11 a.m., mid-May to mid-Sept. Admission is $5 for adults.

Ghost towns are scattered throughout this rugged area, including Stanton, where prospectors are said to have picked up gold nuggets the size of potatoes, and Congress, home of a legendary tunnel that led from the general store to the town's hotel. Hidden Castle Hot Springs, east of Wickenburg, was at one time an exclusive spa where soothing natural hot spring water provided therapeutic relief for an impressive guest list that included President John F. Kennedy.

The city of **Glendale** (623-930-4500 or 877-800-2601; www.visitglendale .com) has some delightful off-the-beaten-path surprises to offer. Historic Downtown Glendale is best known locally as Arizona's antiques capital and includes the **Old Town Glendale,** where you'll find a great antiques shopping area, and the **Catlin Court Historic District,** where the Craftsman bungalow-style homes have been turned into shops and restaurants (streets and alleys are gaslit in the evenings every third Thurs of the month); there's a walking tour leaflet you can use to see the entire neighborhood. A free trolley connects these downtown areas, or it's a short walk through lovely Murphy Park. Kitty-corner from the park is ***The Bead Museum*** (623-931-2737; www.thebeadmuseum.com) at 5754 W. Glenn Dr. The museum features a fascinating collection of beads from around the world, historic to contemporary. Beads come in all shapes and sizes and traditionally have been decorated with various techniques or simply left unadorned. Over the centuries they have been used for trade and currency, as amulets, and, of course, for jewelry and personal adornment. The museum is open Wed through Sat from 10 a.m. to 5 p.m. and Sun from 11 a.m. to 4 p.m. The museum extends evening hours on Thurs until 8 p.m. During the summer admission is free on Thurs from 5 to 8 p.m. and all day Sun. Regular admission is $5.00 for adults and $2.50 for children. Also along the trolley route or a fairly easy walk from Old Town is ***Cerreta Candy Company*** (623-930-1000; www.cerreta.com) at 5345 W. Glendale Ave., a family-operated chocolate factory where you can watch candy being made, buy gift assortments, and enjoy a sample or two. Thirty-minute factory tours are offered Mon through Fri at 10 a.m. and 1 p.m.

trivia

West of Phoenix, the city of Glendale was named by *USA Today* as one of the ten best places in the country to shop for antiques.

In recent years, Glendale has made a play for major league sports venues—acquiring both the NHL Phoenix Coyotes and the NFL Arizona Cardinals. You can watch the Phoenix Coyotes Hockey Club play at the ***Jobing.com Arena*** at the Westgate City Center (623-772-3200 or 623-850-PUCK for tickets; www.phoenixcoyotes.com), and the Arizona Cardinals (www.azcardinals.com) play ball next door at the ***University of Phoenix Stadium,*** (623-433-7100; www.universityofphoenixstadium.com). The stadium, designed by architect Peter Eisenman, is built in the shape of a barrel cactus and seats 63,000. It

University of Phoenix Stadium Fun Facts

- The stadium's 63,400 seats would stretch 18 miles if they were set in a straight line.
- There is enough concrete in the stadium to lay 900 miles of sidewalk, enough to reach from Phoenix to San Francisco.
- The stadium's grass field is the first of its kind in North America. The 18.9-million-pound tray is rolled outside and kept there for optimal grass growth until game day.

opened for the 2006 season and hosted the Super Bowl XLII Championship game in 2008.

The East Valley and Points South

On the opposite side of the Valley, *Tempe,* one of the oldest communities in the area, is known as the home of *Arizona State University* (ASU; 480-965-9011; www.asu.edu). The previously mentioned Grady Gammage Memorial Auditorium is definitely worth your time.

For a different kind of artwork, wander into the ASU campus and head for the *J. Russell and Bonita Nelson Fine Arts Center* (480-965-2787). The 49,700-square-foot center, designed by Antoine Predock, is itself a work of art. The lavender-hued structures that make up the center are boldly geometric yet reflect the shapes you find in the Sonoran Desert. Inside, along with performing arts spaces, are 8,000 works of art in the *ASU Art Museum* (asuart museum.asu.edu), including an extensive collection of contemporary ceramics and Latin American folk and fine art.

ASU, incidentally, is where Jerry Lewis's character worked in his best-loved film, *The Nutty Professor;* you may recognize some of the buildings on campus from the film. *Sun Devil Stadium* was the site of Super Bowl XXX. Tempe, however, doesn't need special events to draw a crowd. The whole downtown area is packed with college hangouts—pizza, Chinese food, coffeehouses, microbreweries. If you can't find something here that tempts your palate, you aren't really hungry.

Just east of Tempe is *Mesa* (480-827-4700 or 800-283-6372; www.visit mesa.com), another surprise in the Valley of the Sun. Graced with a face-lift in recent years, the downtown area is the site of almost everything you might want to see or do. The expanded *Arizona Museum of Natural History* (480-644-2230; www.azmnh.org) at 53 N. Macdonald St. has the largest exhibition of animated, full-scale, "roaring" dinosaurs west of the Mississippi, plus an exhibit of sea life from the Jurassic and Paleozoic periods. A 50-foot waterfall, caves, and re-creations of Hohokam Indian dwellings are also part of the museum's exhibits. The museum is open Tues through Fri from 10 a.m. to 5 p.m., Sat from 11 a.m. to 5 p.m., and Sun from 1 to 5 p.m. Admission is $10 for adults, $8 for students thirteen and older with ID, and $6 for children ages three to twelve. Set among gardens, a half-mile away, the *Arizona Temple Visitors Center* (480-964-7164) at 525 E. Main St. is a well-known landmark in this city that was founded by the Mormons in 1878. Mesa's holiday events are known to draw a big crowd, especially the annual *Easter Pageant,* one of the largest in the world.

Also near the museum is the ***Arizona Wing Commemorative Air Force Aircraft Museum*** (480-924-1940; www.azcaf.org), which is located adjacent to Falcon Field Airport near the crossroads of McKellips and Greenfield Roads. The Arizona Wing displays several of the greats of World War II, restored and maintained not just for display in Arizona but in flying condition and ready for takeoff to events around the country each year. Among their aircraft is the American B-17 *Sentimental Journey,* which is considered the most authentically restored of all the B-17s flying today; plus there is an example of a German Heinkel, and two restored B-25 bombers of the type Jimmy Doolittle flew. The museum is open daily from 10 a.m. to 4 p.m., Oct through May, and Wed through Sun from 9 a.m. to 3 p.m., June through Sept. Admission is $10 for adults and $3 for children ages six to twelve.

The ***Lower Salt River Recreation Area,*** which can be reached easily from Mesa, is a popular summer spot for "tubing" and river rafting trips. Weather permitting, the Salt is crammed with people on inner tubes, drifting lazily while their portable stereos compete for audio dominance. Others take guided tours of the river. A few companies not far from Mesa that provide equipment and transportation are ***Salt River Recreation, Inc.*** (480-984-3305; www.saltrivertubing.com), ***Cimarron River Rafting Co.*** (480-994-1199), and ***Desert Voyagers Guided Raft Trips*** (480-998-7238; www .desertvoyagers.com).

A little farther south in ***Chandler,*** you can visit a piece of the Old West at ***Rawhide Wild West Town*** (480-502-5600; www.rawhide.com) at 5700 W. North Loop Rd. It's a re-created 1880s frontier town, complete with shoot-outs and melodrama; stagecoach, camel, and burro rides; and a number of Old West restaurants and shops.

At the eastern end of the Valley of the Sun sits ***Apache Junction,*** located at the intersection of AZ 88 and US 60. This town boasts several well-attended annual events. Ironically, given the town's name and very southwestern heritage, one of the major yearly amusements is a ***Renaissance Festival*** (520-463-2700; www.royalfaires.com). Held weekends and holidays from mid-February through late March, this 30-acre re-creation of life in sixteenth-century England features performances by jugglers, musicians, dancers, and other entertainers. This merriment is intertwined with jousting matches and falconry demonstrations. There also are more than 200 vendors of food and crafts, and you can even see trained fleas perform. Incidentally, the "sister city" for this event is Sherwood Forest, England. In February, Apache Junction also celebrates its mining heritage with ***Lost Dutchman Days*** (www.lostdutchmandays.org). Legend has it that sometime in the late 1880s Dutch miner Jacob Walz discovered a gold mine in the Superstition Mountains just outside of Apache Junction.

The Superstitions, a 160,285-acre volcanic mountain range, are rocky and rugged throughout. When Walz died in 1891 without revealing the location of his mine, many treasure seekers flocked to the area to hunt for the Dutchman's riches. To this day no one has uncovered the location. Lost Dutchman Days events include a rodeo, a parade, and a carnival.

You can delve into the region's mining history any time of year by following the *Apache Trail,* a circular route into the Tonto National Forest (602-225-5200; www.fs.fed.us/r3/tonto) that takes you to the *Goldfield Ghost Town* (480-983-0333; www.goldfieldghosttown.com) at 4650 N. Mammoth Mine Rd. The re-creation of a 1890s mining town features tours of a former mine, a scenic railroad, and includes the *Superstition Mountain Lost Dutchman Museum.* At the museum you can learn how prehistoric Indians lived in the area, see a model of the entire Superstition Mountain wilderness area, and study exhibits that tell you about natural history—rocks, ores, animals, and reptiles. One exhibit contains photos, furniture, and equipment from a family home; another displays equipment and clothing from the mounted troops that are part of Arizona history; and, perhaps most fun, there are twenty-three maps that show possible locations of the Lost Dutchman Mine. The Goldfield Ghost Town is open daily from 10 a.m. to 5 p.m. The route continues to *Canyon Lake,* where you can ride the **Dolly Steamboat** (480-827-9144; www.dolly steamboat.com) through the inner waterways of the "Junior Grand Canyon" and learn more about plants and animals that live near the lake. To rent a boat of your own, check in at the *Canyon Lake Marina and Campground* (480.288.9233; www.canyonlakemarina.com). Next stop, *Tortilla Flat,* Arizona (480-984-1776; www.tortillaflataz.com), population six, where the combination restaurant, saloon, gift shop, grocery store, and U.S. Post Office is a convenient place to stop for a burger, chili, or an ice-cream cone.

I recommend that you contact a tour company if you'd like to get a close-up look at the Superstition Mountains. Many hikers and prospectors have died because they didn't know the terrain well enough.

Traveling south from Apache Junction on US 60 takes you to *Superior* (520-689-5752; www.superior-arizona.com). Known by several names since the 1880s, the town was a mining center for about one hundred years. Lately Superior has earned a bit of a reputation as a movie set, serving as the setting for *The Prophecy,* a horror flick, and Oliver Stone's *U-Turn.* Word has it that Stone selected the town because it retained a 1950s ambience, and set designers left behind many of the facades they created on the town's main street. Today visitors make the trek to Superior to tour the nearby *Boyce Thompson Arboretum State Park* (520-689-2811 or 520-689-2723; www.azstateparks .com). The arboretum contains more than 1,500 species of plants, as well as many birds and animals. Its specialties are desert and arid-land plants, including cacti and wildflowers of many colorful varieties. Created in 1924, it's the oldest and largest botanical garden in Arizona. There are more than six hiking trails throughout the grounds. Ranging from easy half-mile strolls to moderately rugged 3-mile hikes, these trails are especially popular in the fall and winter when the mild weather in this area encourages people to enjoy the great outdoors. In the vicinity is **Picket Post Mountain,** where in 1927 Colonel Boyce Thompson built a home into the stony face of a cliff. The house is now a museum, maintained just as Thompson, a copper magnate, left it. It's open daily from 8 a.m. to 5 p.m., Sept through Apr, and 6 a.m. to 3 p.m. May through Aug. Dogs are permitted if leashed, and picnic tables are available. Admission is $7.50 for adults and $3.00 for children ages five to twelve.

Also nearby are the **Apache Tears Caves.** The caves contain many fine examples of black obsidian, known in the Southwest as "Apache tears." This dense, glassy volcanic rock is popular in many southwestern jewelry designs. Visitors can chisel off an Apache tear for a small fee. The name Apache Tear comes from a heartbreaking story. Just south of Superior is **Apache Leap** in Queen Creek Canyon. (You can reach this location by taking AZ 177 south from Superior and watching for the turnoff to Apache Leap.) According to legend, it was on this site some 120 years ago that a cavalry detachment from Camp Pinal cornered seventy-five Apache warriors. Rather than submit to capture, they threw themselves off the cliff. Upon hearing of the warriors' fate, the women of the tribe cried tears that turned to stone. Despite the tragic history of this spot, today it's a good place to drive to for a get-away-from-it-all picnic lunch.

If your next destination is the Tucson area, take AZ 177 south and you'll soon enter the tri-city area known as **SMOR (San Manuel, Mammoth, Oracle Region**). This area has a long history as a mining and ranching community, though today SMOR is better known for recreational offerings such as hiking, horseback riding, and bird-watching. North of Oracle on US 79 is the **Tom Mix Monument,** a stone pillar topped by a metal silhouette of a riderless horse. This vaguely macabre statue commemorates the approximate spot where silent-movie western hero Tom Mix was killed when he drove his 1937 Cord automobile off the road. The horse (Tony, Mix's favorite mount) has been stolen from the monument several times over the years, so don't be too surprised if it seems to have moseyed off!

Also near the SMOR is the famous (or, depending upon your perspective, infamous) **Biosphere II** (520-838-6200; www.b2science.org) on AZ 77. The Biosphere II was originally designed by a team of researchers put together by Texas billionaire Edward Bass to create a totally self-contained environment in the form of a giant, pyramid-shaped greenhouse that could be used to study how ecosystems work and also provide a prototype for civilizations of the future (i.e., on other planets). Plagued by personnel problems and dogged by allegations of cultism, the project, which planned to seal a group of researchers inside the facility for two years, became the butt of many jokes. Even the TV series *Cheers* made fun of the concept by putting character Lilith inside such a facility.

In 1993 things came to a head when members of Biosphere II's scientific advisory board resigned, citing concerns over imprecise experiments. The following year, Bass, who reportedly had paid $150 million to build Biosphere II, stepped in and removed key members of the management team. Since then, the University of Arizona, has turned away from the concept of sealing crew members inside the five-story, 7.2-million-cubic-foot greenhouse. Instead they've concentrated on specific experiments dealing with assessing methods of irrigation, creating air-purification products that can be used in homes and commercial buildings, and pursuing other projects that produce tangible results. Today visitors can tour portions of the facility and see environments ranging from a tropical rain forest to a coral reef. You can drop in at a Biosphere II laboratory and see actual experiments or shop in the gift shop and eat lunch or dinner in the restaurant. Biosphere II is open daily 9 a.m. to 4 p.m. Admission is $20 for adults and $13 for children ages six to twelve for a guided tour.

Nearby **Oracle** has a long history as a mining community. In fact, in 1902 Buffalo Bill Cody staked out a gold claim in this area and for a while lived in a cabin above one of his mines. He squandered a large portion of his fortune on what was essentially a hoax (there was virtually no gold, and the tungsten ore he found was not enough for him to recoup his investment).

Like many Arizona towns Oracle has a dedicated group of artists of various disciplines and abilities. The artists range from potters to landscape painters to bronze sculptors. They host an annual weekend **Oracle Festival of Fine Art,** usually in March. During the festival there are tours of the artists' studios, art discussions, and performing arts events. Oracle has a number of galleries and shops that display local artists' work year-round. For information on the SMOR area, contact San Manuel/Mammoth/Oracle Chamber of Commerce (520-385-9322), P.O. Box 416, San Manuel, AZ 85631.

Another off-the-beaten-path route to Tucson is through **Florence** (520-868-9433; www.florenceaz.biz), home to the **Pinal County Historical Museum** (520-868-4382). Florence is also a stone's throw away from such attractions as a group of petroglyphs and coke ovens off Kelvin Road, which is off a four-wheel-drive trail over private property. Check with Greater Florence Chamber of Commerce at P.O. Box 929, Florence, AZ 85232. In town the visitor center is at 234 N. Main St., in the historic district.

The **Pinal County Courthouse,** built in 1891 and located on North Pinal Street between Eleventh and Thirteenth Streets, is a large, rather ornate red-brick building with a clock tower. Incidentally, this is the courthouse where Pearl Hart, the last known stagecoach robber in the United States, was tried in 1899 and sentenced to five years in the Territorial Prison at Yuma. In February guided walking tours of Florence's historic downtown district can be arranged by calling (520) 868-4496.

If you'd like to hang around Florence for a while, check into the **Inn at Rancho Sonora** (520-868-8000 or 800-205-6817; www.ranchosonora.com) at 9198 N. Hwy. 79, a 1930s adobe guest ranch. The comfortable rooms are decorated in classic western fashion, but with the modern comfort conveniences of dual-paned windows and air-conditioning. The inn also has a heated pool and a hot tub. Rooms start at $79 and the suites start at $125.

trivia

If any of the terrain around Florence looks to you like Martians could land and feel right at home, you're not alone in your opinion. The 1953 George Pal–produced film *War of the Worlds* was partially shot here.

From Florence you can take AZ 287 west and AZ 87 south to the **Casa Grande National Monument** (520-723-3172; www.nps.gov/cagr). Casa Grande was a Hohokam settlement built around A.D. 1150. Theories abound, including everything from family dwelling to astronomical observatory, regarding the purpose for the large adobe structure that still stands here in the midst of the desert. It's one of the best-preserved sites of its kind in the state. Stop by the visitor center to get a brochure and take the self-guided tour. If you have the time, stay for one of the informative talks given by a park ranger on the history of the Casa Grande ruins. The visitor center is open daily from 9 a.m. to 5 p.m. Admission is $5 for adults and is good for seven days.

The major annual event for this area is the **O'Odham Tash,** a celebration of Native American culture usually held in February. Festivities are open to the general public. You'll hear traditional music of several varieties, including waila, a kind of rock-and-roll polka. Watch colorful ceremonial dancers compete for awards and browse through arts and crafts, including baskets, rugs, paintings, and jewelry. You can also sample O'Odham cuisine. An all-Indian rodeo rounds out the events. Contact the Casa Grande Chamber of Commerce (520-836-2125 or 800-916-1515; www.casagrandechamber.org) for more information.

Continuing on AZ 87 south takes you past farming communities that sprout forth like an emerald beard across the stubbly face of the desert. AZ 87 merges into I-10 a few miles south of the tiny town of Picacho. Just east of the town is **Picacho Peak State Park** (520-466-3183; www.azstateparks.com), a craggy, saguaro-dotted mountain that in the spring is covered with wildflowers. This is the site of the Battle of Picacho Pass, Arizona's only Civil War battle (military purists insist it was only a skirmish).

In any case, the military engagement took place on April 15, 1862, when Union troops commanded by Lt. James Barrett fired upon Confederate pickets from Tucson. In the ensuing action, Barrett and two Union privates were killed. Fearing that more troops were on the way, both forces retreated. Even though it was a tactical draw, this battle is considered to be the westernmost battle of the Civil War. Activities at Picacho Peak include picnicking, hiking, and camping ($15 to $20). The entrance fee is $6 in the peak winter season and $3 during the hot summer months.

Places to Stay in Central Arizona

GLENDALE

Quality Inn Glendale
7116 N. 59th Ave.
(623) 939-9431 or
(877) 424-6423
www.qualityinn.com
This comfortable inn has an outdoor heated pool and is located near Old Town Glendale and Catlin Court. Inexpensive.

MESA

Phoenix Marriott Mesa
200 N. Centennial Way
(480) 898-8300 or
(800) 228-9290
www.marriott.com
Located near downtown Mesa, this spacious hotel has 265 rooms and 10 suites. Amenities include

a pool and hot tub, business center, fitness center, one restaurant, and a cafe. Inexpensive to moderate.

PHOENIX

Hyatt Regency Phoenix
122 N. 2nd St.
(602) 252-1234 or
(800) 233-1234
www.hyattphoenix.com
Right downtown across from the Civic Plaza, this hotel is renowned for the great views and fabulous cuisine at its revolving Compass Restaurant, which offers 360-degree views of the valley from the hotel rooftop. Moderate to expensive.

Arizona Grand Resort
7777 S. Pointe Parkway
(602) 438-9000 or
(877) 267-1321
www.arizonagrandresort .com
This luxury resort at South Mountain has

championship golf, an athletic club and spa, three restaurants and The Oasis—"Arizona's Ultimate Water Adventure." Moderate to expensive.

SCOTTSDALE

FireSky Resort and Spa
4925 N. Scottsdale Rd.
(480) 945-7666 or
(800) 528-7867
www.fireskyresort.com
This lovely resort is located in downtown Scottsdale near the art galleries and shops in the Old Town District. Expensive.

The Phoenician,
6000 E. Camelback Rd.
(480) 941-8200 or
(800) 888-8234
www.thephoenician.com
Located at the base of Camelback Mountain, this renowned resort offers a golf course, a spa, a tennis garden, nine pools, and ten

WEB SITES FOR CENTRAL ARIZONA

Apache Junction Area Chamber of Commerce
www.apachejunctioncoc.com

Arizona Department of Tourism
www.arizonaguide.com

Carefree/Cave Creek Chamber of Commerce
www.carefree-cavecreek.com

Chandler Chamber of Commerce
www.chandlerchamber.com

Fountain Hills Chamber of Commerce
www.fountainhillschamber.com

Glendale Chamber of Commerce
www.visitglendale.com

Greater Casa Grande Chamber of Commerce
www.casagrandechamber.org

Greater Phoenix Convention and Visitors Bureau
www.phoenixcvb.com

Mesa Convention and Visitors Bureau
www.visitmesa.com

Peoria Chamber of Commerce
www.peoriachamber.com

Scottsdale Area Chamber of Commerce
www.scottsdalecvb.com

Southwest Valley Chamber of Commerce
www.southwestvalleychamber.org

Surprise Regional Chamber of Commerce
www.surpriseregionalchamber.com

Tempe Convention and Visitors Bureau
www.tempecvb.com

Tonto National Forest
www.fs.fed.us/r3/tonto

Wickenburg Chamber of Commerce
www.wickenburgchamber.com

---

restaurants and lounges. Expensive.

TEMPE

Ramada Tempe at Arizona Mills Mall
1701 W. Baseline Rd.
(480) 413-1188 or
(800) 633-8300
www.ramada.com
Right off I-10, this casual hotel is close to all the sights and restaurants in downtown Tempe. Inexpensive.

Places to Eat in Central Arizona

GLENDALE

Haus Murphy's
5739 W. Glendale Ave.
(623) 939-2480
www.hausmurphys.com
Enjoy authentic German food, the Bier Garten, and live music at this popular restaurant on the main street of Old Town

Glendale. Inexpensive to moderate.

Skye
16844 N. Arrowhead Fountain Dr.
(623) 334-0010
www.skye-restaurant.com
Sample exciting cuisine in a modern atmosphere. Skye features weekly live music. Moderate

MESA

Giant Hamburgers
2753 E. Broadway
(480) 733-6542

Enjoy excellent and GIANT hamburgers at this unique American establishment in central Mesa. Also serves breakfast. Inexpensive to moderate.

Mango's Mexican Cafe
44 W. Main St.
(480) 464-5700
mangosmexicancafe.com
Mango's serves Mexican specialties in the heart of downtown shopping not far from Mesa Southwest Museum. Inexpensive to moderate.

PHOENIX

Fry Bread House
4140 N. Seventh Ave.
(602) 351-2345
This small downtown restaurant has some of the best Indian fry bread in town. Inexpensive.

Red Devil Italian Restaurant
3102 E. McDowell Rd.
(602) 267-1036
www.reddevilrestaurant
.com

This Italian restaurant is often voted the best pizzeria in town. Inexpensive to moderate.

SCOTTSDALE

5 & Diner
9069 E. Indian Bend Rd.
(480) 949-1957
www.5anddiner.com
In Scottsdale Pavilions Mall off Pima Road, this fifties diner features jukeboxes playing the oldies and serves up breakfast, burgers, and blue-plate specials. Inexpensive.

North
15024 N. Scottsdale Rd., Ste. 160
(480) 948-2055
www.foxrc.com/north
Part of the national chain of Fox restaurants, North offers an ideal location for shoppers and business executives. The menu features modern cuisine with seasonally fresh food. Moderate to expensive.

TEMPE

My Big Fat Greek Restaurant
227 E. Baseline Rd.
(480) 966-5883
This express version of its Phoenix parent features authentic Greek food at a reasonable price. Inexpensive to moderate.

PF Chang's
740 S. Mill Ave.
(480) 731-4600
www.pfchangs.com
This national restaurant with a modern atmosphere specializes in tasty Asian cuisine. Moderate.

SOUTHERN ARIZONA →

The Southwestern Corner

Yuma (928-783-0071 or 800-293-0071; www.visityuma.com), on I-8, exists among several worlds: It's only a few minute's drive from either the California state line or the Mexican border. It's also in the midst of a desert area, yet it's bordered by the Colorado River and has more than 150,000 acres dedicated to agriculture.

Despite its dichotomies, Yuma has a long, colorful history as a distinctive part of Arizona. It was originally named Colorado City (after the river) and then Arizona City, finally taking the name of the Native American tribe that had long called the area home. Puns were inevitable, and a few years back the suggestion was made that the town adopt the slogan "You'll Love Our Sense of Yuma."

In the nineteenth century the town was a crossing point for the famous Mormon Battalion as well as Kit Carson and California gold seekers. In the 1850s the invention of the shallow-draft steamboat made Yuma a major stop on the Colorado River for boats taking supplies to army posts or mining camps. Its territorial prison, built in 1875, housed some of the

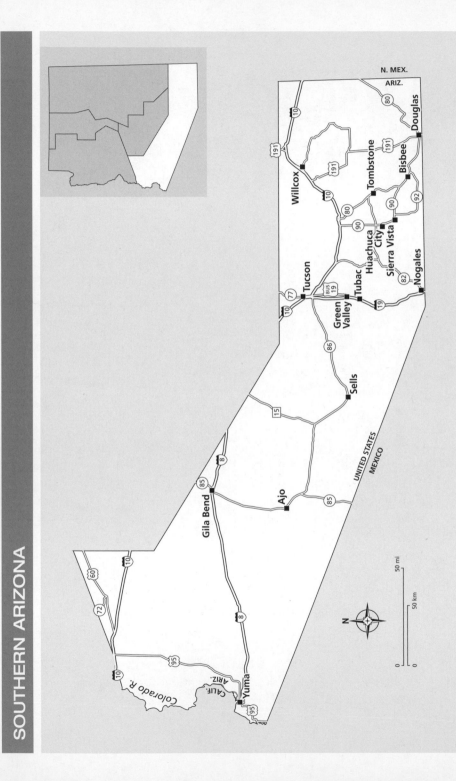

SOUTHERN ARIZONA

West's most notorious desperados, and in modern times the town has become not only an important agricultural center (labor organizer Cesar Chavez grew up here) but also the site for a Marine Corps Air Station and an Army Proving Ground.

For history buffs, Yuma has a number of interesting museums. The *Yuma Crossing State Historic Park* (928-329-0471; www.azstateparks.com) at Fourth Avenue, located beyond the railroad tracks along the river behind City Hall, was a vital distribution point for military equipment from 1864 to 1883. Several original buildings, including the quartermaster's office and the commanding officer's quarters, have been restored. The depot is operated as a living history museum, complete with authentically costumed guides. It's open Thurs through Mon from 9 a.m. to 5 p.m. Admission is $4 for adults and $1 for children ages seven to thirteen.

The *Yuma Territorial Prison State Park* (928-783-4771; www.azstateparks.com) at One Prison Hill Road at the east end of First Avenue is another popular attraction. No film about the Old West is complete without at least one reference to this infamous Iron Bar Hotel. Historians argue over whether the prison, built in 1876, was actually a "hellhole," as it's often depicted. Certainly inmates would have found it cramped, dark, and hot. Yet it had one of the first libraries in the state, electric fans, and many brief prison sentences. There are video presentations on the history of the prison every 35 minutes beginning at 9 a.m. Visit the prison on Sun at high noon and 2 p.m. Oct through Apr, and you can watch Old West shoot-outs staged by the Deguello Gunslingers. It's open Thurs through Mon from 9 a.m. to 5 p.m. Admission is $4 for adults and $1 for children ages seven to thirteen.

One of the strangest bits of history in the area is the *McPhaul Bridge,* 18 miles north of Yuma on US 95. The bridge, sometimes referred to locally

AUTHOR'S TOP PICKS IN SOUTHERN ARIZONA

Arizona-Sonora Desert Museum	Mission San Xavier del Bac
Bisbee	Ramsey Canyon Preserve
Chiricahua Mountains	Sabino Canyon
Club Congress	Tanque Verde Guest Ranch
Kartchner Caverns State Park	Tubac
Kitt Peak National Observatory	

JANUARY

Tucson Gem, Mineral and Fossil Showcase

Tucson

This main event is billed as the "world's largest marketplace gem and mineral show". More than 250 vendors show their wares during the two-week-long festival.
(520) 322-5773 or (800) 638-8350;
www.tgms.org

Wings over Willcox

Willcox

Held on the third week of Jan, this Sandhill Crane Celebration includes guided tours, a "hawk stalk," seminars, workshops, field trips, and bird-watching.
(520) 384-2272 or (800) 200-2272;
www.wingsoverwillcox.com

FEBRUARY

Arizona State Museum's Southwest Indian Art Fair

Tucson

More than 200 Native American artists display their work at Arizona State Museum's most popular event. Other activities include artist demonstrations, ethnic foods, and Native American music and dance performances.
(520) 621-6302; www.statemuseum.arizona.edu

Cochise Cowboy Poetry and Music Gathering

Sierra Vista

On the second weekend in Feb, you can listen to storytellers, reciters, singers and musicians, and nationally recognized artists at this popular event.
(520) 459-3868 or (800) 288-3861;
www.cowboypoets.com

Jaycees Silver Spur Rodeo Parade

Yuma

Running for more than fifty years, this is the largest parade in Yuma.
(928) 344-5451

La Fiesta de los Vaqueros

Tucson

More than eighty years old, this PRCA rodeo is America's largest outdoor, midwinter rodeo.
(520) 741-2233 or (800) 964-5662;
www.tucsonrodeo.com

Territorial Days

Benson

This recently revived event features a mounted shooting event, Wild West show, exhibition shooting, cavalry drills, barrel racing and a historical reenactment.
(520) 419-0050; www.azrangers.org

Tubac Festival of the Arts

Tubac

This event features juried national and international artists, live entertainment, and artist demonstrations.
(520) 398-2704; www.tubacaz.com

MARCH

O'odham Day Celebration

Ajo

Enjoy Native American traditions at the Tohono O'odham basket-weaving demonstration and storytelling on the third Sat in Mar.
520-387-7661

Territorial Days

Tombstone

Relive the Wild West with fire cart championship races, all-pet parade, and gunfight reenactments.
(520) 457-9317 or 888-457-3929

APRIL

La Vuelta de Bisbee
Bisbee
Top amateur men and women cyclists from throughout the United States and abroad wind up and down the roads of historic Old Bisbee in this cycling competition.
(520) 432-5795; www.discoverbisbee.com

Pima County Fair
Tucson
This exciting annual event runs daily for ten days and is free for kids under five. With rides, attractions, and livestock competitions the fair is a great spring outing.
(520) 762-9100; www.pimacountyfair.com

MAY

Cinco de Mayo
Tucson
A celebration of the Mexican holiday commemorating the Puebla battle of May 5, 1862, against France. The event includes ethnic dancing, music, crafts, and food in Kennedy Park and a 10K run through the Tucson foothills.
(520) 719-4863 or (520) 326-9383; www.tucsonchamber.org

Fiber Arts Festival
Bisbee
This special arts festival features a fashion show, fiber animals such as sheep and llamas, displays, demonstrations, workshops, and guest speakers.
(800) 866-2BISBEE; www.bisbeefiberarts.com

Wyatt Earp Days
Tombstone
Gunfights, public hanging, saloon girls, fashion show, parade, dancing, and live country-western music brings back the lifestyle of the Wild West.
(520) 457-3291; www.tombstonevigilantes.com.

JUNE

Diá de San Juan Fiesta
Tucson
A celebration of the "Season of Monsoon Rains" complete with a traditional procession and blessing, *charros* (cowboys) and *escaramuzas* (trick horseback riders), food, and live entertainment.
(520) 792-4806

JULY

Peach Mania Festival
Willcox
Love your peaches with all-you-can-eat breakfasts, wagon rides, pick-your-own peaches, peach products, and a country craft fair.
(520) 384-2084; www.appleannies.com

AUGUST

Southwest Wings Birding Festival
Sierra Vista
Enjoy the day with field trips, displays, lectures, bat stalks, owl prowls, and arts and crafts.
(520) 678-8237; www.swwings.org

Vigilante Day
Tombstone
Get into the spirit of the Old West with shoot-outs, hangings, concerts, a chili cook-off, and performances by saloon girls.
(520) 457-3451; www.tombstone.org

continued

SEPTEMBER

Brewery Gulch Days
Bisbee
Horseshoe and waterball tournament, kiddie carnival, live music, bed races, pet parade, Miz Ol' Biz contest, mining games, and a cakewalk are featured at this annual event.
(800) 866-2BISBEE; www .discoverbisbee.com

Labor Day Rodeo
Sonoita
A western rodeo complete with barrel racing, a wild-horse race, team roping events, and mutton busting at the Sonoita Fairgrounds.
(520) 455-5553; www .sonoitafairgrounds.com

Rendezvous of Gunfighters
Tombstone
This event features shows in the O.K. Corral by the best western groups from around the United States.
(520) 457-9317 or (888) 457-39293548; www.tombstonewildbunch.org.

Santa Cruz County Fair
Sonoita
This county fair includes an old-fashioned carnival, exhibits, and live entertainment.
(520) 455-5553; www.sonoita fairgrounds.com

OCTOBER

Bisbee 1000—The Great Stair Climb
Bisbee
This annual event is not only a fun and popular physical-fitness challenge for all ages and levels of fitness; it also helps to raise money for preservation of the local community.
(520) 266-0401; www.bisbee1000.org

Butterfield Overland Stage Days
Benson
Celebration of overland mail route from St. Louis to San Francisco, reenactments, stage rides, arts and crafts, entertainment, dances, and a car show.
(520) 586-2842; www.cityofbenson.com

Gem and Mineral Show
Bisbee
Dealers display rare minerals at this outdoor show for gem enthusiasts. Field trips are available.
866-2BISBEE; www.discoverbisbee .com

Fall Festival
Patagonia
This southern Arizona community celebrates art and cooling weather with juried arts and crafts, country western, bluegrass, folk, mariachi, Latin jazz, rock 'n' roll, Saturday night dance, and western events.
(520) 394-0060 or (888) 794-0060; www.patagoniaaz.com

Helldorado Days
Tombstone
The oldest celebration in town includes shoot-outs, a fashion show, and street entertainment.
(520) 457-3932; www .tombstonevigilantes.com

as the "swinging bridge to nowhere," was built in 1929 as a route across the Gila River. When the Gila was rerouted for agricultural projects, the bridge was left stranded, straddling only desert. The structure, which resembled a

La Fiesta de los Chiles
Tucson
International cuisine, entertainment, music, artisans and craftspeople highlight this festival held in the Tucson Botanical Gardens.
(520) 326-9686; www.tucsonbotanical.org

Rex Allen Days
Willcox
Celebrate singing cowboy star Rex Allen the first weekend in October.
(520) 398-4583 or (800) 234-4111; www.rexallenmuseum.org

NOVEMBER

Colorado River Crossing Balloon Festival
Yuma
This festival includes sunrise balloon liftoffs, sunset balloon glow, fireworks, and live entertainment.
(928) 276-4803; www.caballeros.org

Festival of Color
Sierra Vista
Annual hot-air balloon rally, held since 1989, gives visitors a great reason to explore the community.
(520) 417-6960; www.festivalofcolor.org

Festival of Lights
Bisbee
Experience a live nativity in historic Bisbee.
(520) 432-5421; www.discoverbisbee.com

Historic Home Tour
Bisbee
Relive eras gone by as you wander through Old Town Bisbee and visit restored historic homes.
866-2BISBEE; www.discoverbisbee.com

DECEMBER

Christmas Apple Festival
Willcox
Judged arts and crafts show, bazaar, craft demos, Santa Claus, tree-lighting ceremony, entertainment, raffles, and door prizes.
(520) 384-2272 or (800) 200-2272; www.willcoxchamber.com

Fourth Avenue Street Fair
Tucson
Arts and crafters, community stage, entertainers, and "Kidstreat" bring visitors to the heart of Tucson.
(520) 624-5004, www.fourthavenue.org

La Fiesta de Tumacácori
Tumacácori
Entertainment and crafts, folklorico and Native American dancing, Mexican, Indian, and old-time Arizona music.
(520) 398-2341; www.nps.gov/tuma

Luminaria Nights
Tucson
Holiday lights and music by local groups and choirs at the Tucson Botanical Gardens.
(520) 326-9686; tucsonbotanical.org

scaled-down version of the Golden Gate Bridge, is named after Harry McPhaul, a former territorial prison guard who ventured into the mining industry and once had claims in this area.

Explore the Colorado River with **Yuma River Tours** (928-783-4400; www .yumarivertours.com) at 1920 Arizona Ave. Group tours and day trips on jet boats and stern-wheelers are offered upriver through the Imperial Wildlife Refuge. Stops along the way include an 1800s mining cabin, Indian petroglyph sites, and historic steamboat landings. Rates start at $48. A more leisurely method of seeing the western edge of Yuma is aboard a stern-wheeler. The **Colorado King I Paddleboat,** which is also owned and operated by Yuma River Tours, is a replica of the craft that used to cruise the Colorado River in Mark Twain's time. Dining tours are available. The paddleboat tours operate October through June.

Numerous restaurant chains populate Yuma, but so do longtime family-operated businesses. One of these is **Lutes Casino** (928-782-2192; www.lutes casino.com) at 221 Main St., which is the oldest continuing pool hall and domino parlor in the state. Lutes offers sandwiches and other fast-food items in a somewhat wacky atmosphere.

Another is the **Yuma Landing Restaurant** (928-782-7427; www.yuma landing.com) at 195 S. Fourth Ave. Along with serving up a hearty menu of homemade meals, this landmark restaurant is decorated with historical photographs and is located near the site of the monument marking the landing site of Robert G. Fowler, who touched down at this location on October 25, 1911, with his Wright model B biplane—the first airplane to land on Arizona soil.

Many national chains are on standby to house road warriors visiting Yuma. Among the top choices are **Best Western Coronado Motor Hotel** (928-783-4453 or 877-234-5567; www.bestwestern.com) at 233 S. Fourth Ave., which

Sand Dune Stand-ins

Arizona's deserts are among the world's most verdant, so visitors looking for a Sahara-like landscape will find more vegetation than bargained for. However, a sandier setting exists west of Yuma. Travel west on I-8 to Gray's Well exit and follow the frontage road. You'll wind up surrounded by sand dunes that have served as stand-ins for Middle Eastern dunes in many TV shows and films, dating back to about 1921 when Valentino's *The Sheik* was filmed here. All three versions of *Beau Geste* were at least partially lensed in these dunes, as well as the Jimmy Stewart movie *The Flight of the Phoenix.* (At the very end of the film, a patched-together plane heads over these dunes and disappears from sight. In real life it crashed just out of camera range, killing the pilot.) The tremendously popular George Lucas film *Star Wars* was partially filmed here, as was the science fiction hit *Stargate.* There are no real markers or landmarks here to photograph—just miles of sand—so bring your imagination and maybe a few props like a light saber or your pet Ewok.

offers rooms with a refrigerator and microwave. In addition to being close to all of Yuma's historical sites, this Spanish-style hotel has two pools, a hot tub, and an exercise room. Rooms start at $78. The **Best Western InnSuites Yuma Mall Hotel and Suites** (928-783-8341 or 800-922-2034; www.bestwestern.com) at 1450 S. Castle Dome Ave. features luxurious suites complete with complimentary breakfast and evening cocktail hour. This pet-friendly hotel also has lighted tennis and basketball courts, a pool and hot tub, and a fitness center. Rates start at $90. Nearby the **Shilo Inn Hotel and Suites** (928-782-9511 or 800-222-2244; www.shiloinns.com) at 1550 S. Castle Dome Ave. offers a free buffet breakfast. Hotel amenities include an on-site restaurant and lounge, one of the largest pools in Yuma, and a fitness center complete with a sauna and steam room. Rates start at $130.

Head east on I-8 to **Gila Bend** (928-683-2002; www.gilabendaz.org). The town got its name from the sharp bend in the Gila River that used to occur at this point before the river was diverted for agricultural purposes.

Today visitors to Gila Bend can step back into history in a variety of ways. Just west of town is petroglyph-covered **Painted Rocks.** You can reach this wildlife area by taking I-8 to exit 102. The exact meaning of these 1,000-year-old Hohokam etchings is unknown. People, reptiles, and geometric doodles cover the black basalt rocks. There's a recreational lake and a picnic area here, so if you have the time, pack a lunch, bring a sketch pad, and try to decode all the combinations of the primitive alphabet depicted on Painted Rocks. The **Agua Caliente Hotel and Hot Springs** ruins are also located just west of town. To reach them, exit from I-8 onto Sentinel Road. The former hotel and surrounding adobe buildings—constructed to take advantage of the area's status as a stage stop as well as the supposed therapeutic values of the water—are still partially standing. You can pose by a crumbling adobe wall and then send copies of the picture to your friends and family. Tell them you've picked out your retirement home. You won't be able to relax in the hot springs, however; they dried up years ago.

In downtown Gila Bend is the **Gila Bend Historical Museum** (928-683-2002) at 644 W. Pima St. Dedicated to the preservation of archaeological and historical finds, it includes information gathered from the Hohokam Ceremonial Platform that's near town. The platform dates from A.D. 800; there are plans to re-excavate and open up some of the area as a state park. The museum is open daily from 8 a.m. to 4 p.m.; donations accepted. The museum is also the visitor information center.

Gila Bend is home to several unusual dwellings. The former **Stout Hotel,** at the corner of Pima and Capitol Streets, is a poured concrete building constructed around 1929 as a first-rate hotel for railroad and automobile travelers.

It had air-conditioning and steam heat and an ice plant in the basement. In its heyday its many famous guests included Clark Gable and Carole Lombard. Incidentally, the pair appears to have been quite fond of Arizona, having been on the guest lists of several other hotels statewide, including the Monte Vista in Flagstaff and Phoenix's San Carlos Hotel and Arizona Biltmore Resort. Now part of the hotel is being used as a general store. The rest is awaiting restoration, but no date has been set to begin yet.

Across an arroyo (a streambed to non-southwesterners), just west of the town's ice plant, is a curious-looking structure built of railroad ties. Constructed in the midst of the Great Depression by **Harvey Brown** (aka "Jungle Jim" because of the pith helmet he wore), this once was a store that sold everything from sandwiches to luggage. Brown's customers were vagrants like himself, and, ironically, the building—whose exact ownership is in question—is now being used by squatters. If you're interested in twentieth-century U.S. history, this unusual building is worth a visit because it represents a typical American's boot-strap response to hard times.

Only a handful of restaurants operate in Gila Bend. A safe bet is a stop at one of the fast-food eateries that beckon hungry travelers or the twenty-four-hour coffee shop at the **Best Western Space Age Lodge** (928-683-2273 or 800-780-7234; www.bestwestern.com) at 401 E. Pima St. Whether you're hungry or not, you have to stop by the kitschy roadside inn. This priceless piece of Americana was built in the early 1960s and has a spaceship attached to the roof.

The Oatman Massacre

South of the hotel ruins on Sentinel Road is the site of the Oatman Massacre. A large, white cross on a nearby plateau stands as a monument to the Oatman family. On Mar 19, 1851, Royce and Mary Ann Oatman and their seven children were part of a Mormon pilgrimage to the Arizona/California border area. They were camped on this spot when a group of Yavapai Indians approached and asked for food and tobacco. Royce complied but, fearful that he wouldn't have enough for his family, refused the Yavapais' request for seconds. The family, with the exception of fifteen-year-old Lorenzo, fourteen-year-old Olive, and her younger sister Mary Ann, was brutally slain. Lorenzo survived by playing dead, while the two girls were taken as captives. Mary Ann died soon after, and Olive was sold to the Mohave Indians and later ransomed back into white society (in a bizarre twist, she became a celebrity as a result of her ordeal, though her story was largely used as anti–Native American propaganda). The actual site of the killings is just east of the roadway, but it can only be reached by a four-wheel-drive vehicle.

Less than an hour south of Gila Bend on AZ 85 is the tiny town of *Ajo* (520-387-7742). Though the word ajo (ahh-ho) is Spanish for garlic and also is used as a mild expletive, some historians believe the town's name actually originated from a similar-sounding Tohono O'Odham word for paint (ore from this area was used for making pigment). In any case Ajo was the oldest-known mine site in the state, and until the 1980s Phelps Dodge ran a sizable copper-mining operation out of here. The mines originally were made profitable during World War I by John C. Greenway, who also gets the credit for building the town's palm tree–shaded *Spanish Colonial Plaza* in Ajo's center. The plaza is a traditional town square created in a Spanish Colonial revival style. In the midst of the plaza is a large, green park and surrounding it are shops, restaurants, and two churches. To the south of the plaza is a Federated church built in 1926. Just north of that structure sits a mission-style Catholic church constructed in 1924.

A number of buildings from the 1920s and before are still standing. *Curley School,* southwest of the plaza on West Vananda Avenue, was constructed in 1919. The Train Depot, directly northeast of the plaza, dates from 1915. *New Cornelia Hotel,* just east of Curley School, was constructed in 1916. The exteriors of these buildings, most done in Spanish Colonial revival, are easily incorporated into a walking tour. Stop by the Ajo Chamber of Commerce on AZ 85 just south of the Plaza and ask for a self-guided tour map.

A building that has been restored is now a charming bed-and-breakfast inn. The *Guest House Inn* (520-387-6133; www.guesthouseinn.biz) at 700 Guest House Rd. was built in 1925 by Phelps Dodge Corporation as a guest-house for its visitors. The inn offers four rooms with private baths. The rooms are furnished in southwestern style, some with Victorian antiques. Breakfast is hearty, and from the patio you can watch a variety of native birds, including quail and cactus wrens. Rates are $89 to $99 for double occupancy. Breakfast is included.

Ajo today is one part retirement community, one part snowbird haven, and one part bedroom community for people who don't mind the two-hour commute to Phoenix or Tucson.

Ajo's gorgeous mountain views and charming Old World architecture are certainly enchanting. For some, however, Ajo is merely a stopping-off point on the way to *Organ Pipe Cactus National Monument* (520-387-6849; www .nps.gov/orpi), located south off AZ 85. If you were to take a giant octopus, turn it upside down, and plant it in the dirt, you would have a rough idea of what an organ pipe cactus looks like. In color and form these cacti resemble saguaros, but unlike saguaros, they have a half-dozen or more long arms reaching out from a center point. They are quite spectacular, especially during their blooming season. This fantastic show typically occurs at dusk from May through July.

The monument, by the way, is the starting point for notorious **El Camino del Diablo**—"the Devil's Highway." Over the years this stretch of godforsaken road has claimed numerous lives (more than 400 during the California gold rush). If you've got a four-wheel-drive vehicle, you may want to attempt this hot, bumpy, desolate trek that ends near Yuma. Because there are no road services along the way, plan on taking plenty of supplies (especially water) for you and your car. A safer, easier drive over a graded dirt road can be taken from near the Organ Pipe National Monument Visitor Center. Called the **Ajo Mountain Drive,** this 21-mile loop will take you through the Diablo Mountain Range to Mount Ajo and back to the visitor center. Along the way you'll see many varieties of cacti and desert creatures. In early spring you may see wildflowers, and in the late spring and early summer months, cactus blossoms dot the landscape. Activities include wildlife watching, camping ($12), and hiking. Admission is $8 per vehicle for seven days.

After the monument take AZ 86 east toward Tucson. Just past the town of Sells, turn south onto AZ 386. This route will lead you 6,900 feet above sea level to the top of Kitt Peak in the Quinlan Mountains. The view, which takes in the neighboring Baboquivari Mountains and long stretches of Sonoran desert, is not only quite spectacular, but this is the site of **NOAO Kitt Peak National Observatory** (520-318-8726; www.noao.edu/kpno). The observatory is home to the world's largest solar telescope and the world's largest collection of telescopes. Though the climb up a paved road to the observatory is a bit steep, if you're interested in astronomy, it's worth the effort. The observatory's McMath solar telescope is the largest aperture solar telescope in the world. The visitor center gives one-hour-long guided tours to either the 4-meter or the 2.1-meter telescope as well as the solar telescope. Picnic grounds with barbecue grills also share space on the peak, and many tourists to Kitt Peak bring lunch. The observatory is located on the Tohono O'Odham Reservation, 56 miles southwest of Tucson, and is open daily from 9 a.m. to 4 p.m. Tours are held at 10 a.m., 11:30 a.m., and 1:30 p.m. and cost $4.00 for adults and $2.50 for children ages six to twelve.

Downtown and East Tucson

From Kitt Peak, **Tucson** (520-624-1817 or 800-638-8350; www.visittucson .org) is the next major stop. Known as the Old Pueblo by locals, Tucson was founded in 1775 and is one of the oldest continually inhabited sites in the United States. Archeologists have discovered Hohokam artifacts that date back thousands of years. The community is an eclectic meld of Native American, Mexican, Spanish, Asian, and European cultures. Consider the fact that the town was founded on the site of an ancient Indian settlement by an Irishman serving in the Spanish Army!

You can reach Tucson from Kitt Peak by taking AZ 86 east. Once you reach the Tucson city limits, AZ 86 turns into Ajo Way. This puts you on the southwest side of the city. Take the I-10 west freeway entrance from Ajo Way, and follow I-10 to the Broadway Boulevard exit. As you exit onto Broadway Boulevard, you'll be driving into downtown Tucson.

While you're cruising on I-10, you'll notice that Tucson is surrounded by mountains. To the west are the Tucson Mountains; to the east, the Rincons. Directly north are the Santa Catalinas, and down south are the Santa Ritas. Some of the peaks are snow-capped in winter, and *Mount Lemmon* in the Catalinas is known for being the southernmost skiable peak in the United States. The community of *Summerhaven* near the top of the mountain is renowned as a cool summer getaway only an hour's drive from the city. Unfortunately, a devastating forest fire burned down most of Summerhaven in June 2003. The town has since been undergoing construction. Despite the ravages of the Aspen Fire, the *Mount Lemmon Ski Valley* (520-576-1400; www.fs.fed.us/ r3/coronado) is open and offers a full season of snow sports. In the off-season the ski lift still runs, providing visitors with great views of the Catalinas.

trivia

Mount Lemmon, in the Santa Catalina Mountains north of Tucson, is the southernmost ski area in the continental United States and is the only mountain in the state named after the first woman who climbed it—Sara Plummer Lemmon.

You can reach Mount Lemmon by taking I-10 north to Grant Road. Follow Grant Road until it reaches the far east side of Tucson. The road will become Tanque Verde Road. Stay on Tanque Verde Road until you reach the Catalina Highway. Turn left onto the Catalina Highway and drive north. The road will take you all the way up Mount Lemmon.

Mountains are very important to Tucsonans. For one thing, they provide landmarks. While you're traveling anywhere on the northwest side of Tucson, glance to the west and you'll notice a small peak with an "A" whitewashed onto the rocks. *Sentinel Peak* ("A" Mountain to locals) is where the community called Chukson ("spring at the foot of the black mountain") began. The "A"—whitewashed every year by University of Arizona freshmen—has been a prominent monument since 1914. There is a narrow, paved road that takes you all the way up Sentinel Peak. The view of the city from the peak, especially as the sun sets and lights begin to twinkle on, is quite spectacular. To reach Sentinel Peak take the Congress Street exit from I-10 and head west toward the peak. One note of caution: You probably don't want to linger on the peak after dark; Sentinel Peak at night becomes a favorite "parking" and hang-out spot for high-schoolers and others.

trivia

Tucson has more than 150 Mexican restaurants.

From Sentinel Peak you can reach the downtown by simply driving east on Congress Street. Less than two decades ago, downtown Tucson was dead: mortally wounded by new, centrally located shopping malls that forced the downtown department stores to close up. Downtown—roughly bounded by Fourth Avenue on the east, Church Avenue on the west, Council Street on the south, and Twelfth Street on the north—became a graveyard that no one wanted to whistle past after dark.

Today the once-silent area, together with neighboring districts such as the university area, is as vibrant and exciting as a jazz sax solo. On *First Fridays* the cafes, art galleries, and boutique shops that line both sides of Congress Street, Broadway Boulevard, and other downtown routes stay open late. Street musicians play in the square, and you'll see everything from strolling Shakespearean actors to aging hippies selling tie-dyed T-shirts. For example, members of the Tucson Symphony Orchestra sometimes play short concerts aimed at getting kids interested in music. You don't have to wait for a special day, however, to enjoy the galleries, performance venues, and cafes. The following paragraphs direct you to some of the area's most unique and interesting attractions.

Dinnerware Artspace (520-792-4503; www.dinnerwarearts.com) at 264 E. Congress St. always has interesting exhibits. One month the gallery might pair a sculptor who creates realistic images of people with an installation by a performance artist who will display a dining room set wrapped in newspaper. You'll discover as you visit these and the other downtown galleries that art in Tucson is very diverse. Some of it is heavily influenced by the Southwest. Much of it, however, is cosmopolitan. You'll see abstract and impressionist and pop art that would look right at home in a New York high-rise apartment as well as pieces that portray coyotes, Native Americans, Spanish missions, and other classic symbols of Tucson's history.

Within walking distance of the downtown galleries is the newly renovated and expanded *Tucson Museum of Art and Historic Block* (520-624-2333; www.tucsonarts.com) at 140 N. Main Ave. The museum, considered to be a mini-Guggenheim in its interior design, houses numerous permanent collections, including a large exhibit of pre-Columbian art. The courtyard in front of the museum is often used for events, including blues and jazz concerts as well as block-party-style fund-raisers for the museum. The museum is open Tues through Sat from 10 a.m. to 4 p.m. and Sun from noon to 4 p.m. Admission is $8 for adults and $3 for children age thirteen and up. The museum offers free admission on the first Sun of each month.

Across the courtyard from the Tucson Museum of Art is the historic **Stevens/Duffield House** at 150 N. Main Ave. On the **Presidio** square are other historic houses—the **Romero House** from the 1860s, the **Corbett House** built in 1907, and **La Casa Cordova** built in the pre– and post– Civil War years. The **Fish House** (aka Goodman Pavilion) built in 1867 now houses a collection of western art.

Tucson has truly emerged as a hot spot for haute cuisine. Great choices include **Barrio Bar & Grill** (520-629-0191) at 135 S. Sixth Ave., a downtown bistro, and **Anthony's in the Catalinas** at 6440 N. Campbell Ave. (520-299-1771; www.anthonysinthecatalinas .com), which features more than 1,700 wines and a Continental menu.

> ## trivia
>
> The sun shines 340 days a year in Tucson.

As you might suspect of a town located smack-dab in the heart of Old West territory, quite a few rough-and-tumble incidents took place in the downtown area. At the corner of Church and Pennington Streets, a couple of blocks south of North Main Avenue, a bizarre shooting involving two prominent members of the community occurred in 1891. C. Handy, the chief surgeon for the Southern Pacific Railroad (and one-time chancellor for the nascent University of Arizona) shot and killed Francis J. Heney, the lawyer representing Handy's wife in their divorce.

A few blocks farther south on Main Avenue and Simpson Street beyond the Convention Center, in the neighborhood known as **Barrio Historico,** stands an adobe wall with a plaque dedicated to **El Tiradito** ("the little castaway"). One version of the story goes that many years ago, a young sheepherder who lived with his wife and his in-laws on a ranch outside of town fell in love with his wife's mother. While meeting in town for an adulterous liaison, they were caught by the sheepherder's father-in-law, who killed the young man and buried him. Because the sheepherder was buried in unconsecrated ground, he was forever doomed as a sinner—a castaway. Today, locals light candles and leave hand-printed prayers at this wishing shrine. It is said that if your candle burns the whole night through, your dream will come true.

Next to El Tiradito is **El Minuto Cafe** (520-882-4145; www.elminutocafe .com) at 354 S. Main Ave. It's a very popular Mexican restaurant featuring authentic versions of Sonoran cuisine. During weekdays it's difficult to get a table at lunch. It's equally busy in the evening if there's an event at the nearby Tucson Convention Center or the Arizona Theatre Company Temple of Music and Art.

A brief jog to the north is **Old Town Artisans** (520-623-6024 or 800-782-8072; www.oldtownartisans.com) at 201 N. Court Ave. It's a collection of fine art, jewelry, and crafts shops that sit in the area of the original Spanish presidio. Two front rooms contain adobe blocks dating back to the 1860s. For a bite to eat, enjoy dining in the cantina or courtyard of **La Cocina** (520-622-0351), which serves up southwestern specialties and American favorites Mon through Sat from 4 to 9 p.m.

On Congress Avenue there's lots to see and do. You might want to peruse the many antiques and secondhand shops. At the end of the street is the historic **Hotel Congress** (520-622-8848 or 800-722-8848; www.hotelcongress .com) at 311 E. Congress St. A funky sort of place, the hotel provides basic accommodations and houses the **Club Congress,** which features live alternative music on weekends. The **Cup Cafe,** where you can get gourmet coffee and a bite to eat, is also within the hotel complex. The club and cafe are considered the "be-seen" hot spots in downtown Tucson.

At 330 S. Scott Ave. is the **Arizona Theatre Company Temple of Music and Art** (520-884-8210 or 520-622-2823 for tickets; www.arizonatheater.org), a beautiful complex that includes a cabaret theater, a main auditorium, a cafe, and an art gallery. Performances by the Arizona Theatre Company are held here, as are concerts and other cultural events. The Arizona Theatre Company's season is usually September through May. Tickets may be purchased online.

About a three-minute drive east of downtown is **Fourth Avenue** (Merchants Association, 520-624-5004; www.fourthavenue.org), a lively strip of real estate that has the atmosphere (and the history) of San Francisco's Haight-Ashbury neighborhood. In the 1960s and 1970s, the businesses in this sleepy residential area were dominated by head shops and smoky bars where (nearly) free love and illegal drugs flowed. Today Fourth Avenue has really cleaned up its act. The eclectic mix of shops includes **Bison Witches Bar and Deli** (520-740-1541; www.bisonwitches.com), a restaurant and bar at 326 N. Fourth Ave.; **Native Seed Search** (520-622-5561; www.nativeseeds.org) at 526 N. Fourth Ave.; and **Arroyo Design** (520-884-1012; www.arroyo-design.com), a shop at 224 N. Fourth Ave. featuring custom furniture made from desert wood including mesquite and ironwood. Other shops specialize in antique clothing, such as **How Sweet It Was** (520-623-9854; www.howsweetitwas.com) at 419

N. Fourth Ave. and *Desert Vintage & Costume* (520-620-1570) at 636 N. Fourth Ave.

Lots of restaurants to choose from guarantee that you won't go hungry. *Caruso's Italian Restaurant* (520-624-5765; www.carusositalian.com) at 434 N. Fourth Ave. has been serving Italian food to Tucsonans since it first opened in the 1930s. Across the street, *Delectables* (520-884-9289; www.delectables .com) at 533 N. Fourth Ave. offers a variety of gourmet items, including fruit and cheese plates. If your sweet tooth gets the better of you, stop at the corner of Sixth Street and Fourth Avenue to find the *Chocolate Iguana* on Fourth Avenue (520-798-1211; www.chocolateiguanaon4th.com) at 500 N. Fourth Ave. It sells all sorts of candy, baked goods, and coffee drinks. It also has an interesting selection of greeting cards.

Fourth Avenue is best known locally for its two annual weekend street fairs—one usually runs in early December, and one is in late March or early April. Besides arts, crafts, and food booths (where you can sample some wonderful Tohono O'Odham fry bread), the fairs feature street entertainers and representatives from all sorts of worthy human rights/animal rights groups. During a typical street fair, Fourth Avenue is blocked off between University Boulevard and Ninth Street, and exhibitors' booths are set up down the center of the avenue. Additionally, the sidewalks are taken over by people doing face painting and hair weaving and musicians playing everything from folk standards to doo-wop ballads. These events are extremely popular and draw Tucsonans of every background and visitors from every state. Expect to park at least four or five blocks away from Fourth Avenue—and to part with a few bucks for a spot. The fairs usually start Friday afternoon.

trivia

Tucson has thrived under four flags—the Spanish, Mexican, Confederate, and United States—and is the oldest continually inhabited site in the United States, with artifacts found in the area dating back to before Christ.

To leave Fourth Avenue you can simply drive out of the neighborhood via University Boulevard, or you can take the trolley. The *Old Pueblo Trolley* (520-792-1802; www.oldpueblotrolley.org), reinstalled just a few years ago (it originally ran from 1906 to 1930), takes riders down University Boulevard past shops and restaurants to the main gate of the University of Arizona. On Tucson's fairly flat urban streets, it isn't quite the hair-raising, white-knuckle trip that San Francisco's streetcars take up Powell Street, but it is a lot of fun. The trolley runs Fri from 6 to 10 p.m., Sat from noon to midnight, and Sun from noon to 6 p.m. One-way fares on Fri and Sat are $1 for adults and 50 cents for children ages six to twelve. On Sun the one-way fare is 25 cents. The all-day pass ($2.50 for adults and $1.50 for children ages six to twelve) lets you get on and off.

Known internationally for its optical sciences department, the **University of Arizona** (520-621-2211; www.arizona.edu) also has a number of other outstanding programs, including its basketball team, the Wildcats, which have had the nation's highest winning percentage since 1987. The school has produced such NBA stars as Sean Elliott, Brian Williams, and Steve Kerr. The older part of the campus, just through the main gate on University Boulevard, contains a number of interesting buildings and museums. Among them are **Centennial Hall,** which is a performing arts venue, **Old Main,** which is the school's first classroom, and the **Center for Creative Photography** (520-621-7968), which holds an archive of photographs from Ansel Adams and Alfred Steiglitz and features rotating and traveling exhibits. The Center for Creative Photography is open Mon through Fri from 9 a.m. to 5 p.m and Sat and Sun from 1 to 4 p.m.

The **University of Arizona Museum of Art** (520-621-7567; artmuseum. arizona.edu) at 1031 N. Olive Rd. on the University of Arizona campus has an impressive collection that ranges from pre-Renaissance to twentieth century, including works by Dürer, Rembrandt, Matisse, Picasso, O'Keeffe, and Audubon. The museum is open weekdays from 9 a.m. to 5 p.m. and Sun from noon to 4 p.m. Call for summer hours. Admission is $5 for adults. Founded in 1893, the **Arizona State Museum** (520-621-6302, 1013 E. University Blvd.; www .statemuseum.arizona.edu) is also part of the university. It specializes in American Indian cultures of the Southwest and northern Mexico and is recognized as one of the world's finest resources for artifacts (100,000 plus). More than 25,000 ethnographic objects also make up the collection. The museum is open Mon through Sat from 10 a.m. to 5 p.m. Donations are accepted.

Just west of campus is the **Arizona History Museum** (520-628-5774; www.arizonahistoricalsociety.org) at 949 E. Second St. Run by the Arizona Historical Society, this museum features permanent and rotating exhibits on the state's past. There are also user-friendly archives available for those who want to look up any arcane lore about Tucson. The historical society holds several annual events, including *La Fiesta de San Agustin,* a two-day celebration of Tucson's patron saint. The fiesta, held in fall, features Mexican and Native American music and entertainment, games for adults and kids, and food. The museum is open Mon through Sat from 10 a.m. to 4 p.m. Admission is $5 for adults and $4 for students ages twelve to eighteen. Admission is free on the first Sat of each month.

East of campus is the **Arizona Inn** (520-325-1541 or 800-933-1093; www .arizonainn.com), which is on the National Register of Historic Places, across

Campbell Avenue at 2200 E. Elm St. This 1930 hacienda-style hotel not only exudes charm but has the dual advantages of being near the center of town yet isolated enough to provide peace and quiet to its guests. It's a good place to visit in spring and fall just to stroll through the flower-bedecked inner courtyard. The inn is a popular spot for weddings and formal dinners. Visiting celebrities who want to eschew the big resorts often bunk here. Rooms start at $169.

If you seek not celebrities but celebrated food with a Spanish accent, take a quick trip to **South Tucson,** a separate 1-square-mile city within Tucson's borders. Head south on Tucson Avenue until you can exit onto Twenty-Second Street, then go west on Twenty-Second Street until you reach South Fourth Avenue and head south.

There are several Mexican restaurants and cafes in this area, including **Guillermo's Double L Restaurant** (520-792-1585) at 1830 S. Fourth Ave. This establishment features Sonoran cuisine, a hybrid created by the indigenous peoples of Northern Mexico using Native American and Spanish influences. If you're bored with bland, fast-food-style tacos, enchiladas, and the like, you'll be pleasantly surprised at the variety of flavors Sonoran cuisine employs. One caveat for diners: Expect crowds on Friday and Saturday night. Hosts or hostesses may tell you there is a twenty-minute wait—it may actually be closer to forty minutes. You can spend your wait watching the colorful low-riding cruisers out on the boulevard. The restaurant is closed Sunday.

The east side of Tucson has its own **Saguaro National Park Rincon Mountain District** (520-733-5153; www.nps.gov/sagu). To reach Saguaro National Park, take Broadway east to Old Spanish Trail and follow the signs. It doesn't offer the dramatic sunset views of Saguaro National Park Tucson Mountain District, but it's nearly 50,000 acres larger than the west side park. Stop at the Saguaro National Park Rincon Mountain District visitor center (open from 9 a.m. to 5 p.m. daily) and ask about the condition and difficulty of the trails before doing any hiking here. There are some easy loop trails, but others are quite difficult. Restrooms and picnic areas are available at both the east side and west side parks. During times of drought when the desert brush is especially dry, you may be asked not to use the barbecue grills. The road is open from 7 a.m. to sunset. Admission is $10 per vehicle for seven days.

The east side also has a wonderful, hidden arboreal getaway called **Sabino Canyon** (520-749-2327 or 520-749-2861; www.sabinocanyon.com). Drive east on Tanque Verde Road to Sabino Canyon Road, go north and keep driving, and you'll wind up in the parking lot. Sabino Canyon has roadrunners that are so tame they eat out of your hand and tram rides that can take you through the canyon (no other vehicles are allowed). Trams leave every thirty minutes.

(The tram also runs in the moonlight three nights a month from Apr through June and Sept through Nov.) Tram rides are $8 adults and $4 for children ages three to twelve. Parking is $5. Experienced hikers who visit Sabino Canyon often choose to make the trek to Seven Falls—occasionally quite a spectacular swimming hole, depending on the rain. It's only about a 5-mile hike, but the ground can be quite rocky and the underbrush treacherous. A quicker way to get there is to ride the tram to the start of Bear Canyon Trail and then hike the last 2 miles.

Incidentally, Tanque Verde Road could probably win an award as one of the strangest-looking streets in Arizona. It has a variety of weird statuary along its route: a life-size Tyrannosaurus rex at the Kolb intersection; an ersatz castle at Golf 'n' Stuff; a sculpted metal fish jumping out of the dry Tanque Verde wash (river) onto the street; and a wagon sitting on top of boulders at Trail Dust Town (home to the **Dakota Cafe** (520-298-7188) at 6541 E. Tanque Verde Rd.—a great place to get nouvelle cuisine with a southwestern flair). Not far from the Tanque Verde strip is the **Tanque Verde Guest Ranch** (520-296-6275 or 800-234-3833; www.tanqueverderanch.com) at 14301 E. Speedway. It's an authentic, Old West–style dude ranch that was even used as the location for the Nickelodeon series *Hey Dude*. It has stables, tennis courts, and gourmet dining. Accommodations here are surprisingly luxurious, and the foothills setting is incomparable.

Tucson's West Side

From south Tucson, backtrack to Speedway Boulevard and head west. Pretty soon you'll notice that the cacti begin to outnumber the houses. Speedway becomes Gates Pass Road, and suddenly you're in the heart of **Saguaro National Park Tucson Mountain District** (928-733-5158; www.nps.gov/sagu), a terrific place to watch sunsets and take pictures, especially in the spring when the saguaro's white blossoms open. The park was created to preserve the majestic saguaro cactus, which only grows in the Sonoran Desert. It can take a saguaro ten years to reach an inch in height and fifty-plus years before it grows arms. It's not unusual for a saguaro to be more than one hundred years old, although they're frequently killed off by frost, fire, and bacterial infection. State laws protect these mighty cacti from damage or theft. Several hiking or biking trails run through the park. They range from easy to moderately difficult. Before you start off on any of them, stop by the visitors center and talk to a park ranger. If you've never hiked in the desert before, it presents its own set of challenges. The road is open from 7 a.m. to sunset. Admission is $10 per vehicle for seven days.

An interesting attraction on this side of the city is the ***Arizona-Sonora Desert Museum*** (520-883-2702; www.desertmuseum.org) at 2021 N. Kinney Rd. It features only plants and animals native to the Sonoran Desert. You can see everything from mountain lions and javelinas to bark scorpions. The museum also has an extensive mineral collection. During summer the museum often holds special evening events so that visitors can get a look at bats, night-blooming cacti, and other nocturnal phenomena. Museum hours vary; call for information. Admission is $9.50 for adults and $2.25 for children ages six to twelve, June through Aug, and $13.00 for adults and $4.25 for children ages six to twelve, Sept through May.

trivia

The multiarmed saguaro cactus only grows in the Sonoran desert.

Tucson is also brimming with entertaining options for experiencing the best of the Old West. Located just down the road from the Arizona Sonora Desert Museum, ***Old Tucson Studios*** (520-883-0100; www.oldtucson.com) was once known as the "Hollywood of the Desert." More than 250 movies have been filmed at this 1880s frontier town set. This working film set also doubles as a place for cowpokes and wannabes to enjoy western-themed buildings, rides and games, set tours, dining, shopping, and shows.

If casino gambling is your sort of amusement, you're in luck—and you're also adhering to a Tucson tradition. Wyatt Earp and Doc Holliday used to play faro here in the 1880s. Take Valencia Road west, and turn south onto Camino de Oeste. You're now on the ***San Xavier*** (depending upon your facility with Spanish, you can try to pronounce the first syllable or simply say "Hah-veer") Indian Reservation. This is Pascua Yaqui land, and the tribe operates the ***Casino of the Sun*** (800-344-9435; www.casinodelsol.com) at 7406 S. Camino de Oeste, an enterprise that includes 500 gaming machines, high stakes bingo, and live keno, poker, and blackjack. And if you're hungry, the casino offers an all-you-can-eat prime rib buffet.

The reservation also is the location of ***Mission San Xavier del Bac*** (520-294-2624; www.sanxaviermission.org) at 1950 W. San Xavier Rd. The fabled "White Dove of the Desert" is one part museum (containing artifacts and paintings that are several hundred years old) and one part Jesuit church, with regular services and many weddings. It's common to run into a wedding party while you're visiting the mission. You can take a self-guided tour of the church if there isn't a mass or other service going on. Also venture across the courtyard, and you'll find shops selling Native American crafts and vendors offering fry bread and other goodies. The Mission is open daily from 7 a.m. to 5 p.m.

On the east side of the reservation, on land deeded to the Tohono O'Odham Indians, sits the *Desert Diamond Casino* (520-294-7777 or 866-332-9467; www.desertdiamond.com) at 7350 S. Nogales Hwy. It has nearly everything the Casino of the Sun has including blackjack and poker. Both casinos have slots with progressive jackpots and opportunities to win vehicles. Both have fast-food eateries.

Closer to town, off Oracle and Ina Roads, is *Tohono Chul Park* (520-742-6455; www.tohonochulpark.org) at 7366 N. Paseo del Norte. This preserved site of natural Sonoran Desert has an easy-to-follow trail through forty-nine acres that contain about 500 species of plants and animals. Wrens, quails, roadrunners, and other birds frequent the park, and you may see a black-tailed jackrabbit or two. Year-round the park hosts demonstrations on low-water landscaping, lectures on southwestern history, and seasonal events. Tohono Chul also has an art gallery that shows southwestern artists and a tearoom in a hacienda-style home with a plant-filled courtyard. The park is open from 8 a.m. to 5 p.m., with occasional after-hours events. Admission is $7 for adults, $3 for students with ID, and $2 for children ages five to twelve.

Santa Cruz County

Mexico is only about an hour's drive south from Tucson, and to get there you pass through the tail end of Pima County into *Santa Cruz County* (520-287-3685; www.nogaleschamber.com), an area with an oxcart load of history and rustic charm. The state's name actually originated in this region, where the Tohono O'Odham Indians called the land Arizonac, meaning "place of little springs."

Take the Nogales Highway off-ramp from I-10, and you'll merge onto I-19. For part of the next 20-mile stretch—where signs begin to show both miles and kilometers—there isn't much to see out the window: shrubs, sand, and an occasional patch of intense greenness where palo verde and mesquite have taken root. The scenery, however, zips by quite quickly, delivering motorists to the town of *Green Valley* (520-625-7575 or 800-858-5872; www.greenvalley chamber.com). As the name implies, Green Valley is as verdant as a garden show. Set into a valley created by the Santa Rita Mountains, this Pima County community of about 20,000 was started nearly fifty years ago as a retirement haven. The close-knit nature of Green Valley is in evidence everywhere. You won't find graffiti, litter, or abandoned buildings. The streets are clean, and the people are friendly. Lots of shops for groceries, restaurants—such as *Manuel Mexican Restaurant* (520-648-6068) at 121 W. Duval Rd. and the long-established *Arizona Family Restaurant* (520-625-3680) at 80 W.

Esperanza Blvd.—and a half-dozen golf courses make the town appealing to vacationers.

Just north of Green Valley is also the site for the **Titan Missile Museum** (520-625-7736; www.pimaair.org), a National Historic Landmark on Duval Mine Road. In the early 1980s, when the Titan II missile silos were deactivated, all but this one were destroyed. Green Valley's silo is the same today (minus the warhead, of course) as it was when it was part of America's defense program. Guided tours are available of the control room, the crew living quarters, and the missile launch area. The museum contains aircraft and mockups of early space capsules. The museum is open daily from 8:45 a.m. to 5 p.m., with the last tour leaving at 4 p.m. Admission is $9.50 for adults and $6.00 for children ages six to thirteen.

About 10 miles south on I-19 is Santa Cruz County and the tiny town of **Amado,** a ranching community with a few shops and restaurants.

A favorite restaurant in the area is **Cantina Romantica** (520-398-2914 or 800-547-2696; www.rexranch.com) at the Rex Ranch, which is located at 131 Amado Montosa Rd. Chef Stephanie Leonard whips up an extraordinary menu of creative cuisine, all served up in the gorgeous restaurant at this historic landmark. The restaurant is open for dinner Wednesday through Sunday. Reservations are required.

Another five minutes or so away on I-19 is **Tubac** (520-398-2704; www .tubacaz.com), the oldest city in the state—established in 1752 as a Spanish settlement and, today, sort of Arizona's answer to the artists' colony of Santa Fe, New Mexico. The attractions in this community are close together, and

trivia

In the film *Tin Cup,* Kevin Costner was shown teeing off at the Tubac Golf Resort in southern Arizona.

walking or bicycling is the best way to get around. Park your car in one of the lots just off I-19 and stroll down Tubac's narrow streets. Shops and art galleries like **C. Curry Studio & Gallery** (520-398-3304) and **Lee Blackwell Studio** (520-398-2268; www.leeblackwellstudio.com) offer handcrafted jewelry and crafts items. The community has a yearly arts festival in winter and a fall historic re-enactment of the trek of Juan Bautista de Anza, the Spanish officer who passed through the area before he founded what would later become San Francisco. Be sure to see the **Tubac Presidio State Historic Park** (520-398-2252; www.azstateparks.com) on Burruel Street on the east side of town. The crumbling adobe remains of the original presidio wall (before the fort was relocated to Tucson) are here, along with an 1885 schoolhouse and a museum with exhibits detailing Spain's influence in this area. Also stop by

St. Ann's Church, built in 1920 by a Bavarian carpenter. The park is open Thurs through Mon from 9 a.m. to 5 p.m. Admission is $3 for adults and $1 for children ages seven to thirteen.

When hunger pangs strike check out *Wisdom's Cafe* (520-398-2397) at 1931 E. Frontage Rd. This Mexican restaurant, established in 1944, is a favorite among visiting celebrities.

And if you need a cozy place to rest your head, try the *Tubac Secret Garden Inn* (520-398-9371 or 888-399-9371; www.tubacsecretgarden.com), a Spanish Colonial bed-and-breakfast located in Tubac's historic area at 13 Placita de Anza. Rooms start at $80.

Heading south on I-19 takes you to another historic spot: *Tumacácori National Historic Park* (520-398-2341; www.nps.gov/tuma), a collection of three Spanish colonial missions, including the *Tumacácori Mission.* Many visitors stop off just to photograph the mission, built by Franciscan friars and Native Americans in the early 1800s. Standing inside the weathered adobe rooms, you can see that the people who built this mission, which was an integral part of life in the Santa Cruz Valley during the 1800s, put a tremendous effort into the construction. Tumacácori National Historic Park also offers guided tours of the nearby *Missions San Cayetano de Calabazas and Los Santos Ángeles de Guevavi* every Tues from Feb through Apr. To make a reservation for these tours, contact *Spirit Steps Tours* (520-398-2655 or 866-508-0094; www.spiritsteps.org). These tours are limited and range from $20 to $36. The park is open daily from 9 a.m. to 5 p.m. Admission is $3 for adults and is good for seven days.

The best cultural experience of this trip may be 15 miles down the road in the city of *Nogales* (520-287-3685; www.nogaleschamber.com). Nogales (the word means "walnut") is a town with a split personality. On the American side of the border, it seems like a sleepy bedroom community tucked into rolling hillsides. Here and there are spots of industry or commerce, especially along Grand Avenue, the city's main drag. The town has had more than its share of problems: political squabbles, pollution problems, and an economy that's especially dependent on the Mexican peso. Yet Nogales keeps plugging along, partly because many of the residents have family, friends, and business partners on the other side of the border. For a look at the border town's history, check out the exhibits at the *Pimería Alta Historical Museum* (520-287-4621), which is housed in the 1914 Old City Hall. In addition to the exhibits, you can see period rooms including the mayor's office, the fire department, and the sheriff's office complete with two holding cells. Hours are Mon through Fri from noon to 4 p.m. and Sat and Sun from 11 a.m. to 4 p.m.

It's what's south of the border that some visitors come to see. It is possible to cross over into Nogales, Mexico, without a visa, passport, or birth certificate if you stay within the border zone. Be advised, however, that if you want to go farther south into Mexico, you will need some documentation, and you may have to put up a bond to take a vehicle or boat into the country. You should also be aware that American auto insurance is not honored in Mexico. You should purchase relatively inexpensive Mexican insurance if you are taking your car across the border. There are a number of clearly marked insurance agencies on the American side where you can buy the necessary policy before taking your vehicle into Mexico. You may also consider parking your vehicle on the American side (you may have to pay a few dollars for a space) and walking across the border.

Nogales, in the Mexican state of Sonora, is definitely another world. The streets are narrow, and often the paving bricks are cracked or uneven. Much of the city isn't accessible to people in wheelchairs. Throughout the city you'll see many vendors clustered together under one awning. Everything is for sale here: jewelry, blankets, leather goods, electronics, arts and crafts, and liquor—especially the ever-popular Mexican specialties like tequila (made from the root of the agave cactus), kahlua (coffee liqueur), and cerveza (beer to you gringos and gringas). Luxury items like Cartier watches also are available here at duty-free rates. You can fill prescriptions here quickly and cheaply, and many Arizonans drive to Nogales to stock up on allergy medications and other drugs that are significantly pricier in the States. American currency is readily accepted and is often preferred over pesos.

Some of the products for sale are illegal in the States. Fireworks, switchblades (most made in Germany or Italy), and illegal drugs are among the most notable contraband. Mexican customs officials will detain and search you if they think your behavior is suspicious. If you get into trouble on the Mexican side, don't expect the American guards to help you. Buyer (smuggler) beware!

Although you'll find a lot of friendly people (and some great bargains on glassware and silver jewelry if you're willing to haggle a little), you should be aware that shopkeepers eschew subtle sales tactics for the direct approach. They can be a bit forward at times, and some of the merchants think nothing of touching female customers in a manner considered inappropriate in the United States. There is also a dark side to Nogales. In recent years the problem of street kids mugging tourists has reared its ugly head. To play it safe, stay on well-traveled avenues and don't display any signs of wealth such as flashy jewelry, rolls of bills, expensive clothes, and camcorders. Keep away from the kids who approach you offering to do favors. Recently Nogales began using bilingual students to provide guidance to tourists, and the city has also beefed up police patrols in an effort to keep muggers away from the border area.

As for dining south of the border, it's wise to follow the standard rules for touristas: Don't drink the water unless it's in a restaurant advertising purified water, don't eat anything that's been undercooked, and don't purchase food from street vendors. You'll find Sonoran cuisine a little different from the Americanized version of Mexican food. Cheese is often goat cheese; the chili peppers tend to be hotter (even the innocent-looking habanéro, also known as "the gringo killer"); and a lot of seafood entrees are flavored with fresh lime juice. Prices at the better Nogales restaurants are about the same as in Arizona.

trivia

Arizona Wines have complemented meals served at the White House since 1989.

Did you know that Arizona has a *wine country?* Actually the history of grape growing in southeastern Arizona dates back to the Spanish missionaries who planted vines here in the seventeenth century. After you've visited south of the border, you may want to explore a different side of the Grand Canyon State. Instead of taking I-19 back toward Tucson, take the freeway entrance to AZ 82 east. You'll head north toward the town of *Patagonia* (520-394-0060 or 888-794-0060; www.patagoniaaz.com). For nature lovers, this area is in itself a delight. The Nature Conservancy's *Patagonia-Sonoita Creek Preserve* (520-394-2400; www.nature.org) is a cottonwood-willow riparian forest with trees as old as 130 years and as tall as 100 feet. More than 260 species of birds call the preserve home, including the gray hawk, green kingfisher, and violet-crowned hummingbird. There are also whitetail deer, javelina, and coyote. Many species of fish inhabit a perennial stream that runs through the preserve. Guided tours are held at 9 a.m. every Saturday. The preserve is open Wed through Sun from 6:30 a.m. to 4 p.m. Admission is $5 for adults.

Continuing north on AZ 82, you'll find that while the state doesn't yet have the number of wineries and vineyards (www.arizonawine.org) in California's wine country, the former ranch lands of *Sonoita* and *Elgin* are doing quite nicely in their current incarnations as grape fields. The vineyards that dot the hillsides of this gently rolling terrain include Callaghan, Charron, Dos Cabezas, Sonoita, and Village of Elgin. Among the wineries, *Callaghan Vineyards* (www.callaghanvineyards.com) is known for its Buena Suerte Cuvees. Many different varieties of table wine grapes are grown here. Approximately 20,000 cases of wine are produced annually by the winemakers in this region.

Depending on the time of year you visit, you may be able to watch a crush (usually in August), where you can see the grapes being stomped. April is the month for the Annual Wine Festival, when the fields are blessed by a coalition of clergy members. Whatever the month, you can drop by the ***Chapel of Santa Maria,*** an adobe territorial-style nondenominational shrine located in Elgin, just a tiny detour off AZ 82.

This entire region was the site for many mines (copper, lead, silver, and gold), some of them in operation until the 1930s. Surrounding these mines were small communities, which sprang up in the 1850s to the 1880s. All long abandoned, these towns are little but crumbling adobe, not even worth the trouble to try to find. Many are on private property, so check with the Nogales/Santa Cruz Chamber of Commerce (520-287-3685; www.nogaleschamber.com) before wandering off. They can provide you with information on road conditions and which sites might still be worth visiting. One final word of caution if you do set off on your own: If you happen to come across a mine shaft, under no circumstances should you enter. Cave-ins are common; snakes and other creatures often take up residence in these locations; and caches of old, unstable dynamite have been found in shaft corridors.

Tombstone Area

Just east of Santa Cruz County is ***Cochise County,*** once the stomping ground (and I mean that in the most literal sense) of Johnny Ringo, Wyatt Earp, and Doc Holliday. If your base of operations is Tucson, you can reach the historic towns of Benson, St. David, Tombstone, Sierra Vista, Bisbee, and Douglas by taking I-10 east until you reach AZ 80, then heading south. You can also reach them from Santa Cruz County by taking AZ 82 (which runs through Patagonia and Elgin) east to AZ 80. Depending upon which direction you come from, you either arrive at Benson first (coming from Tucson) or Tombstone (from Sonoita).

For the sake of simplicity, let's assume you've driven down from Tucson.

Just before the Benson turnoff, you'll see a sign marked J–SIX RANCH ROAD/MESCAL. ***Mescal,*** to the north toward the mountains, is a dream factory. Since 1968 this make-believe town—a series of dirt streets and wooden buildings—has been the location for countless western movies, TV shows, and commercials. Originally built for the Lee Marvin film *Monte Walsh,* it has since been used for the features *High Plains Drifter, Tom Horn, Tombstone,* and *The Quick and the Dead,* as well as the series *The Young Riders.* Unfortunately Mescal is strictly a closed set. Uninvited visitors are not allowed, and guards are posted to see to it that none show up. However, you can drive up the access road to the keep-out sign and with a good pair of binoculars you can easily make out many of the buildings. For a look at a western movie town that you can walk through, head north to the *Gammons Gulch Ghost Town Movie Set* (520-212-2831; www.gammonsgulch.com). This set of a 1890s mining town is open for tours from Wed through Sun from 9 a.m. to 4 p.m., Sept to May. Because this is a working film set, be sure to call ahead before visiting. Admission is $7 per person.

Just down the road a bit is *Benson* (520-586-2842; www.bensonchamber az.com), situated in the San Pedro Valley. The scenery here is sporadically lush, with vistas that often include snowcapped mountains.

Fourteen miles east of Benson on I-10, you'll come to the turn-off to scenic *Texas Canyon,* which is known for its strange and spectacular rock formations. If you want to explore the canyon by foot or on horseback, you may want to check into the *Triangle T Guest Ranch* (520-586-7533; www .azretreatcenter.com). The ranch offers your choice of casitas and has cabins and also a restaurant and saloon. Activities include horseback riding and jeep tours. Rooms start at $149.

trivia

The San Pedro River in southeastern Arizona's Cochise County actually flows northward into the United States from Mexico.

South on AZ 90, between Bisbee and Sierra Vista, you'll find another natural jewel at the *San Pedro Riparian National Conservation Area* (520-586-3467; www.blm.gov/az). This area protects 40 miles of riparian habitat of the San Pedro River, which supports more than 350 species of birds—making this a prime bird-watching destination. Other recreational activities here include camping ($2), hiking, fishing, and bow hunting.

If you head south towards Sierra Vista from Benson, you'll come to *Kartchner Caverns State Park* (520-586-2283; www.azstateparks.com). These pristine caves are considered to be some of the most beautiful and unusual "living" cave formations in the world. The crystalline underground garden takes shape in an array of unusual formations or "speleothems"—shields, stalactites, stalagmites, columns, cave pearls, soda straws, flowstone, popcorn, rimstone dams, and cave cotton. One of the reasons that Kartchner Caverns is world-renowned is that it is a living cave, where all of the glorious speleothems are still growing. The Throne Room and Rotunda Room, the first rooms open for tours, feature the longest soda straw formation in the United States at 21 feet and 2 inches, and the largest column in the state reaching to an impressive height of 58 feet. The Big Room also has some notable features—the world's most extensive formation of brushite moonmilk, the first reported occurrence of turnip shields, and the first noted occurrence of birdsnest needle formations. The Big Room is also the nursery roost for female cave myotis bats from Apr through Sept, during which time the Big Room is closed in an effort to foster the cave's unique ecosystem. The tours for the Rotunda and Throne Rooms are $18.95 for adults and $9.95 for children ages seven to thirteen, Oct through July, and $16.95 for adults and $8.95 for children ages seven to thirteen, Aug and Sept. Big Room tours are $22.95 for adults and $12.95 for children ages seven to thirteen. Reservations are required. Other activities at the park include wildlife watching, hiking, and camping ($22). Admission to the park is $5 per vehicle.

Bibliophiles may want to take a slight detour to the ***Singing Wind Ranch Bookshop*** (520-586-2425), north of I-10 via Ocotillo Road (turn at Singing Wind Road and look for the green gate with a chain). The bookshop's numerous offerings are grouped helter-skelter within a southwestern ranch house, where hunting for buried treasures is as much fun as finding them. The bookshop is open daily from 9 a.m. to 5 p.m. A treat for Benson's visitors is a stop at the ***Horseshoe Cafe*** (520-586-3303), 154 E. Fourth St. Burgers are mouthwatering, and the Mexican fare is good. The Horseshoe's giant cinnamon rolls are killer. It's a great spot for watching the trains go by and enjoying some down-home cooking.

Heading south on AZ 80 takes you through more riparian areas to the tucked-away town of ***St. David.*** Like much of southeastern Arizona, this peaceful little village was booming when nearby mines were open. Today, you can enjoy browsing in antiques shops or visiting the ***Holy Trinity Monastery*** (520-720-4642; www.holytrinitymonastery.org). The monastery has a gift shop, library, meditation garden, museum, and other areas that are open to the public.

Tombstone (888-457-3929; www.tombstone.org), "the town too tough to die," is only a few miles away from St. David on AZ 80. The story goes that the burg's founder (a prospector) was told that the only thing he would find in southern Arizona would be his tombstone—and the name stuck. The town had a much harder time sticking around than did the name. It was a prosperous mining community in the early 1880s, but by 1909 the community had fallen on hard times. It became prohibitively expensive to pull ore out of the nearby mines, which had flooded after miners had struck underground streams.

Driving into town, high on a hill to your left, you'll see the grave sites of infamous ***Boot Hill*** (520-457-3300), where the victims of the gunfight at OK Corral were buried. This wasn't, however, the original location for the cemetery; it was moved when the road was built. You can take a self-guided tour of the cemetery, photograph the sometimes comical markers (HERE LIES LESTER MOORE / FOUR SHOTS FROM A .44 / NO LES, NO MORE), and shop in the gift shop. The cemetery is open from 7:30 a.m. to 6:30 p.m.

The community of Tombstone is rightfully proud of its place in American history. About $37 million in various ores was removed from the mines in its environs before they ceased operation. Even in the wild and woolly 1880s, the town of nearly 10,000 residents (now 1,500) had cultural activities, including literary societies, theater, and musical groups. Important mine-related events that occurred here were reported all over the country. Today Tombstone survives primarily because tourists who are fascinated with the Old West want to (as one sign puts it) WALK WHERE THEY [western outlaws like the Clantons] FELL.

Allen Street in the heart of the historic section of Tombstone actually looks very much like a movie location, and this effect is heightened by staged gunfights that occur at regular times during *Helldorado Days* (usually Oct), *Nellie Cashman Rose Festival* (usually Apr), and other popular celebrations the town holds. Both sides of the boardwalk get crammed with camcorder-wielding tourists, as actors in 1880s attire shoot it out with black-powder firearms. Ironically the town has had a few problems with visitors brandishing real guns on the streets. So, as was the case in the days of Wyatt Earp, wearing firearms in town has been banned. Re-enactors are exempt.

A number of souvenir shops line Allen Street, selling everything from T-shirts to Navajo jewelry.

On Allen and Sixth Streets sits the *Bird Cage Theatre* (520-457-3421 or 800-457-3423), a notorious gambling hall, saloon, and cathouse that operated from 1881 until 1889. The atmosphere was so wild in here that there are 140 bullet holes in the walls from gun battles. The Bird Cage Theatre is open daily for tours, and it's worth seeing as a good example of the type of place where frontier men entertained themselves. Hours are from 8 a.m. to 6 p.m. Theatre tours cost $10 for adults and $8 for children ages eight to eighteen.

While you're on Allen Street, you may be tempted to pay the fee to walk around in the *OK Corral* (520-457-3456; www.ok-corral.com) at 308 Allen St. The live daily show is at 2 p.m., with an additional show at 4 p.m. on Fri and Sat. In all fairness it's worth a peek. You can tour exhibits of photographs of early Tombstone and read original newspaper accounts of the famous gunfight between the Clantons and the Earps. Inside the corral you can see life-size statues of the Earps and the Clantons arranged to represent the real participants of the shoot-out. The corral wasn't, however, the actual site of their armed altercation. The gunfight took place in 1881, in a vacant lot around the corner, across the street from where Fly's Boarding House once stood. The shooting lasted about a minute and occurred at nearly point-blank range. The final score: Morgan and Virgil Earp were seriously wounded; Doc Holliday was grazed by a round (he allegedly ran away in hysterics—a vicious killer, he was neither a good shot nor a brave man); Billy Clanton and Tom and Frank

McLaury were shot dead. An excellent book on the subject is Paula Mitchell Marks's *And Die in the West,* which is available in bookstores on Allen Street. Admission is $9 per person.

On a happier note, Tombstone is also home to the **world's largest rose tree** (planted in 1885), located at the **Rose Tree Museum** (520-457-3326), just a short walk from Allen Street on Fourth and Toughnut Streets. The Lady Banksia rose tree is in the courtyard of a home that once belonged to Amelia Adamson, grown from a shoot given to her by the wife of a Scottish immigrant. The roses bloom from mid-March to mid-April, and even when the bush is dormant, you can enjoy the museum displays within the converted home. The displays recount life in early Tombstone. The museum is open daily from 9 a.m. to 5 p.m. Admission is $5 for adults.

If hunger pangs get the better of you, try the **Nellie Cashman Restaurant** (520-457-2212) at Fifth and Toughnut Streets. Located in a historic building and named after one of the town's leading citizens of the 1880s, this traditional American restaurant has western memorabilia on the walls and a menu that includes salads, sandwiches, steaks, chicken, hamburgers, and homemade pie. The **Longhorn Restaurant** (520-457-3405) at Fifth and Allen Streets also offers American cuisine in addition to a little peek at history: Virgil Earp was shot and killed by a gunman firing from one of the Longhorn's second-story windows.

If you decide to stay in Tombstone, try the **Tombstone Boarding House Bed and Breakfast Inn** (520-457-3716 or 877-225-1319; www.tombstone-boardinghouse.com) at 108 N. Fourth St. This bed-and-breakfast is a restored Victorian home that's been decorated in period splendor. Rooms range from $99 to $119. Likewise, the **Tombstone Bordello Boarding House** (520-457-2394) on Allen Street is a historic adobe home that reflects a time when the West was wilder. Rates start at $89. The town's newspaper is the *Tombstone Epitaph* and is considered Arizona's oldest newspaper. Featured prominently in TV series like *Wyatt Earp* and *Bat Masterson,* the more than one-hundred-year-old paper is published by the University of Arizona's journalism department. However, if you want to take a different look at frontier life and the Old West, you can pick up a map of the area's ghost towns at the Tombstone Chamber of Commerce (888-457-3929).

Bisbee, Douglas, and Sierra Vista

Continuing south on AZ 80 takes you to another historic place: **Bisbee** (520-432-3554 or 866-2-BISBEE; www.bisbeearizona.com), formerly a mining town and now best known as an artists' community and a retreat for celebrities. It has been heralded by *Travel and Leisure* magazine as one of the "Best New American Destinations," comparing the century-old town with such world-renowned arts destinations as Aspen and Santa Fe. Set in the Mule Mountains, the older section of Bisbee (which can easily be covered on foot but is not particularly accessible for wheelchairs) may remind you a bit of San Francisco. The wooden Victorian buildings that dot the hillside and line the narrow main street have maintained their quaint charm. To find your way around, park in the first lot you come to as you enter town on AZ 80, and walk across the street to the chamber of commerce office. They can give you maps of the area, as well as information on any events—poetry readings, music festivals, art openings—that may be taking place that day.

Next, you may want to wander into the ***Bisbee Mining and Historical Museum*** (520-432-7071; www.bisbeemuseum.org) on Main Street (just look for the train out front). The museum, situated in the 1897 Copper Queen Consolidated Mining Offices, details Bisbee's mining history and has displays of minerals that were found in and around the Mule Mountains. It also offers a glimpse into the town's past by describing its transition from boom to bust. The museum is open daily from 10 a.m. to 4 p.m. Admission is $7.50 for adults and $3.00 for children ages three to sixteen.

While in the older section of Bisbee, you may want to take the underground tour of the ***Queen Mine*** (520-432-2071 or 866-432-2071; www.queen minetour.com) on Arizona Street. The tour guides are former Queen Mine workers who take visitors deep into the defunct mine aboard original miniature train cars. Bring a jacket: The mine stays a cool 47 degrees Fahrenheit year-round! Tours leave at 9 and 10:30 a.m., noon, and 2 and 3:30 p.m. Admission is $12 for adults and $5 for children ages four to fifteen. Be sure to stop by the grand ***Copper Queen Hotel*** (520-432-2216; www.copperqueen.com) on Howell Avenue, where Theodore Roosevelt once stayed and which continues to operate as a hotel and a restaurant. Rumor has it that a few friendly spirits inhabit the rooms of this classic hotel. For that matter, walking through the antiques shops lining Main Street is a trip back in time. Basic rooms start at $89 and the specialty suites start at $159.

Antiques buffs and visitors looking for one-of-a-kind treasures will find Bisbee's winding streets a virtual paradise. Galleries, boutiques, gem shops, and antiques stores are plentiful, offering everything from locally mined Bisbee Blue turquoise to original art—much of it is created by local artisans.

Christina Plascencia's ***55 Main Gallery*** (520-432-4694) at 55 Main St. displays original art, clothing, and handcrafted jewelry. She even brings in psychics to entertain browsers in the gallery she describes as "a holistic venue for showing the essence of Bisbee . . . something for mind, body, and spirit." **Óptimo Custom Hatworks** (520-432-4544 or 888-FINE-HAT; www.optimohatworks.com) at 47 Main St. sells Panama straw hats from Ecuador. While walking the main drag, you might want to stop and sample the eclectic mix of honey products at The **Killer Bee Guy** (520-432-2938 or 877-2-B-SWEET; www.killerbeeguy.com) at 18 Main St. In addition to the fabulous array of honey butters, you'll also find the spicy "Smooth Horserad-ish Honey Mustard," which won the 2005 Napa Valley World Mustard Com-petition bronze award and the 2008 bronze award for their "Smooth Orginal Honey Mustard."

Dining is equally eclectic in this historic hillside burg. **Cafe Roka** (520-432-5153; www.caferoka.com) is gaining a well-deserved reputation for its gourmet fare presented in a historic storefront along the main drag at 35 Main St. Reservations are recommended.

Besides the aforementioned Copper Queen, there are several comfortable, unique places to stay in town. The **School House Inn Bed and Breakfast** (520-432-2996 or 800-537-4333; www.schoolhouseinnbb.com) at 818 Tomb-stone Canyon Rd. is, as the name implies, a former schoolhouse. It has airy yet cozy rooms with private bathrooms. Rooms start at $89. The **Oliver House** (520-432-1900) at 24 Sowles Rd. is a bit of a hike from the main drag but has a lot of Victorian charm. Rooms start at $94.

For nostalgia fanatics perhaps the only logical lodging choice would be the **Shady Dell Vintage Trailer and RV Park** (520-432-3567; www.theshadydell .com). This cluster of restored vintage Airstream trailers ranges from a 1949 Airstream to a 1951 Royal Mansion and is located near the town's traffic circle. Each RV is furnished with period artifacts, chenille bedspreads, and radios tuned to swing music. Rates are from the past, as well, with accommodations available for $55 to $124. Adjacent to the Shady Dell is another period treasure, an actual refurbished diner that serves up the standard diner grub.

From Bisbee you can either continue along AZ 80 to Douglas (520-364-2477), almost on the Mexican border, or you can backtrack north on AZ 80 and take AZ 90 west to Sierra Vista.

Let's consider **Douglas** (520-364-2477) first. One reason for making the drive to Douglas is to cross the border for a shopping trip in Agua Prieta (*ah-wah pree-etta,* meaning "dark water"); others are to romp in the surrounding Coronado National Forest or to visit the Gadsden Hotel.

Agua Prieta, a city of about 100,000, is headquarters to many maquila-dras (Mexican factories built by American companies) and features the same sort of Old World shopping you'll find in Nogales. If you're suffering from buyer's remorse because you passed up a *gonga* (bargain), you have a second shot at it.

On the north side of the border, the **Coronado National Forest** (520-388-8300; www.fs.fed.us/r3/coronado) is an area ringed with mountain ranges, most notably the Dragoons to the northwest, the Peloncillo mountains to the east, and the Chiricahuas to the northeast. The Dragoons are the location of the fabled Cochise Stronghold, the last battle site for the legendary Native American leader. The Chiricahuas are known for being a bird-watcher's paradise, providing haven for varieties like the elegant trogon.

History buffs can take a detour on the Geronimo Trail to the restored **Slaughter Ranch** (520-558-2474), about 16 miles east of Douglas—and truly off the beaten path! John Slaughter, a former Texas ranger, was the sheriff of Cochise County during the late 1880s. He is credited with running a lot of the riffraff out of the area. The **Slaughter Ranch Museum** is open Wed through Sun from 10 a.m. to 3 p.m.

If comfort and a certain early twentieth-century elegance are what you're looking for in lodgings, check into The **Gadsden Hotel** (520-364-4481; www .hotelgadsden.com) on G Avenue. The Gadsden was built in 1907 as a grand hotel for cattle barons and other well-heeled travelers, including Wilford Brimley, Paul Newman, Eleanor Roosevelt, Amelia Earhart, Johnny Depp, Faye Dunaway, Lee Marvin, and Jerry Lewis. Natasia Kinsski and Charlie Sheen called the Gadsden home during the filming of *Terminal Velocity*. It, too, is rumored to be inhabited by a few friendly ghosts! It boasts a lobby with an Italian marble staircase and four marble columns decorated in fourteen-karat gold leaf. This hotel, listed on the National Register of Historic Places, is a completely modern facility with air-conditioned rooms, apartments, and executive suites with kitchenettes, and convention facilities. Rates range from $60 to $150.

Church Square on East E Avenue is believed to be the only place in the world with four churches on four corners in the same block. Once you've seen Douglas, you can either head west to Sierra Vista or north up to Willcox.

The city of **Sierra Vista** (520-417-6960 or 800-288-3861; www.visitsierra vista.com) can be reached by taking I-10 east from Tucson to AZ 90, or by taking AZ 80 west to AZ 90. Those who think of southeastern Arizona as vast stretches of vacant desert are in for a shock when they near Sierra Vista. The area around the town has not only the mountain views its name promises but also long expanses of palo verde, mesquite, and grasslands. A short distance

trivia

Dueling deities: **Church Square** in the city of Douglas is believed to be the only place in the world with four churches on four corners in the same block.

from Sierra Vista are Garden Canyon and Ramsey Canyon Preserve. **Garden Canyon,** on the nearby Fort Huachuca property, is usually open for visitors and is a good place for bird-watchers to spot elegant trogons, Montezuma quail, and even northern pygmy owls. **Ramsey Canyon Preserve** (520-378-2785; www.nature.org), which is protected by the Nature Conservancy, is a great place for hummingbird watching and just one of the many reasons Sierra Vista is known as the "Hummingbird Capital of the World." This proliferation of winged wonders (fourteen species) is the cornerstone of the annual South-west Wings (www.sabo.org) birding festival that takes place every August in Sierra Vista and surrounding habitats. The preserve is open daily from 8 a.m. to 5 p.m. Admission is $5 for adults. At the preserve's entrance, the **Ramsey Canyon Inn Bed and Breakfast** (520-378-3010; www.ramseycanyoninn.com) has modern accommodations and freshly baked pies. Space in these facilities books fast! This lovely bed-and-breakfast does not allow children under the age of sixteen. Rooms start at $135. Just outside the preserve is the nonprofit **Arizona Folklore Preserve** (520-378-6165; www.arizonafolklore.com). There Arizona's Official Balladeer, Dolan Ellis, entertains visitors with the songs, legends, and poetry of the Old West, accompanied by stunning photographic images he has collected. The Arizona Folklore Preserve is open on weekends for performances by Ellis (a former member of the New Christy Minstrels) and other folk artists and is dedicated to the collection, presentation, and preservation of Arizona folklore.

Fort Huachuca (520-533-5736) is just a few minutes west of Sierra Vista. An army base that today serves as headquarters for the U.S. Army's Intelligence Center and Information Systems Command, the fort's history stretches back to the 1870s, when it was established as a camp to protect settlers against Apache raiders. It has had an interesting history as a base for the soldiers who tracked down Geronimo and the troops who battled Pancho Villa, as well as home for the African-American cavalry units that came to be known as the "buffalo soldiers." The fort had its ups and downs after World War II. It even closed for a while. In 1954 it was turned into the army's electronic proving ground. One former soldier who served at the fort in the 1950s is a well-known speaker on the UFO circuit. He claims that he saw the army test extraterrestrial aircraft there, though no proof of his claims exists. The **Fort Huachuca Museum** is dedicated to the various incarnations of Fort Huachuca.

Modern accommodations and charming bed-and-breakfast inns are plentiful in Sierra Vista, with nearly 900 rooms available. The nicest full-service hotel is the 148-room **Windemere Hotel & Conference Center** (520–459–5900 or 800–825–4656); www.windemerehotel.com) at 2047 S. Hwy. 92, located a few miles from the turnoff for Ramsey Canyon. Room rates start at $98.

Northern Cochise County

You can reach historic sites like the Chiricahua National Monument and the adobe ruins of Fort Bowie by taking US 90 from Sierra Vista; take I-10 to Willcox, and then follow US 186 to *Chiricahua National Monument* (520-824-3560; www.nps.gov/chir). Here are many hoodoos (huge stone towers) surrounded by pine and juniper forests. Take the Bonita Canyon Drive through the monument, and you'll reach the top of Massai Point. You can park here and get a terrific view of the Chiricahua Mountain range, known as the "Wonderland of Rocks." Picnic tables, camping sites ($12), and restrooms are available at marked areas within the monument. The visitor center is open daily from 8 a.m. to 4:30 p.m. Admission is $5 for adults. North of the monument is *Fort Bowie National Historic Site* (520-847-2500; ww.nps.gov/fobo). It was established in 1862 to protect travelers from Apache raids. Today all that remains of the fort are crumbling adobe walls. A museum on the grounds displays exhibits illustrating the fort's history. An easy 1.5-mile walk from the parking lot to the fort travels past the ruins of a Butterfield Stage Coach Station and a cemetery where the son of Apache leader Geronimo is buried. The visitor center is open daily from 8 a.m. to 4:30 p.m. The Ruins Trail is open from sunrise to sunset.

If you take AZ 181 heading northwest, the next town you reach is *Willcox* (520-384-2272 or 800-200-2272; www.willcoxchamber.com), located in the Sulphur Springs Valley, an agricultural paradise. More than two dozen farms grow everything from apples to chilis to pecans. Harvest seasons vary, but many range from late July through late September or early October. Some of these farms allow you to pick your own produce, and you can write for or pick up a brochure with a list of the farms and a map from Willcox Chamber of Commerce, 1500 N. Circle I Rd., Willcox, AZ 85643. For a historic look at the area, stop by the *Chiricahua Regional Museum* (520-384-3971), which chronicles the area's rich history and agriculture-based economy. The museum is at 127 E. Maley St. and is open Mon through Sat from 10 a.m. to 4 p.m. Admission is $3 per person.

If you'd prefer to sample nature's bounty without risking throwing your back out, you may want to drop by the nearby *Stout's Cider Mill* (520-384-3696; www.cidermill.com) at 1510 N. Circle I Rd. It can be reached by taking exit 340 from I-10. The mill offers apple cider, ice cream, a variety of condiments and snacks, and several very tempting types of apple pie, including one with no added sugar or artificial sweeteners. Stout's Cider Mill is open daily year-round.

West of Willcox just off I-10 resides the museum housing the infamous *Thing.* This "Thing" isn't the hand from *The Addams Family* series or the

Cowboy Singer Rex Allen

Willcox's favorite son unquestionably is cowboy singer Rex Allen, whose film, television, and recording career is celebrated at the *Rex Allen Arizona Cowboy Museum* (520-384-4583; www.rexallenmuseum.org) at 150 N. Historic Railroad Ave. The museum also contains exhibits about frontier settlers and the cowboy way of life. The museum is open daily from 10 a.m. to 4 p.m. Admission is $2 per person, $3 per couple, or $5 for the entire family. Willcox hosts an annual Rex Allen Days festival the first weekend in October. Featured events include a rodeo, a parade, and stage shows.

creature from either the John Carpenter or the Howard Hawks science fiction films. It's the *other* thing. The one advertised on the giant yellow billboards you can't help but see unless you drive through southeastern Arizona with your eyes closed. The "museum" (for want of a better description) housing "The Thing?? Mysteries of the Ages" is a barnlike building that for about three-and-a-half decades also has contained a variety of antiques. Its proud centerpiece is a mummy-like figure encased in glass. No one knows for certain if this is a genuine mummy. (It's possible: Some cliff-dwelling Native American tribes, including the Anasazi, tucked their dead away in places out of reach of scavengers, and more than a few of these bodies have been recovered.) In any case, you can get in for less than a buck, and I recommend the museum to Stephen King aficionados, lovers of roadside Americana, and anyone who grew up in the 1950s or 1960s who read EC or Warren horror comics ("Look, Johnny—that thing is moving! EEYYYIII!").

Even if you're not wrapped up in mummies, you'll find that the scenery around Willcox is quite lovely. In places this high-desert community barely resembles the Southwest. Nowhere is this more apparent than on the marshlike *Willcox Playa Wildlife Refuge,* just south of town. Bird-watchers may want to plan a visit to occur between late October and mid-February to catch a glimpse of the sandhill cranes that nest in the playa. Sandhill cranes are believed to be one of the oldest species of birds. Standing 4 feet tall with a 5-to-7-foot wingspan, they are quite spectacular. Each January, Willcox stages a major celebration of the cranes' arrival (by the thousands) during the *Wings over Willcox* event (800-200-2272; www.wingsoverwillcox.com).

Also south of Willcox on FR 84 is *Cochise Stronghold* (520-364-3468; www.fs.fed.us/r3/coronado). This national monument is the site where the legendary chief of the Chiricahua Apaches made his final stand against the U.S. Army. He is buried within the monument, though no one knows the exact location. The area, both rugged and serene, is home to a variety of wildlife and offers a number of picnic areas and campsites ($10). Hiking trails are well marked but can be quite difficult because of the elevation and the rocky nature of the terrain. For romance and relaxation, you might want to check in to the ***Cochise Stronghold Bed and Breakfast*** (520-826-4141; www.cochise strongholdbb.com). This wilderness retreat is close to hiking trails and is a great place for wildlife watching. Room choices include a luxury room, a yurt, and a cozy cottage. Rates run from $129 to $209 and include a full gourmet breakfast.

Places to Stay in Southern Arizona

GREEN VALLEY

Viscount Suite Hotel
4855 E. Broadway
(520) 745-6500
Microwaves and refrigerators in all suites; three restaurants. Inexpensive.

PEARCE

Grapevine Canyon Ranch
P.O. Box 302
Pearce AZ; 85625
(520) 826-3185 or
(800) 245-9202
www.gcranch.com
Open year-round. Eleven rooms nestled in a picturesque canyon in rugged Dragoon Mountains 80 miles southeast of Tucson. Moderate to expensive.

TUBAC

Tubac Country Inn
13 Burruel St.
(520) 398-3178
www.tubaccountryinn.com

Five suites with private entrances in historic downtown Tubac. No children under twelve. Moderate.

Tubac Resort and Spa
One Ave. de Otero
(520) 298-2211
www.tubacgolfresort.com
This resort is part of Historic Hotels of America and features structures dating back more than a century. Each hotel room is uniquely designed and features plush beds with updated bathrooms. The resort is adjacent to 26-holes of golf and two gourmet restaurants. Moderate to expensive.

TUCSON

Hampton Inn Tucson
1375 W. Grant Rd.
(520) 206-0602
All rooms have microwaves and refrigerators. The hotel also features a breakfast bar and a heated pool. Inexpensive.

The Hilton Tucson East
7600 E. Broadway Blvd.
(520) 721-5600

This full-service atrium hotel has spacious rooms with mountain views. Inexpensive.

Westin La Paloma
3800 E. Sunrise Dr.
(520) 742-6000 or
(800) 677-6338
www.westinlapalomaresort
.com
This vast property in north Tucson has 487 rooms, a spa, a pool with a waterslide, five restaurants, and stunning views. Moderate.

YUMA

Clarion Suites
2600 S. Fourth Ave.
(928) 726-4830 or
(800) 333-3333
www.choicehotels.com
Hotel amenities include a pool and hot tub, plus a coin-operated laundry. Moderate.

Places to Eat in Southern Arizona

BISBEE

The Bisbee Grill
#2 Copper Queen Plaza
(520) 432-6788
This dining room has a reputation for having the best burgers in town. Other menu items include salads, sandwiches, Mexican specialties, pasta, salmon, and steaks. Reservations are recommended. Inexpensive to moderate.

Cafe Cornucopia
14 Main St.
(520) 432-4820
This local favorite serves homemade soups, salads, and sandwiches in a casual setting until 5 p.m. Inexpensive.

TOMBSTONE

Lamplight Room
108 N. Fourth St.
(520) 457-3716 or
(877) 225-1319
www.tombstoneboarding house.com.
Located in the Tombstone Boarding House, this fine-dining establishment serves up French and Mexican cuisine for dinner. Reservations are recommended. Moderate.

TUBAC

The Artist's Palate
40 Avenida Goya, Plaza de Anza
(520) 398-3333
Soup, salads, sandwiches, pasta, pizza, steak, and seafood. Open from 6 a.m. to 10 p.m. daily. Moderate to expensive.

Melio's Trattoria
2261 E. Frontage Rd.
(520) 398-8494
Italian food created in the Roman tradition. Moderate.

Stables
One Ave de Otero
(520) 398-2211
www.tubacgolfresort.com
The restaurant in the Tubac Resort and Spa features savory steak and

WEB SITES FOR SOUTHERN ARIZONA

Arizona Department of Tourism
www.arizonaguide.com

Benson-San Pedro Valley Chamber of Commerce
www.bensonchamberaz.com

Bisbee Chamber of Commerce and Visitor Center
www.bisbeearizona.com

Greater Sierra Vista Area Chamber of Commerce
www.sierravistachamber.org

Green Valley Chamber of Commerce
www.greenvalleychamber.com

Metropolitan Tucson Convention & Visitors Bureau
www.visittucson.org

Nogales-Santa Cruz Chamber of Commerce
www.nogaleschamber.com

Northern Pima County Chamber of Commerce
www.the-chamber.com

Patagonia Area Business Association
www.patagoniaaz.com

Tombstone Chamber of Commerce
www.tombstone.org

Tubac Chamber of Commerce
www.tubacaz.com

Yuma Convention and Visitors Bureau
www.visityuma.com

fish entrees with artistic desserts and excellent service. Diners can enjoy the summer nights under the starry sky near the trickling sounds of the local river. Live music on the weekends. Moderate to Expensive

TUCSON

Blue Willow Restaurant
2616 N. Campbell Ave.
(520) 327-7577
Family owned for more than thirty years, Blue Willow is rated as one of Tucson's "Best for Breakfast and Outdoor Dining." The menu features simple, fresh food day and evening. Inexpensive to Moderate

El Charro Mexican Cafe & Gift Shop
311 N. Court Ave.
(520) 622-1922
www.elcharrocafe.com
Oldest family-operated Mexican restaurant in the United States, with a long tradition of spicing things up! Inexpensive to moderate.

Elle Wine Country Restaurant
3048 E. Broadway Blvd.
(520) 327-0500
www.ellerestaurant.com
With a seasonally changing menu and fresh fare, Elle offers a unique setting, centrally located in Tucson. Moderate

Sweet Tomatoes
6202 E. Broadway Blvd.
4420 N. Stone Ave.
(520) 747-4137 or (520) 293-3343
All you care to eat from a buffet of fresh salads, from-scratch soups, and hot muffins. Inexpensive.

YUMA

Bella Vita
2755 S. Fourth Ave.
(928) 344-3989
This family-owned Italian spot is known locally for its huge portions and delicious, authentic fare. Don't let its "hole-in-the-wall" location fool you. It's worth a stop for a modestly priced meal. Inexpensive.

The Crossing
2680 S. Fourth Ave.
(928) 726-5551
Talk about selection! From steak and prime rib to burgers, seafood, and pasta, The Crossing has a little something for everyone at prices that won't break the bank. Inexpensive.

Martinez Lake Restaurant and Cantina
West end of Martinez Lake Road
(928) 783-0253
www.martinezlake.com
The restaurant overlooks the water and features a full menu and live music every Sunday. It's worth the thirty-minute drive from downtown Yuma. Inexpensive to moderate.

River City Grill
600 W. Third St.
(928) 782-7988
www.rivercitygrillyuma.com
This delightful restaurant serves Caribbean and South American cuisine with a focus on trendy fish dishes. Moderate to expensive.

Index

About the Author

Carrie Miner Frasure has been writing about Arizona and the Southwest for more than a decade. She loves exploring new places with her twin teenage sons Hayden and Blake. Together they have rafted the Colorado River through the Grand Canyon, explored cotton fields in Graham County, and visited with a Navajo medicine man. Carrie's work has been featured in national and regional publications including *Arizona Highways, Las Vegas Review Journal,* and the *Dallas Morning News.*